P9-CAM-090

# THE EVERYTHING.
## VEGAN BAKING COOKBOOK

When I moved away from home at nineteen years old, my cooking skills were limited to preparing boxed macaroni and cheese, or cake from a packaged mix. I quickly realized that if I wanted to enjoy good food, the way my mother made it, I needed to learn to cook . . . and fast! Thus began a several-year quest. Even greater challenges loomed over the next twenty-five years as I embraced vegetarian, vegan, and raw vegan cuisines. As a registered dietitian, I began doing cooking demonstrations to teach others.

Still, in spite of years of cooking experience, baking—with its specific measurements and chemical reactions—seemed so scientific, so mysterious. And what about the prospect of baking without eggs and dairy products? I thought vegan baking must certainly require some kind of magic or fairy dust! But after learning a few basic principles I discovered that perfect loaves of bread, and sweet, delicious cupcakes were easy to make. My friends and family still seem to think there's magic involved . . . I let them! It is my pleasure to offer you the recipes in this book, so you can impress your friends and family with baked goodies they'll love. Work your "magic"!

*Lorena Novak Bull, RD*

# Welcome to the EVERYTHING® Series!

These handy, accessible books give you all you need to tackle a difficult project, gain a new hobby, comprehend a fascinating topic, prepare for an exam, or even brush up on something you learned back in school but have since forgotten.

You can choose to read an Everything® book from cover to cover or just pick out the information you want from our four useful boxes: e-questions, e-facts, e-alerts, and e-ssentials.

We give you everything you need to know on the subject, but throw in a lot of fun stuff along the way, too.

We now have more than 400 Everything® books in print, spanning such wide-ranging categories as weddings, pregnancy, cooking, music instruction, foreign language, crafts, pets, New Age, and so much more. When you're done reading them all, you can finally say you know Everything®!

**QUESTION**

Answers to common questions

**FACT**

Important snippets of information

**ALERT**

Urgent warnings

**ESSENTIAL**

Quick handy tips

PUBLISHER Karen Cooper

DIRECTOR OF ACQUISITIONS AND INNOVATION Paula Munier

MANAGING EDITOR, EVERYTHING® SERIES Lisa Laing

COPY CHIEF Casey Ebert

ASSISTANT PRODUCTION EDITOR Melanie Cordova

ACQUISITIONS EDITOR Hillary Thompson

ASSOCIATE DEVELOPMENT EDITOR Hillary Thompson

EDITORIAL ASSISTANT Matthew Kane

EVERYTHING® SERIES COVER DESIGNER Erin Alexander

LAYOUT DESIGNERS Erin Dawson, Michelle Roy Kelly, Elisabeth Lariviere, Denise Wallace

Visit the entire Everything® series at www.everything.com

# THE
# EVERYTHING®
# VEGAN BAKING
# COOKBOOK

Lorena Novak Bull, RD

Aadamsmedia

Avon, Massachusetts

*For my Mama and the "Charlie Brown" sandwiches . . .*

Copyright © 2012 by F+W Media, Inc. All rights reserved.
This book, or parts thereof, may not be reproduced
in any form without permission from the publisher; exceptions
are made for brief excerpts used in published reviews.

An Everything® Series Book.
Everything® and everything.com® are registered trademarks of F+W Media, Inc.

Published by Adams Media, a division of F+W Media, Inc.
57 Littlefield Street, Avon, MA 02322 U.S.A.
*www.adamsmedia.com*

ISBN 10: 1-4405-2997-3
ISBN 13: 978-1-4405-2997-9
eISBN 10: 1-4405-3043-2
eISBN 13: 978-1-4405-3043-2

Printed in the United States of America.

10 9 8 7 6 5 4 3 2 1

**Library of Congress Cataloging-in-Publication Data**
is available from the publisher.

This publication is designed to provide accurate and authoritative information with regard to the subject matter covered. It is sold with the understanding that the publisher is not engaged in rendering legal, accounting, or other professional advice. If legal advice or other expert assistance is required, the services of a competent professional person should be sought.
—From a *Declaration of Principles* jointly adopted by a Committee of the American Bar Association and a Committee of Publishers and Associations

Many of the designations used by manufacturers and sellers to distinguish their products are claimed as trademarks. Where those designations appear in this book and Adams Media was aware of a trademark claim, the designations have been printed with initial capital letters.

Contains material adapted and abridged from *The Everything® Vegan Cookbook*, by Jolinda Hackett with Lorena Novak Bull, RD, copyright © 2010 by F+W Media, Inc., ISBN 10: 1-4405-0216-1, ISBN 13: 978-1-4405-0216-3; and *The Everything® Bread Cookbook*, by Leslie Bilderback, CMB, copyright © 2010 by F+W Media, Inc., ISBN 10: 1-4405-0031-2, ISBN 13: 978-1-4405-0031-2.

Photography by Stephen J. Payne

*This book is available at quantity discounts for bulk purchases.*
*For information, please call 1-800-289-0963.*

# Contents

# Introduction

HAVE YOU MISSED THE intoxicating aroma of cinnamon rolls baking in the oven on a chilly morning? Or longed for a flaky tart crust filled with sweet fruit and custard? When considering a vegan lifestyle, you may have thought that the egg- and dairy-free diet wouldn't allow you to enjoy savory breads, decadent brownies, and sweet pies. And you aren't likely to be happy about shelling out $8 for a vegan cupcake, if you're even lucky enough to find a vegan bakery. Baking cakes and cookies without eggs or dairy products? Is that even possible? Yes! Now you can make your own tempting breads and delicious desserts with this incredible cookbook! With 300 irresistible vegan recipes, you will be able to prepare all the treats you've missed, from Old-Fashioned Peanut Butter Cookies to Pineapple Upside-Down Cake.

No matter what reason you chose to go vegan—for health, ethical, spiritual, or earth-friendly reasons—you won't have to sacrifice the baked goods you love. With fresh recipes and step-by-step instructions, you will be like a kid in a candy shop . . . a *vegan* candy shop! Whether you are a seasoned vegan baker or a novice, you will find recipes to suit your needs and experience level. The recipes in this book are designed to give you the opportunity to explore baking everything from simple flatbreads and pies to the more complex yeasted breads and cakes, as well as recipes from a variety of regions and cultures. Try your hand at making fresh flour tortillas from Mexico, socca from France, naan from India, and potato bolani from Afghanistan. Or play around with fermentation—experiment by making a loaf of Sourdough Bread! And don't forget about the sweets! With this guide, you will be baking up a vegan storm in no time. And when that first beautiful loaf of bread comes out of the oven, or that yummy, home-baked vegan cupcake hits your lips, you'll have a smile on your face and a twinkle in your eye!

# Acknowledgments

I wish to thank Danny R. Bull for his encouragement and confidence in my ability to tackle this project, as well as many other major milestone undertakings in my life, from college to martial arts to becoming a registered dietitian. Thank you to my wonderful baking instructor, who showed me that baking is heart AND science! You are missed. My sincere appreciation goes to my associate editor, Hillary Thompson, for her patience, flexibility, and assistance as I learned and worked within this process. I owe a huge debt to my coworkers for their willingness to honestly critique my kitchen conjurings, gaining weight with me along the way. Thank you, Steve "Paynie" Payne, photographer phenom, for making everything look amazing! Finally, my deep gratitude goes to Christopher D. Kirkpatrick, for surrounding me with the environment, support, and laughter necessary to make this pursuit happen.

## CHAPTER 1

# Vegan Baking Basics

Welcome to vegan baking! Vegan baking uses fun, fresh, and innovative methods to create delicious baked goods that are much healthier for you—and for the planet. But how can you create your favorite cakes and breads without eggs and dairy products? The answer lies in vegan baking's simple substitutions and healthy alternatives. This chapter will familiarize you with essential baking ingredients and their vegan substitutes. The trick is to relax. Accept that not every recipe attempt will be met with a round of applause, but know that you'll enjoy the earth-friendly, sinfully sweet process! To help ensure your success, begin by selecting recipes that match your experience and comfort level. Then as your confidence grows, branch out and try making something a little more challenging. And if you already have mad ninja baking skills, jump in with a recipe that's new to you. But whatever you do, have fun in the kitchen!

# An Ingredients Introduction

Understanding ingredients is critical in baking, and even more so in vegan baking! Learning the function of fat in a pie crust, of sugar in a cake, and of flour in a loaf of bread will make all the work that goes into baking a joy. All the major players are given attention here, including flours, sweeteners, and leavening agents, just to mention a few. You will find that some commonly used baking ingredients are not covered. This is because their purpose in baking is related more to taste than actual function. Spices like cinnamon, nutmeg, and cloves, and add-ins like nuts and dried fruits, make baked goods taste and look good, but they tend to be self-explanatory.

# Flours

As a main ingredient in baking, flour has several functions, with different varieties having characteristics that make them well-suited to certain types of recipes. For example, flour provides structure, body, and texture to baked goods through the formation of a protein known as gluten. Strands of gluten trap bubbles of gas and air, providing "lift" as the structure of a cake or bread sets. As bread dough is kneaded, more and more gluten is formed, which makes the dough elastic and gives the finished bread that wonderful chewiness. For that reason, using a flour containing a higher percentage of protein is beneficial for making bread, but probably would not work so well when you're making a cake where a tender crumb is desired. A tough, chewy cake wouldn't taste very pleasant! The protein content of wheat flours ranges from 5–15 percent. Most types of flour also contribute flavor and varying amounts of fiber to baked goods. Flour should be stored in an airtight container.

## Measurements Matter

Measuring flour can be a bit tricky in baking! Flour can be placed into a measuring cup in a manner that causes the flour to be very compact and heavy, or it may be measured into the same cup in such a way that it is light and airy. The difference in the actual amount of flour between the two measurements may be huge even though the same cup was used in both instances, and may seriously affect the final product. Another confounding factor related to flour measurements in baking is that the amount of flour called for in a recipe is often written as a range due to the fact that the amount of humidity in the air on the day that you're baking can affect the stickiness or dryness of your dough. This means that you may have to add more or less flour to achieve the desired texture. These uncertainties may make baking a little—or very—daunting to the inexperienced baker. To understand how a dough should feel, learning firsthand is a great idea. Or you could try taking baking classes at a local culinary school. In lieu of firsthand experience, online videos are also a tremendous resource.

**ALERT**

A friend or relative who is an avid baker would probably love to make a few of their old family recipes with you. And it's a great opportunity to spend time with your mother or grandmother and to record some of those recipes to share with future generations, before they're lost forever.

## All-Purpose Flour

All-purpose flour is a combination of both hard and soft wheat and is available bleached or unbleached. It is the most commonly used flour in the United States, having a medium protein content of about 9–12 percent, which makes it suitable for most baking needs. The bran of the wheat grain is removed during processing, so all-purpose flour is lower in fiber than a whole-grain flour where the bran is retained. The nutritional value of all-purpose flour is reduced by the removal of the germ; therefore most all-purpose flour is enriched by the manufacturer, by adding back a portion of the nutrients that were lost in processing.

## Whole-Wheat Flour

Whole-wheat flour contains all the components of the wheat grain, including the bran, which makes the flour higher in fiber than all-purpose flour. Along with the fiber comes an increased level of fat-soluble vitamins, like vitamin E. Due to the high fiber content, products made with only whole-wheat flour are dense and heavy, but you can replace some of the whole-wheat flour with all-purpose flour for a lighter texture, if desired.

## Bread Flour

The chewy texture of baked goods such as breads and pizza crust is achieved through the development of gluten from proteins in the flour. All-purpose flour will produce an acceptable bread; however, bread flour is designed to have a higher protein content than all-purpose flour, leading to more gluten development and producing a bread with a better texture. The protein content of bread flour is 12–13 percent.

## Pastry Flour

Pastries, pie crusts, and any other baked good that is meant to be tender or flaky may call for pastry flour, which is lower in protein, and therefore gluten, than all-purpose flour. The protein content of pastry flour is 8–9 percent. Recipes using pastry flour usually involve only minimal handling of the dough in order to limit the amount of gluten production, because the more gluten that is produced, the tougher the crust or pastry will be!

## Cake Flour

Cake flour has the lowest protein content of all the wheat flours, at only 5–8 percent, which gives cakes their delicate texture. When cake flour is not available, you can approximate it by the following process. Measure 1 cup of all-purpose flour, and replace 2 tablespoons of the flour with 2 tablespoons cornstarch. The amount of protein in this flour will still be higher than in cake flour, but the added cornstarch will work to inhibit some of the gluten formation. It may be a "work-around," but it works in a pinch!

**ESSENTIAL**

Measuring flour correctly is a major key to success in baking. First, fluff the flour in its container with a spoon. Then lightly spoon the flour into your measuring cup until it is overflowing. Now run the back edge of a knife across the top of the cup to level off the flour. It's that easy!

## Self-Rising Flour

Self-rising flour is a convenient blend of all-purpose flour, baking powder, and salt. Recipes that call for self-rising flour do not usually include additional salt or leavening agents in the ingredient list because it's already combined with the flour. To make your own self-rising flour, add 1 teaspoon baking powder and ¼ teaspoon salt to 1 cup of all-purpose flour.

## Rye Flour

Rye flour is lower in gluten than wheat flour and is commonly used to make breads, such as rye and pumpernickel. Because it has less gluten, rye flour is often combined with all-purpose flour in recipes. Rye gives bread a distinct flavor.

**QUESTION**

**Should I use *organic* flour?**

In general, if you prefer to use organic products, and you can afford them, then use them! Be advised, however, that there may be little difference between conventional products and those labeled as "organic." According to the United States Department of Agriculture (USDA), products labeled "organic" may likely contain a lower level of pesticide contamination than conventionally grown foods; but there is not an absolute guarantee that they are completely free of pesticides, and they are generally more expensive to purchase. Visit *www.nal .usda.gov/afsic/pubs/ofp/ofp.shtml* for more information.

## Spelt and Kamut Flours

Spelt and kamut are related to wheat and are considered to be "ancient grains," as they have remained unmodified and unchanged over hundreds or even thousands of years. These two flours are sometimes thought to be acceptable alternatives to wheat flour in a gluten-free diet; however, this is not the case as they do both actually contain gluten.

## Gluten-Free Flours

For individuals with the unfortunate inability to tolerate gluten, there are several alternative flours available for use in gluten-free baking. They include amaranth, buckwheat, corn, millet, quinoa, rice, sorghum, teff, and wild rice. Oats are also technically gluten-free; however, they are often cross-contaminated with gluten-containing grains during the growth and harvesting processes. Avoid oats or look for labeling on packages of oats that specifies that the contents are gluten-free.

# Granulated Sugar and Other Sweeteners

To paraphrase William Shakespeare, a sugar by any other name would taste as sweet! Granulated sugar is a refined table sugar derived from sugar cane or sugar beets. Sugar is nearly 100 percent sucrose, which is a combination of two simple sugar molecules: glucose and fructose. Sugar is a great, basic sweetener, adding no flavor or aftertaste to food except when caramelized. In baking, sugar also contributes to tenderness, texture, color, and volume. The browning of baked goods is a result of the Maillard reaction, in which the sugar and proteins react chemically with the heat to produce that beautiful, golden brown color that is so pleasing! The quality of sugar to attract moisture allows it to act as a preservative, helping keep foods fresh longer. Nutritionally, sugar provides calories from carbohydrates, but little else of value.

**ALERT**

Granulated sugar is filtered during the refining process through the use of carbon, the source of which may include charred animal bone. If this offends your vegan sensibilities, you can use an unrefined cane sugar, an alternative sweetener such as stevia, or take care to purchase granulated sugar from manufacturers who verify that charred bone is not the source of carbon used in the processing of their product.

### Evaporated Cane Juice

To produce evaporated cane juice, sugar cane is pressed or "juiced" to separate the sweet syrup from the fibrous pulp. This syrup is then allowed to dry until all the moisture has evaporated, leaving behind sucrose crystals that retain some of the molasses and perhaps a small amount of trace minerals that are absent from the more processed granulated table sugar. Use just like sugar. Evaporated cane juice varies little in nutritional value from sugar, providing carbohydrates from sucrose along with a bit of trace minerals.

### Demerara Sugar

Demerara sugar is a large-grain sugar that is considered unrefined, as it is less processed than granulated sugar. In a production process slightly different than that of evaporated cane juice, demerara sugar is made by pressing sugar cane to extract the cane juice, which is then reduced through boiling or steaming to form a thick syrup. The thickened syrup is allowed to dry until large crystals form. Demerara sugar is nutritionally similar to evaporated cane juice, with calories coming from the carbohydrate, sucrose. Use in baking recipes where a large sugar crystal is desired.

### Rapadura and Sucanat Sugars

Two more sweeteners made from evaporated cane juice are rapadura and Sucanat. Both sugars retain molasses. Either may be used like granulated sugar in baked goods; however, the higher molasses and somewhat lower sucrose content may affect the final product, giving foods a strong, distinct flavor and possibly an altered texture.

### Muscovado Sugar

With a coarse crystal texture, dark color, and high molasses content, muscovado sugar is similar to brown sugar. Due to the amount of molasses present, this sugar has a strong, distinct flavor, but may be used in baking like brown sugar.

## Turbinado Raw Sugar

This unrefined sugar is a product of the first pressing of the sugar cane and maintains some of the molasses, making it more flavorful than processed granulated sugar. The crystals of turbinado sugar are large and light brown in color. Turbinado raw sugar has become quite popular and is available in individual packets alongside sugar, honey, and artificial sweeteners for sweetening coffee and tea at many stores and restaurants.

**FACT**

Granulated and powdered sugars attract moisture, which is beneficial for tenderizing the crumb texture of cakes, but not so beneficial for storage, leading to the formation of hard clumps in the sugar. Sugar and powdered sugar are best stored in a dry, cool area, not in the refrigerator. In contrast, brown sugars harden when exposed to the air and should be stored in a cool, moist area in an airtight container.

## Powdered Sugar

Powdered sugar is also known as confectioners' or icing sugar. This sweetener is granulated sugar that has been ground to a fine powder and mixed with cornstarch to keep it flowing and to prevent clumping. Powdered sugar works well in certain types of cookie recipes, makes a beautiful decoration when dusted or stenciled over the top of a sweet bread or cake, and is terrific for making delicious icings and glazes!

## Crystalline Fructose

Fructose is referred to as a monosaccharide, being comprised of a single saccharide molecule, in contrast to the disaccharide, sucrose, or table sugar, which is comprised of two saccharide molecules, including fructose plus glucose. Due to its simpler structure, fructose is about 20–50 percent sweeter than granulated table sugar, so less fructose is needed in a recipe than sugar. This means that when sugar is replaced by the appropriate amount of fructose, the food will have fewer calories! As an ingredient in baked goods, fructose contributes to the Maillard reaction, or the browning of the food, more rapidly than sugar, so foods may need to be shielded with foil in the oven at some point during the baking process in order to avoid excessive browning.

## Liquid Sweeteners

Maple, agave, molasses, and brown rice syrup are all acceptable liquid sweeteners for vegan baking. While the origins of maple and brown rice syrups are obvious, agave and molasses may be less familiar. Molasses is a simply a byproduct of sugar refinement, and agave is the nectar of the succulent plant of the same name. There are many varieties of agave plants; the nectar from blue agave is popular for its high carbohydrate content. Honey is also a wonderful liquid sweetener in baked goods, but many vegans choose not to use honey because of the exploitation of the bees, as well as the cruel treatment that may occur in certain phases of honey production and harvesting. If you are unsure of your own position on the consumption of honey in your diet, do the research and make a decision that suits your lifestyle and philosophy.

**QUESTION**

**What is the difference between "enriched" foods and "fortified" foods?**
The processing of foods sometimes results in a loss of inherent nutrients, resulting in the final product having less nutritional value than the whole food. When wheat grains are milled to produce all-purpose flour, nutrients from the bran and germ are removed, so the manufacturer adds a percentage of what was lost back into the flour, creating an enriched food. Fortified foods are foods in which the manufacturer has added nutrients that are not inherent in the food; for example, adding calcium and vitamin B12 to soymilk, or folic acid to bread.

## Stevia

Stevia is a powerful natural sweetener that is extracted from the stevia plant, dried, and turned into a powder. At around 300 times the sweetness of sugar, stevia has zero carbohydrates and therefore contains zero calories.

Some people detect a distinct aftertaste when a large amount of stevia is used.

## Artificial Sweeteners

People have varied concerns and opinions about the use and safety of artificial or non-nutritive sweeteners, such as aspartame, sucralose, acesulfame potassium, and saccharin. On the positive side, artificial sweeteners are often hundreds of times sweeter to taste than sugar and contain little to no calories. However, according to the Kansas State University Research and Extension, aspartame loses its sweetness when baked, and while saccharin does not lose sweetness, it may leave an unpleasant aftertaste. If you choose to use artificial sweeteners, sucralose, which does not lose its sweetness when heated, is a great option for baking! Sucralose is also equal to sugar by volume, meaning that 1 teaspoon of sucralose has the same sweetening power as 1 teaspoon of sugar, making it simple to use. Sucralose is made when chloride molecules are used to replace three oxygen-hydrogen groups on a molecule of sucrose, or table sugar.

Many people have expressed fears or beliefs that the consumption of these products may cause a plethora of health issues, ranging from headaches to fibromyalgia to multiple sclerosis to cancers; however, the artificial sweeteners mentioned here have undergone rigorous testing regarding their safety for human consumption and have all received approval from the Food and Drug Administration (FDA) for use in the United States. Educate yourself on these products and make an informed choice within your personal comfort zone.

## Fats and Fat Replacements

The amazing Julia Child said, "Fat gives things flavor." She was so right! Of course, she also said, "If you're afraid of butter, use cream," neither of which will be found anywhere in this book, at least not the animal-based versions that Julia referred to! But the truth is that fats are extremely important, not only in helping you feel satiated, but also as flavor carriers and flavor enhancers. This became quite apparent during the diet craze of the 1980s and 1990s, when fats were castigated as the cause of obesity and other health ills and manufacturers raced to produce and market fat-free diet foods. To make up for the lack of fats, manufacturers had to greatly increase the amount of carbohydrates in snack cakes and cookies, mostly in the form of sugars, resulting in foods that were cloyingly sweet and not at all satisfying. This dissatisfaction, paired with the delusion that you could eat as much of these foods as you wanted because they were fat-free, led many consumers to seriously overeat these foods and gain even more weight!

Fats also contribute to browning and function as shorteners in doughs and batters, working to inhibit the formation of long gluten strands, resulting in "shortened" strands. This keeps biscuits and pie crusts nice and tender!

## Margarine

As a replacement for butter in vegan baking, margarine works great in recipes where you want that butter flavor! Be sure to use a margarine that is truly vegan, such as Earth Balance or Nucoa, and use only the stick variety. Tub margarines tend to have a higher ratio of water to fat in them than stick margarines and will therefore not work as well in baking. Another consideration when using margarine is the salt content. When you use margarine in recipes calling for unsalted butter, you may want to reduce or eliminate the amount of salt listed in the ingredients. Many baking recipes will instruct you to use the margarine cold, softened, or melted. Pay close attention to this detail, as it can make or break your recipe! Cold margarine is most often used for baked goods like biscuits, shortbread cookies, and pie crusts where you want a shortened (or tender) dough. Softened or room temperature margarine is usually called for in recipes where it will be creamed with sugar until fluffy, adding air to the batter or dough. For melted margarine, heat margarine until just melted. Cool slightly if margarine becomes very hot, unless the recipe directs you to do otherwise.

## Vegetable Shortening

Unlike butter and margarine, shortening is 100 percent fat, which gives baked goods a lighter texture but contributes no flavor. When a buttery flavor is desired, you will need to use margarine or a combination of margarine and shortening. Margarine has a lower melting point than shortening, which will make cookie dough spread out faster and farther before the cookie bakes than if it was made with shortening, causing a flat cookie. With short-ening, the same cookie dough will spread out less before it sets, and there-fore produce a cookie that is less flat. For that reason, shortening is often the preferred ingredient. Besides being an artificially hydrogenated fat, which is a health no-no, hydrogenated fats may also contain trans fats, which are an even bigger health no-no! Fortunately, there are some brands of vegetable shortening on the market that claim and appear to be trans-fat free, such as Spectrum Naturals.

**ALERT**

Not all products that claim to be trans-fat free are actually free of all trans fats! Read nutrition and ingredient labels carefully. Foods con-taining partially hydrogenated fats will contain trans fats, even though the label says zero grams of trans fats per serving. This is due to the fact that the nutrition labeling requirements allow manufacturers to claim a food is trans-fat free even when the food may actually contain up to .5 grams of trans fat per serving.

## Oils

Oils are carriers of flavor, so your choice of oil can be critical to the final flavor of a recipe. Canola, safflower, and vegetable oil all have a neutral fla-vor making them suitable for your general baking needs. Olive oil may have a relatively mild flavor or a very strong flavor, depending on both the brand and the pressing that the oil came from. In general, the less processed the oil is, the more flavor it will have. Extra-virgin olive oil is bottled after the first pressing, so it usually has a stronger flavor than regular olive oil, which has gone through additional pressings and processing.

## Fat Replacements

When you're attempting to reduce the fat and calories in baked goods, you can often use ⅓ less of the fat called for in the recipe without causing any noticeable difference in the end product. To cut back the fat even fur-ther, you can often replace ½ to ¾ of the fat with puréed fruit or squash, such as prunes, applesauce, apple butter, bananas, sweet potatoes, or pumpkin.

Be sure to take the flavor of the ingredient into consideration when making your decision about which replacement to use. Replacing all of the fat is possible in some recipes, but may result in a texture that is more dense than expected or desired.

# Leavening Agents

Leavening is the process that "gives rise" to breads and cakes. Leavening agents, or leaveners, are ingredients that cause bubbles of either air or carbon dioxide to be formed and incorporated into a dough or batter. These bubbles become trapped within the gluten structure of the cake or bread as it bakes, causing it to rise and creating the holes that become part of the finished texture. Leavening may occur as a result of biological or chemical agents, or through mechanical actions.

## Biological Leavening Agents

Yeasts and bacteria are living microorganisms that are used to leaven baked goods through fermentation and the subsequent release of carbon dioxide gas, which makes the dough rise. Active dry yeast requires proofing prior to being used in a recipe, which involves mixing the yeast with water and waiting 5–10 minutes until the mixture is bubbly. If the mixture doesn't bubble it should be discarded. Instant, rapid rise, and bread machine yeasts do not need to be proofed prior to being added to a recipe. Another type of yeast, fresh yeast, is sold in the form of compressed cakes.

Sourdough breads are made with a fermented sourdough starter, which is a flour and water mixture combined with a commercial sourdough starter product. Some bakers prefer to make their own starter from scratch by exposing a flour and water mixture to the air in order to attract wild yeasts along with the bacteria known as lactobacillus. Sourdough starters must periodically be fed flour and water to keep the culture alive. A properly cared for sourdough starter can live for many years! Other types of biological leavening agents include beer, ginger beer, and kefir.

## Chemical Leavening Agents

The success of chemical leavening is based on the chemical reaction between an acidic and an alkaline compound. A great example of this is the use of baking powder, which contains an acid, and baking soda, which is a base, or alkaline. Baking soda and vinegar can be used to mimic the leavening power of eggs. See the "Egg Replacements" section for more information.

**ESSENTIAL**

There are two types of baking powder commonly used in baking. Single-acting baking powder begins producing gas bubbles as soon as it comes in contact with water. Double-acting baking powder also produces bubbles upon contact with water; however, there is a second reaction when the dough or batter is heated.

## Mechanical Leaveners

Mechanical leavening occurs when air is incorporated into a batter or dough; for example, through the creaming of shortening and sugar until it is fluffy, prior to adding the rest of the ingredients. Steam is also considered to be a mechanical leavener. When a loaf of bread is baked at a high temperature, the water in the dough can quickly turn to steam, causing the dough to expand and rise. This is known as oven spring—the steam causes the bread to "spring" up in the oven!

# Egg Replacements

Eggs have two major purposes in baking: providing structure, or leavening, from the protein in the egg white; and functioning as a binding agent. Eggs are also useful for the texture they can impart to a dish—for example, the silkiness of a custard—as well as for their ability to act as a thickener, and for the color that the yolk can add to a dish. Choose egg replacements based on their ability to provide the desired function. For example, a cake relies on the protein in the egg white to add structure to the cake, so an egg replacement such as a mixture of baking soda and vinegar can be used to provide structure or lift to help give the cake a light texture. Egg replacements are used most successfully in recipes calling for no more than 1–3 eggs.

## Commercial Egg Replacement Products

Health food stores, high-end grocery stores, and many regular grocery stores now sell packaged egg replacements, such as EnerG Egg Replacer and Orgran No Egg Natural Egg Replacer. These products are convenient and easy to use! For most recipes, follow the directions on the box to combine the appropriate amounts of egg replacer and water and allow to sit for a few minutes to thicken before adding to the rest of the ingredients. Read on to learn about several egg replacements. For additional options and tips, go to *www.peta.org/living/vegetarian-living/egg-replacements.aspx*.

## Baking Soda and Vinegar

When eggs are used as a leavening agent, a combination of baking soda and vinegar can do the trick!

One egg = 1 teaspoon baking soda + 1 tablespoon vinegar

The chemical reaction that occurs when baking soda is mixed with vinegar causes the release of bubbles of carbon dioxide gas, which works great for providing lift to a cake or cupcake batter. The baking soda and vinegar mixture often works best when gently stirred into the batter as the final ingredient. The reaction will start right away, so be careful not to stir the batter any more than needed, or too many of the gas bubbles will burst and the cake won't rise! Once mixed, the batter should then be quickly poured into the desired pans or cupcake tins and immediately placed in the preheated oven to bake according to the recipe directions. Use either white distilled vinegar or apple cider vinegar.

## Flaxseeds

1 egg = 1 tablespoon ground flaxseeds + 3 tablespoons water

Flaxseeds become quite thick and gooey when ground into a meal and mixed with water. Flaxseeds will add a nutty flavor, and the ground-up bits may be visible in the finished product, so they may be best used in heartier recipes, such as whole-wheat bread.

### Silken Tofu

1 egg = ¼ cup silken tofu

For quiches and fillings, such as puddings, curds, cheesecake, and custards, silken tofu is a wonderful substitute for eggs! Tofu should be well drained and wiped off with paper towels to remove any excess moisture before being blended for your recipe.

### Bananas and Applesauce

Just as these fruits are good fat replacers, they also function pretty well as egg replacers in sweet recipes. Add an extra ½ teaspoon of baking powder to your recipe to help keep the texture of the baked good lighter. For 1 egg, mash ½ of a ripe banana, or use ¼ cup applesauce.

## Dairy Replacements

When it comes to shopping for vegan dairy products today, there have never been more choices! Dairy products such as milk serve to contribute flavor and moisture to baked goods. Other dairy products used in baking include cream, nonfat dry milk powder, sour cream, cream cheese, yogurt, evaporated milk, sweetened condensed milk, and buttermilk.

### Milk

Milk can be replaced with any number of alternatives, such as soy, almond, hemp, rice, and coconut milks; however, soymilk is the most similar in protein content and other nutrients and will perform more like milk than other substitutes.

### Cream or Half-and-Half

Nondairy creamers, such as Silk and Organic Valley brands, are thick and rich, making them a fantastic substitute for cream!

### Nonfat Dry Milk Powder

There are two options for replacing nonfat dry milk powder in your recipes. First of all, you can purchase a can of soymilk powder, such as the brand Better Than Milk. Use it in the recipe as you would the nonfat dry milk powder. The second option is to first calculate the amount of milk that would be reconstituted from the amount of nonfat dry milk powder required by the recipe, and then replace that amount of liquid from the recipe with the same amount of soymilk. Since the ratio of nonfat dry milk powder to water is usually 1 to 4, if a recipe called for 1 tablespoon of nonfat dry milk powder, that would mean that you would need 4 tablespoons or ¼ cup of water to reconstitute that milk. So you would reduce the amount of liquid in your recipe by ¼ cup and add the ¼ cup soymilk.

### Sour Cream and Cream Cheese

Sour cream is easily replaced with a vegan sour cream. Tofutti has a delicious, cool, and creamy sour cream called Sour Supreme. Tofutti also offers a good cream cheese substitute called Better Than Cream Cheese.

### Yogurt

There are a variety of soy and other nondairy yogurts on the market these days. Look for brands that contain live cultures! As with replacing milk with soymilk, soy yogurt is likely to more closely resemble the nutrition profile of dairy yogurt than some of the other nondairy yogurt options.

### Evaporated Milk and Sweetened Condensed Milk

Evaporated milk is like taking 1 cup of water and adding twice as much dry milk powder as needed to make 1 cup of milk. In other words, it's double strength! To make one cup of vegan evaporated milk, simply measure 1 cup of water and add two times the soymilk powder needed to make 1 cup of regular-strength soymilk.

For sweetened condensed milk, make 1 cup of vegan evaporated milk, as described above. Then add 1½ cups sugar and stir over medium heat until sugar is dissolved.

## Buttermilk

Buttermilk's functions in baking are very important! First of all, buttermilk contributes to leavening. Buttermilk is acidic, and when mixed into a recipe along with baking soda or baking powder, the acid of the buttermilk will react with the alkalinity of the baking soda or baking powder, producing the carbon dioxide bubbles that help baked goods rise. Buttermilk also adds flavor. To make 1 cup of vegan buttermilk, place 1 tablespoon of vinegar or lemon juice in the bottom of a measuring cup. Add enough soymilk to make 1 cup. Stir and allow to thicken or "curdle" for 10–15 minutes. Your "buttermilk" is now ready to use!

# Baking Equipment

Fortunately, you won't need a lot of expensive, specialized equipment for baking. Here is a list of the usual essential items for baking:

- Mixing bowls of various sizes
- Dry and liquid measuring cups
- Measuring spoons
- A whisk
- A handheld electric mixer
- A blender
- A food processor
- Spoons
- Rubber and metal spatulas
- A pastry cutter or a large fork
- Cake and cookie pans
- Baking sheets
- Muffin tins
- Pie pans
- Oven mitts
- Cooking thermometers

There isn't really much else that you absolutely need. If you already own or choose to buy a heavy-duty mixer with a dough hook attachment for making bread, that's great! It makes baking a little easier and quicker. But there is something to be said for getting your hands right down into a dough and kneading it until your muscles ache, and then kneading it some more! It is a very soul-satisfying experience to hold a beautiful, fresh-baked loaf of bread and know that it was created by your hands. Now, get to baking!

**CHAPTER 2**

# Breakfasts

# Pancakes

*For a cool treat, liberally spread fruit jam over leftover pancakes
that have been chilled in the refrigerator. Roll up and enjoy!*

**INGREDIENTS | SERVES 4**

2 cups flour

1 tablespoon baking powder

¼ cup sugar

½ teaspoon salt

Egg replacement equal to 2 eggs

2 cups soymilk

⅓ cup canola oil

1. Sift dry ingredients together in a large bowl. In a separate bowl, whisk egg replacer, soymilk, and oil. Stir wet ingredients into flour mixture, taking care not to overmix.
2. Heat griddle to 375°F, or set to medium-high heat. Pour batter by ¼ cupful onto the ungreased griddle. Cook until golden brown on the bottom and bubbles form across the top, approximately 2–3 minutes. Carefully flip over and cook for another 1–2 minutes.
3. Serve immediately. Store unused portions in the refrigerator in an airtight container.

**PER SERVING** Calories: 489 | Fat: 20 g | Protein: 10 g | Sugar: 16 g | Fiber: 2 g | Carbohydrates: 67 g

# Blueberry Pancakes

*Blueberries out of season? Use frozen blueberries that have been thawed and drained.*

**INGREDIENTS | SERVES 4**

1 tablespoon lemon juice or apple cider vinegar

1 cup soymilk, less 1 tablespoon

1¾ cups all-purpose flour

2 teaspoons baking soda

¼ teaspoon salt

Egg replacement equal to 2 eggs

3 tablespoons vegan margarine, melted

1 cup blueberries

1. Preheat griddle over medium heat. Place lemon juice in a measuring cup and add soymilk up to the 1 cup mark. Allow to sit for 10 minutes.
2. Whisk flour, baking soda, and salt together in a medium bowl. Whisk egg replacement, margarine, and soymilk mixture in a large bowl. Stir dry ingredients into wet ingredients until just mixed.
3. Pour by ¼ cupful onto hot griddle and top each pancake with several blueberries. When pancakes are browned on the bottom and bubbles have formed across the top, approximately 2–3 minutes, flip over and cook for 1–2 more minutes.

**PER SERVING** Calories: 326 | Fat: 10 g | Protein: 8 g | Sugar: 5 g | Fiber: 2 g | Carbohydrates: 51 g

# Oat Waffles

*These are delicious smeared with peanut butter and a dash of cinnamon.*

**INGREDIENTS | SERVES 8**

½ cup whole-wheat flour

½ cup all-purpose flour

1 cup oat flour

4 teaspoons baking powder

¼ teaspoon cinnamon

1 tablespoon rapadura or Sucanat

½ teaspoon salt

Egg replacement equal to 2 eggs

1¾ cups soymilk

3 tablespoons canola or vegetable oil

1 teaspoon vanilla extract

### Keeping Pancakes and Waffles Warm

When cooking for a crowd, keep finished pancakes or waffles warm in a 200°F oven for up to 15 minutes. Stack pancakes on a baking sheet and cover with aluminum foil. Waffles can be placed directly on the oven racks in a single layer.

1. Preheat waffle iron according to manufacturer directions for desired browness.
2. In a large bowl, combine whole-wheat flour, all-purpose flour, oat flour, baking powder, cinnamon, rapadura or Sucanat, and salt. In a separate bowl, mix egg replacement, soymilk, oil, and vanilla extract. Add wet ingredients to flour mixture and stir until just mixed.
3. Pour batter into waffle iron and bake according to manufacturer's directions.
4. Serve immediately. Unused portions may be stored in the refrigerator in an airtight container.

**PER SERVING** Calories: 397 | Fat: 15 g | Protein: 12 g | Sugar: 6 g | Fiber: 4 g | Carbohydrates: 54 g

# Cinnamon Rolls

*Instead of vanilla glaze, try using your favorite cream cheese frosting for an even more decadent treat!*

**INGREDIENTS | YIELDS 24 ROLLS**

1 package active dry yeast

3 tablespoons warm water (110°F–115°F)

½ cup plus 2 teaspoons sugar, divided use

1 cup soymilk

¼ cup vegan margarine

1 teaspoon salt

3 cups all-purpose flour

2 tablespoons vital wheat gluten

Egg replacement equal to 1 egg

2½ tablespoons cinnamon

½ cup raisins

1 batch Vanilla Glaze (see Chapter 14)

1. Combine yeast with warm water and 2 teaspoons sugar in a small bowl. Allow to sit until yeast is bubbly. Heat the soymilk, 2 tablespoons margarine, and salt over low heat until margarine is just melted. Remove from heat and allow to cool.

2. Whisk flour and gluten together in a large bowl. Set aside. Stir the egg replacement into the soymilk mixture, then add the yeast mixture. Add wet ingredients to the flour mixture and stir until a dough begins to form.

3. Turn dough out onto a floured surface and knead for 10 minutes, or until dough is satiny and elastic. Place in a lightly oiled bowl, turning once. Cover and allow to rise until doubled in size, approximately 2 hours. Punch the dough down and allow to rest for 10 minutes. Roll dough out on a floured surface into a 12" × 16" rectangle.

4. Melt remaining 2 tablespoons margarine and spread over dough. Combine cinnamon with remaining ½ cup sugar and sprinkle evenly over dough. Sprinkle raisins evenly over the cinnamon mixture. Begin rolling up dough tightly along the long edge into a log-shaped roll. Cut into 1" slices, and place on a lightly greased baking sheet 1" apart. Cover and allow to rise for approximately 45 minutes.

5. Preheat oven to 350°F. Bake 25–30 minutes, or until golden brown. Allow to cool 10 minutes. Frost with Vanilla Glaze.

**PER SERVING** Calories: 145 | Fat: 2 g | Protein: 3 g | Sugar: 14 g | Fiber: 1 g | Carbohydrates: 29 g

# Johnnycakes

*These are hearty, fried cornmeal cakes. Serve with homemade apple butter.*
*They taste great with margarine and maple syrup, too!*

**INGREDIENTS | SERVES 2**

¼ cup all-purpose flour

¾ cup cornmeal

¾ teaspoon salt

½ teaspoon sugar

1 teaspoon baking powder

½ cup soymilk

Egg replacement equal to 1 egg

1 tablespoon vegan margarine, melted

Water, as needed

1. Preheat griddle over medium heat.
2. Whisk flour, cornmeal, salt, sugar, and baking powder in a medium bowl. Stir in soymilk, egg replacement, and melted margarine. Batter should be fairly thick, but add water to thin, if needed.
3. Drop by tablespoonful onto lightly greased, preheated griddle. Cook 2–3 minutes on each side until golden brown.

**PER SERVING** Calories: 362 | Fat: 7 g | Protein: 8 g | Sugar: 4 g | Fiber: 3 g | Carbohydrates: 65 g

## Homemade Apple Butter

Place 3 pounds of cooking apples that have been cored, peeled, and sliced in a slow cooker. Stir in 3 cups sugar, 2½ teaspoons cinnamon, ½ teaspoon nutmeg, ¼ teaspoon cloves, a dash of salt, ¼ cup apple cider vinegar, and ½ cup water. Cover and cook on high for 3 hours, stirring occasionally. Cook an additional 5–6 hours on low, or until mixture is dark and thick. Press through a sieve for a smoother texture. Freeze or can any apple butter that will not be used within a week or two.

# Monkey Bread

*Also known as pull-apart bread and bubble bread, this sticky, cinnamon treat is great fun to eat!*

**INGREDIENTS | SERVES 12**

1 package active dry yeast

3 tablespoons warm water (110°F–115°F)

¾ cup plus 2 teaspoons sugar, divided use

1 cup soymilk

½ cup plus 2 tablespoons vegan margarine, divided use

1½ teaspoons salt

3 cups all-purpose flour

1 tablespoon vital wheat gluten

Egg replacement equal to 1 egg

2 teaspoons cinnamon

½ cup brown sugar, packed

1. Combine yeast with warm water and 2 teaspoons sugar in a small bowl. Allow to sit until yeast is bubbly. Heat the soymilk, 2 tablespoons margarine, and salt over low heat until margarine is just melted. Remove from heat and allow to cool.

2. Whisk flour and gluten together in a large bowl. Set aside. Stir the egg replacement into the soymilk mixture, then add the yeast mixture. Add wet ingredients to the flour mixture and stir until a dough begins to form.

3. Turn dough out onto a floured surface and knead for 10 minutes, or until dough is satiny and elastic. Place in a lightly oiled bowl, turning once. Cover and allow to rise until doubled in size, approximately 2 hours. Punch the dough down and allow to rest for 10 minutes.

4. Combine remaining ¾ cup sugar and cinnamon in a large bowl. Cut dough into 1" pieces. Toss dough pieces with cinnamon mixture to thoroughly coat. Layer dough in a lightly greased bundt pan, being careful to fill in any gaps. Cover bundt pan with plastic wrap and allow to rise another 1–2 hours until dough is 1"–2" from the top of the pan.

5. Preheat oven to 350°F. Combine brown sugar and remaining ½ cup margarine in a medium saucepan and heat over medium-high heat until margarine is melted and brown sugar is dissolved. Pour evenly over the top of the dough.

6. Bake at 350°F for 30–35 minutes. Cool 10 minutes before serving.

**PER SERVING** Calories: 294 | Fat: 10 g | Protein: 5 g | Sugar: 22 g | Fiber: 1 g | Carbohydrates: 47 g

# Cocoa Crepes with Strawberries and Bananas

*Now you can enjoy chocolate and fruit . . . for breakfast!*

**INGREDIENTS | SERVES 4**

½ cup soymilk

¾ cup water

¼ cup vegan margarine, melted

½ teaspoon vanilla extract

2 tablespoons agave syrup

1 cup all-purpose flour

2 tablespoons unsweetened cocoa powder

1 tablespoon sugar

¼ teaspoon cinnamon

Pinch salt

1 cup strawberries, hulled and sliced

1 cup bananas, sliced

⅓ cup chocolate syrup

Powdered sugar for dusting, optional

1. Whisk soymilk, water, margarine, vanilla extract, agave, flour, cocoa powder, sugar, cinnamon, and salt together in a large bowl. Cover and chill overnight.
2. Lightly grease a crepe pan or small 5"–6" skillet, and heat over medium heat. Pour 3 tablespoons of batter into the pan and tilt to evenly distribute. Cook for 1 minute, or until batter sets. Flip and cook for 1 more minute.
3. Stack finished crepes with parchment paper between them. To serve, evenly divide fruit and fill each crepe, drizzle with chocolate syrup, and roll up. Dust with powdered sugar, as desired.

**PER SERVING** Calories: 388 | Fat: 13 g | Protein: 6 g | Sugar: 23 g | Fiber: 4 g | Carbohydrates: 57 g

## Creative Crepes Bar

For your next brunch, try a crepes bar where your guests can build crepe creations of their choosing. Stock your bar with plain, sweet, and chocolate crepes along with a variety of fillings and toppings. Offer fresh fruit, fruit sauces, and vegan whipped topping for the sweet and chocolate crepes. Whip up some quick veggie, herb, and tofu stir-fry combinations for the plain crepes.

# Blueberry Breakfast Cake

*This is a moist, sweet cake—perfect for brunch!*

**INGREDIENTS | SERVES 8**

¼ cup plus 3 tablespoons vegan margarine, softened, divided use

1¼ cups sugar, divided use

Egg replacement equal to 1 egg

1 teaspoon vanilla extract

2⅓ cups all-purpose flour, divided use

2 teaspoons baking powder

1 teaspoon salt, divided use

½ cup soymilk

2½ cups blueberries

1. Preheat oven to 375°F.
2. Cream ¼ cup margarine, ¾ cup sugar, and egg replacement in a large bowl. Stir in vanilla extract. In a separate bowl, whisk 2 cups flour, baking powder, and ½ teaspoon salt. Add flour mixture to wet ingredients in batches, alternating with soymilk. Mix well. Fold in blueberries. Spread into a greased 8" × 8" baking pan.
3. For the topping, combine remaining ½ cup sugar, ⅓ cup flour, ½ teaspoon salt, and 3 tablespoons margarine. Mix well and sprinkle evenly over top.
4. Bake 20–25 minutes, or until a toothpick comes out clean when inserted into the center of the cake.

**PER SERVING** Calories: 377 | Fat: 10 g | Protein: 5 g | Sugar: 36 g | Fiber: 2 g | Carbohydrates: 67 g

# Fruity Skillet Bake

*You'll love this moist cake filled with peaches. It's like bread pudding!*
*Try making this with a mixture of fruits, such as peaches, pears, and raisins.*

**INGREDIENTS | SERVES 8**

¼ cup vegan margarine

½ cup whole-wheat flour

½ cup all-purpose flour

½ cup sugar

1 teaspoon baking powder

⅛ teaspoon salt

1 cup soymilk

2 (15-ounce) cans sliced peaches, drained

1. Preheat oven to 450°F.
2. Melt margarine over medium heat in a 10" cast-iron skillet. In a large bowl, whisk together whole-wheat flour, all-purpose flour, sugar, baking powder, and salt.
3. With an electric mixer on medium speed, beat soymilk into dry ingredients for 2 minutes. Pour batter into skillet and arrange sliced peaches on top.
4. Place skillet in oven and bake for 20–25 minutes, or until golden brown. Slice into wedges to serve.

**PER SERVING** Calories: 276 | Fat: 6 g | Protein: 3 g | Sugar: 37 g | Fiber: 2 g | Carbohydrates: 54 g

# Buttermylk Pancakes

*A sprinkling of vegan chocolate chips in the batter will thrill kids of all ages!*

**INGREDIENTS | SERVES 6**

1¾ cups soymilk

1 tablespoon plus 2¼ teaspoons lemon juice

2 cups all-purpose flour

2 teaspoons baking powder

1 teaspoon baking soda

½ teaspoon salt

2 tablespoons sugar

Egg replacement equal to 2 eggs

½ cup canola oil

1. Preheat griddle over medium heat. Combine soymilk and lemon juice in a small bowl. Allow to sit for 10 minutes.
2. Whisk flour, baking powder, baking soda, salt, and sugar together in a large bowl. In a separate bowl, stir together soymilk mixture, egg replacement, and oil. Stir soymilk mixture into dry ingredients until just mixed.
3. Pour by ¼ cupful onto lightly greased, preheated griddle. When bottom of pancakes have browned and bubbles have formed across the top, approximately 2–3 minutes, flip over and cook an additional 1–2 minutes.

**PER SERVING** Calories: 361 | Fat: 19 g | Protein: 6 g | Sugar: 6 g | Fiber: 1 g | Carbohydrates: 40 g

# Maple-Glazed Doughnuts

*Maple-Glazed Doughnuts are sugary and fried . . . perfect for that "hate-my-diet" moment!*

**INGREDIENTS | SERVES 8**

2 cups all-purpose flour

½ cup sugar

2 teaspoons baking soda

½ teaspoon salt

Egg replacement equal to 1 egg

½ cup applesauce

½ cup soymilk

1½ tablespoons vegetable shortening, melted

Canola or vegetable oil for frying

1 batch Maple Glaze (see Chapter 14)

1. In a large bowl, whisk flour, sugar, baking soda, and salt together. In a separate bowl, whisk egg replacement, applesauce, and soymilk. Stir wet ingredients into flour mixture until smooth. Add shortening and mix well.
2. Pour oil 4" deep in a deep pot and heat to 375°F, over medium to medium-high heat.
3. Carefully drop batter by the tablespoon, a few at a time, into the hot oil and fry until golden brown, about 2–3 minutes, turning once. Drain on paper towels.
4. While still warm, dip in Maple Glaze on one side and set on a wire rack to cool. Cool completely and store in an airtight container.

**PER SERVING** Calories: 366 | Fat: 12 g | Protein: 4 g | Sugar: 37 g | Fiber: 1 g | Carbohydrates: 62 g

# Mexican Griddle Cakes

*Mexican Griddle Cakes are savory, spicy pancakes made with corn and chiles.*
*Try roasted poblano (sometimes called pasilla) chiles for wonderful flavor without a lot of heat.*

**INGREDIENTS | SERVES 4**

1½ cups soymilk, less 1½ tablespoons

1½ tablespoons lemon juice

1 cup all-purpose flour

¼ cup cornmeal

¼ cup masa harina

1 teaspoon baking powder

½ teaspoon baking soda

1 teaspoon sugar

½ teaspoon salt

Egg replacement equal to 1 egg

½ onion, minced

1 clove garlic, minced

3 scallions, thinly sliced

1 tablespoon cilantro, minced

1½ cups corn, thawed if frozen

1–2 tablespoons roasted green chile pepper, peeled, seeded, and minced

Diced avocado, to taste, optional

Vegan sour cream, to taste, optional

1. Preheat griddle over medium heat. Combine soymilk and lemon juice in a small bowl and allow to sit for 10 minutes.
2. Whisk together flour, cornmeal, masa harina, baking powder, baking soda, sugar, and salt in a large bowl. In a separate bowl, combine the soymilk mixture and egg replacement.
3. Stir the soymilk mixture into the flour mixture until just mixed. Fold in the onion, garlic, scallions, cilantro, corn, and chile.
4. Pour batter by ¼ cupful onto the hot, lightly greased griddle. When pancakes are browned on the bottom and bubbles have formed across the top (approximately 2–3 minutes) flip over and cook another 1–2 minutes. Serve with diced avocado and a dollop of vegan sour cream, if desired.

**PER SERVING** Calories: 391 | Fat: 3 g | Protein: 12 g | Sugar: 7 g | Fiber: 5 g | Carbohydrates: 80 g

## Roasting Bell Peppers and Chile Peppers

Place whole bell peppers and chiles directly on a gas burner over medium-high flame for about 1 minute until skin blisters and chars. Using tongs, turn peppers over and repeat until all sides are charred. Immediately place peppers in a paper bag, close the bag, and allow peppers to sit for 15 minutes. Remove peppers from the bag and remove the peel, which will come off quite easily. Cut off the stems and remove seeds. For extra heat, leave seeds in chile peppers! The peppers and chiles are now ready to use.

# Walnut Coffee Cake

*Cinnamon and nuts are in every bite of this tasty breakfast favorite!*

**INGREDIENTS | SERVES 10**

¾ cup sugar

¼ cup vegetable shortening

½ cup soymilk

1 teaspoon vanilla extract

1½ cups plus 1 tablespoon all-purpose flour, divided use

2 teaspoons baking powder

¼ teaspoon salt

Egg replacement equal to 2 eggs

2 tablespoons vegan margarine

½ cup brown sugar, packed

1 teaspoon cinnamon

1 cup walnuts, chopped

1. Preheat oven to 350°F.
2. In a large bowl, cream sugar and shortening with an electric mixer until fluffy. Add soymilk and vanilla extract and mix well. In a separate bowl, whisk together flour, baking powder, and salt. Add flour mixture to the wet ingredients and beat for 2 minutes. Add egg replacement and beat for 2 more minutes. Spread half of batter in a greased and floured 9" cake pan.
3. In a medium bowl, combine margarine, brown sugar, cinnamon, and walnuts. Sprinkle half the walnut mixture over the top of the batter in the pan. Add remaining batter and sprinkle with the rest of the walnut mixture on top.
4. Bake for 30 minutes, or until a toothpick comes out clean when inserted into the center of the cake.

**PER SERVING** Calories: 296 | Fat: 15 g | Protein: 3 g | Sugar: 26 g | Fiber: 1 g | Carbohydrates: 38 g

# Apple Fritters

*These irresistible fritters are crunchy on the outside and tender on the inside.*

## INGREDIENTS | SERVES 4

¾ cup all-purpose flour

¼ cup whole-wheat flour

¼ cup sugar

1½ teaspoons baking powder

¾ teaspoon salt

1½ teaspoons cinnamon

Pinch nutmeg

⅓ cup plus 2 teaspoons soymilk, divided use

Egg replacement equal to 1 egg

1 cup apple, diced small

Canola oil, for frying

½ cup powdered sugar

1. In a large bowl, whisk together the flours, sugar, baking powder, salt, cinnamon, and nutmeg. Stir in ⅓ cup soymilk and egg replacement until just mixed. Fold in apples. Pour oil 1½" deep in a deep skillet and heat to 375°F, over medium-high heat.

2. Carefully place dough in oil by heaping tablespoonful, a few at a time. Cook until browned, about 2 minutes. Flip and continue cooking on other side for another 1–2 minutes until browned. Drain excess oil from fritters on paper towels.

3. Mix powdered sugar with 1–2 teaspoons soymilk and drizzle over apple fritters while still warm.

**PER SERVING** Calories: 367 | Fat: 15 g | Protein: 5 g | Sugar: 29 g | Fiber: 2 g | Carbohydrates: 55 g

## Storing Doughnuts

Unfilled doughnuts should be kept in a plastic bag or wrapped in foil or plastic wrap. They will keep for up to 2 days at room temperature, up to 1 week in the refrigerator, and up to 3 months in the freezer. Use a freezer bag when freezing doughnuts. Filled doughnuts will keep in the refrigerator for up to 2 days, but should not be frozen or left at room temperature.

# Raised Doughnuts

*These doughnuts are lighter and fluffier than a cake doughnut.*
*It's well worth the time it takes for the dough to rise!*

**INGREDIENTS | MAKES APPROXIMATELY 2 DOZEN DOUGHNUTS**

1 package active dry yeast
½ cup water, lukewarm
¼ cup vegetable shortening
½ cup sugar
½ cup boiling water
⅓ cup soymilk, warmed
Egg replacement equal to 2 eggs
½ teaspoon salt
4 cups all-purpose flour
Canola or vegetable oil for frying
1 batch Vanilla Glaze (see Chapter 14)

1. Stir yeast into ½ cup lukewarm water in a large bowl and set aside for 5 minutes. In a medium bowl, stir shortening and sugar into the ½ cup boiling water until dissolved. Add the soymilk, egg replacement, and yeast mixture to the sugar mixture.
2. Mix in salt and 2 cups flour. Gradually mix in additional flour until you have a soft dough. Place dough on a floured surface and knead until smooth, approximately 5 minutes. Place in a lightly greased bowl, cover, and set aside for 1 hour, until doubled in size.
3. Punch the dough down and place on a lightly floured surface. Roll dough to ½" thick and cut out 2"–3" circles with a doughnut cutter or the rim of a drinking glass. Place dough circles on parchment paper and allow to rise for 1 hour.
4. Pour oil 4" deep in a deep pot and heat to 375°F over medium to medium-high heat. Fry doughnuts, a few at a time, turning once, until golden brown, about 2 minutes per side. Drain on paper towels.
5. While doughnuts are still warm, dip in Vanilla Glaze on one side and place on wire racks to cool. Cool completely and store in an airtight container.

**PER 1 DOUGHNUT** Calories: 279 | Fat: 16 g | Protein: 2 g | Sugar: 15 g | Fiber: 1 g | Carbohydrates: 31 g

# Sour Cream Coffee Cake

*Sour cream makes this cake rich and moist!*

**INGREDIENTS | SERVES 8**

2 cups all-purpose flour, divided use

½ cup sugar

1 teaspoon baking powder

½ teaspoon baking soda

½ teaspoon salt

2 teaspoons cinnamon, divided use

Egg replacement equal to 1 egg

½ cup vegan sour cream

⅓ cup canola oil

1 teaspoon vanilla extract

½ cup light brown sugar, packed

¼ cup vegan margarine, cold and cut into small pieces

1. Preheat oven to 350°F.
2. In a large bowl, whisk together 1½ cups flour, sugar, baking powder, baking soda, salt, and 1 teaspoon cinnamon. In a separate bowl, combine egg replacement, sour cream, oil, and vanilla extract with an electric mixer on low speed until smooth.
3. Add sour cream mixture to dry ingredients and mix until just blended. Spread batter in a greased 8" × 8" pan.
4. In a medium bowl, add the remaining ½ cup flour, 1 teaspoon cinnamon, brown sugar, and margarine. Cream with a large fork or pastry cutter until combined and crumbly. Sprinkle evenly over the top of the batter.
5. Bake 30–35 minutes or until a toothpick comes out clean when inserted into the center of the cake.

**PER SERVING** Calories: 392 | Fat: 17 g | Protein: 4 g | Sugar: 27 g | Fiber: 1 g | Carbohydrates: 56 g

# Chocolate Doughnuts

*If you like nuts on your chocolate doughnuts, allow glaze to harden for a moment and then press the glazed side of the doughnuts into crushed peanuts.*

### INGREDIENTS | SERVES 8

2 cups all-purpose flour

½ cup sugar

2 teaspoons baking powder

½ teaspoon salt

¼ cup unsweetened cocoa powder

Egg replacement equal to 1 egg

¾ cup applesauce

½ cup soymilk

2 tablespoons vegetable shortening, melted

Canola or vegetable oil for frying

½ cup Chocolate Ganache (see Chapter 14)

## Brown Sugar Outage?

Next time you're out of brown sugar, try making your own by combining 1 cup sugar with 2 tablespoons molasses or dark corn syrup! Who knew it was so simple?

1. In a large bowl, whisk flour, sugar, baking powder, salt, and cocoa powder together. In a separate bowl, whisk egg replacement, applesauce, and soymilk. Stir wet ingredients into flour mixture until smooth. Add shortening and mix well.
2. Pour oil 4" deep into a deep pot and heat to 375°F, over medium to medium-high heat.
3. Carefully drop batter by tablespoon into hot oil, a few at a time, and fry until golden brown, 1–2 minutes per side, turning once. Drain on paper towels. Place on wire racks to cool completely.
4. Lightly dip doughnuts in Chocolate Ganache on one side. Place doughnuts ganache-side up and allow ganache to set before serving. Store in an airtight container.

**PER SERVING** Calories: 352 | Fat: 17 g | Protein: 5 g | Sugar: 20 g | Fiber: 3 g | Carbohydrates: 48 g

# Pear Coffee Cake

*This breakfast cake also makes a great dessert topped with vegan whipped topping!*

**INGREDIENTS | SERVES 8**

1¾ cups all-purpose flour, divided use

2¼ teaspoons baking powder

½ cup sugar

¼ teaspoon salt

2 teaspoons cinnamon, divided use

Egg replacement equal to 1 egg

¼ cup vegetable shortening, melted

½ cup soymilk

½ teaspoon vanilla extract

¼ teaspoon almond extract

2 ripe pears, cored and chopped

½ cup light brown sugar, packed

¼ cup vegan margarine, cold and cut into small pieces

1. Preheat oven to 350°F.
2. In a large bowl, whisk together 1¼ cups flour, baking powder, sugar, salt, and 1 teaspoon cinnamon. In a separate bowl, combine egg replacement, shortening, soymilk, and vanilla and almond extracts. Blend on low speed with an electric mixer until smooth. Add wet ingredients to flour mixture and beat on low speed for 1 minute until well mixed. Fold in chopped pears. Spread batter in a greased 8" × 8" pan.
3. In a medium bowl, combine remaining ½ cup flour, 1 teaspoon cinnamon, brown sugar, and margarine. Cream with large fork or pastry cutter until crumbly. Spread in an even layer over the batter.
4. Bake for 30–35 minutes or until a toothpick comes out clean when inserted into the center of the cake.

**PER SERVING** Calories: 342 | Fat: 12 g | Protein: 3 g | Sugar: 31 g | Fiber: 2 g | Carbohydrates: 56 g

# Pecan Rolls

*Here you'll find all the sticky, nutty goodness you've wished for.
Even Princess Leia would want these buns!*

**INGREDIENTS | SERVES 16**

1 package active dry yeast

3 tablespoons warm water, (120°F–130°F)

¼ cup plus 2 teaspoons sugar, divided use

1 cup soymilk

¾ cup vegan margarine, divided use

1 teaspoon salt

3 cups all-purpose flour

2 tablespoons vital wheat gluten

Egg replacement equal to 1 egg

½ cup brown sugar, packed

2 cups pecans, coarsely chopped

2½ teaspoons cinnamon

### Maple-Spiced Pecans

Maple-Spiced Pecans are a great snack for the holidays . . . or any day! In a medium bowl, stir together 2 cups pecan halves, 2 teaspoons melted coconut oil, 4 table-spoons maple syrup, 1 teaspoon salt, ½ teaspoon cinnamon, and ¼ teaspoon each of nutmeg and cloves. Pour nuts in a single layer on a baking sheet and bake at 350°F for 15 minutes, or until browned. Shake or stir nuts every 5 minutes. Store in an air-tight container.

1. Combine yeast with warm water and 2 teaspoons sugar in a small bowl. Allow to sit until yeast is bubbly. Heat the soymilk, 2 tablespoons margarine, and salt over low heat until margarine is just melted. Remove from heat and allow to cool.

2. Whisk flour and gluten together in a large bowl. Set aside. Stir the egg replacement into the soymilk mixture, then add the yeast mixture. Add wet ingredients to the flour mixture and stir until a dough begins to form.

3. Turn dough out onto a floured surface and knead for 10 minutes, or until dough is satiny and elastic. Place in a lightly oiled bowl, turning once. Cover and allow to rise until doubled in size, approximately 2 hours. Punch the dough down and allow to rest for 10 minutes. Roll dough out on a floured surface into a 9" × 16" rectangle.

4. Spread entire surface of dough with 2 tablespoons margarine. Mix the remaining ¼ cup sugar and cinnamon together and sprinkle evenly over the dough. Begin rolling up dough tightly along the long edge into a log-shaped roll. Cut into 1" slices.

5. Melt remaining ½ cup margarine in a 9" × 13" pan. Sprinkle brown sugar and pecan pieces evenly in the pan. Place pecan rolls over pecans in the pan. Cover and allow to rise for approximately 45 minutes, until doubled in size.

6. Preheat oven to 375°F. Bake 25–30 minutes. Immediately invert onto a serving platter or cookie sheet.

**PER SERVING** Calories: 307 | Fat: 19 g | Protein: 5 g | Sugar: 11 g | Fiber: 2 g | Carbohydrates: 31 g

# Crepes with Stewed Fruit

*Thin pancakes topped with soft, delicious fruits are perfect for a
light breakfast in the garden on a lovely spring morning!*

**INGREDIENTS | SERVES 8**

½ cup soymilk

2 cups water, divided use

¼ cup vegan margarine, melted

½ teaspoon vanilla extract

1 cup plus 2 tablespoons sugar, divided use

1 cup all-purpose flour

¼ teaspoon cinnamon

Pinch salt

1 tablespoon orange zest

½ cup apple, peeled, cored, and cut into 1" chunks

½ cup peaches, pitted, peeled, and cut into 1" chunks

½ cup dried plums, pitted and halved

½ cup dried apricots, quartered

1. Whisk soymilk, ½ cup water, margarine, vanilla extract, 2 tablespoons sugar, flour, cinnamon, and salt together in a large bowl. Cover and chill overnight.
2. Lightly grease a crepe pan or a small 5"–6" skillet, and heat over medium heat. Pour 3 tablespoons of batter into the pan and tilt to evenly distribute. Cook for 1 minute, or until batter sets. Flip and cook for 1 more minute. Stack finished crepes with parchment paper between them.
3. To make stewed fruit, bring remaining 1 cup sugar and 1½ cups water to a boil in a large saucepan. Add orange zest and fruits, heat to boiling again, then reduce heat and simmer for 20–30 minutes until fruit is soft and liquid has become syrupy.
4. To serve, roll each crepe and place on plate. Spoon ¼ cup of stewed fruit over the top.

**PER SERVING** Calories: 280 | Fat: 6 g | Protein: 3 g | Sugar: 39 g | Fiber: 2 g | Carbohydrates: 56 g

## Fruit Compote

The word "compote" is a French word meaning "mixture" and is commonly used in the culinary world as the term to describe a mixture of fruits that are stewed in a syrup. Fruit compote may consist of a combination of fresh or dried fruits, sugar, spices, and sometimes wine or other alcoholic beverages, which is cooked until the fruits are soft and the liquid has a thick syrup- or jam-like consistency.

# Biscuits and Scones

# Quick Biscuits

*Hot, delicious biscuits in a half hour or less!*
*Split them open while they're warm and spread fruit jam in the middle.*

**INGREDIENTS | SERVES 6**

2 cups all-purpose flour

1 tablespoon baking powder

¼ teaspoon salt

6 tablespoons vegan margarine or shortening, cold

¾ cup soymilk

## Soy, Almond, and Rice Milks

Though soymilk is the most common, vegans can also choose from almond and rice milk substitutes. Rice milk is thinner and sweeter than soymilk, and almond milk has a grainier texture. For baking, soy or almond milk is best, and in savory casseroles and sauces, use soymilk for its neutral flavor. Choose brands fortified with vitamin D, B12, and calcium, particularly if you've got kids.

1. Preheat oven to 425°F.
2. In a large bowl, whisk together flour, baking powder, and salt. Cut cold margarine into small pieces and using a pastry cutter or large fork, cut the margarine into the flour until you have pea-sized pieces of margarine.
3. Stir the soymilk into the flour mixture, being careful not to overmix. Form the dough into a ball with your hands, but don't knead.
4. Place dough on a lightly floured surface and roll out into a sheet about ¼" thick. Use a biscuit cutter or the rim of glass to cut dough into rounds. Arrange dough rounds in an ungreased 9" round cake pan so that they are just touching. Bake 13–15 minutes until golden brown.

**PER SERVING** Calories: 264 | Fat: 12 g | Protein: 5 g | Sugar: 1 g | Fiber: 1 g | Carbohydrates: 33 g

# Raisin Scones

*Scones are similar in taste and texture to biscuits, but with more class!*
*Serve for breakfast or for an afternoon tea break.*

**INGREDIENTS | SERVES 12**

1¾ cups plus 1 teaspoon all-purpose flour, divided use

1½ teaspoons cinnamon

1 cup raisins

1 tablespoon baking powder

¼ cup sugar

¼ teaspoon salt

⅓ cup vegan margarine, cold and cut into pieces

Egg replacement equal to 2 eggs

3 tablespoons vegan creamer

2 tablespoons soymilk (optional)

Additional cinnamon and sugar to sprinkle on top (optional)

1. Preheat oven to 400°F.
2. In a small bowl, combine 1 teaspoon flour, cinnamon, and raisins. Set aside. In a large bowl, whisk together 1¾ cups flour, baking powder, sugar, and salt. Using a pastry cutter or large fork, cut cold margarine into flour mixture until margarine is pea-sized.
3. Add egg replacement, creamer, and raisin mixture, stirring until just mixed. Place dough on a floured surface and divide into 2 equal pieces. Form each piece into a 6" disk, ¾" thick. Place on an ungreased baking sheet and cut into 6 wedges. If desired, brush with soymilk and sprinkle with additional cinnamon and sugar.
4. Bake 13–15 minutes, until lightly browned.

**PER SERVING** Calories: 170 | Fat: 5 g | Protein: 2 g | Sugar: 11 g | Fiber: 1 g | Carbohydrates: 29 g

# Blueberry Scones

*Blueberries give these scones delightful bursts of juicy, sweet flavor.*

**INGREDIENTS | SERVES 12**

1¾ cups plus 2 teaspoons all-purpose flour, divided use

1 teaspoon cinnamon

1 cup blueberries

1 tablespoon baking powder

¼ cup sugar

¼ teaspoon salt

⅓ cup vegan margarine, cold and cut into pieces

Egg replacement equal to 2 eggs

3 tablespoons vegan creamer

2 tablespoons soymilk (optional)

Additional cinnamon and sugar to sprinkle on top (optional)

1. Preheat oven to 400°F.
2. In a small bowl, combine 2 teaspoons flour, cinnamon, and blueberries. Set aside. In a large bowl. whisk together 1¾ cups flour, baking powder, sugar, and salt. Using a pastry cutter or large fork, cut cold margarine into flour mixture until margarine is pea-sized.
3. Add egg replacement, creamer, and blueberry mixture, stirring until just mixed. Place dough on a floured surface and divide into 2 equal pieces. Form each piece into a 6" disk, ¾" thick. Place on an ungreased baking sheet and cut into 6 wedges. If desired, brush with soymilk and sprinkle with additional cinnamon and sugar.
4. Bake 13–15 minutes, until lightly browned.

**PER SERVING** Calories: 140 | Fat: 5 g | Protein: 2 g | Sugar: 5 g | Fiber: 1 g | Carbohydrates: 21 g

## A Cup of Tea for Your Health!

Have you heard the news that tea is good for you? Studies have shown that there may be many health benefits from the regular consumption of both green and black teas. This is due to the flavonoids in tea, which may play a role in reducing heart disease, reducing stroke and cancer risk, lowering cholesterol, and boosting the immune system, as well as a whole host of other health benefits. The types of flavonoids differ between green and black teas, so drink both! Either hot or iced, tea is a great beverage to enjoy with scones, muffins, and sweet desserts.

# Sweet Potato Biscuits

*Light, fluffy, and slightly sweet, these biscuits are a great addition to your vegan Thanksgiving table. Serve them warm with vegan margarine, or use to dip in your favorite stews.*

### INGREDIENTS | SERVES 8

⅔ cup soymilk

2 teaspoons lemon juice or white vinegar

1¾ cups all-purpose flour

2 tablespoons sugar

2½ teaspoons baking powder

½ teaspoon baking soda

1 teaspoon salt

6 tablespoons vegan margarine, cold and cut into pieces

¾ cup mashed cooked sweet potato, cold

2–3 tablespoons vegan margarine, melted

1. Preheat oven to 425°F. Combine soymilk and lemon juice in a measuring cup and allow to sit for 10 minutes. In a large bowl, whisk flour, sugar, baking powder, baking soda, and salt. Using a pastry cutter or large fork, cut cold margarine into the mixture until it forms pea-sized pieces.
2. In a separate bowl, whisk together sweet potato and soymilk mixture. Combine wet ingredients with flour mixture until just mixed. Knead slightly to shape into a disk, then pat dough to a 1" thickness. Using a 2" biscuit cutter or the rim of a drinking glass, cut dough into rounds and place 2" apart on a lightly greased baking sheet. Brush tops with melted margarine.
3. Bake 22–24 minutes, or until golden brown.

**PER SERVING** Calories: 243 | Fat: 12 g | Protein: 4 g | Sugar: 5 g | Fiber: 2 g | Carbohydrates: 30 g

# Buttermylk Biscuits

*These biscuits are made tender by the combination of soymilk and lemon juice, which acts like buttermilk.*

### INGREDIENTS | MAKES 20 BISCUITS

1 cup soymilk

1 tablespoon lemon juice

⅓ cup vegetable shortening

1 tablespoon sugar

1⅔ cups all-purpose flour

1½ teaspoons salt

¼ teaspoon cream of tartar

½ teaspoon baking soda

1. Preheat oven to 475°F. Combine soymilk and lemon juice in a small bowl and allow to sit for 10 minutes. In a large bowl, cream shortening and sugar together.
2. In a separate bowl, whisk together flour, salt, cream of tartar, and baking soda. Stir flour mixture, alternately with soymilk, into the creamed mixture. Mix well.
3. Turn dough onto a lightly floured surface and roll to ½" thickness. Using a biscuit cutter or the rim of a drinking glass, cut rounds and place on an ungreased baking sheet. Bake for 10 minutes, or until browned.

**PER 1 BISCUIT** Calories: 74 | Fat: 4 g | Protein: 1 g | Sugar: 1 g | Fiber: 0 g | Carbohydrates: 9 g

# Irish Scones

*These scones are lovely served with fresh fruit for breakfast,
or pair with your afternoon tea for a delicious pick-me-up.*

**INGREDIENTS | SERVES 16**

1 cup soymilk, plus more as desired

1 tablespoon lemon juice

2¾ cups all-purpose flour

2 teaspoons baking powder

½ teaspoon salt

½ cup olive oil

½ cup sugar

Egg replacement equal to 1 egg

1. Preheat oven to 500°F.
2. Combine 1 cup soymilk and lemon juice in a small bowl and allow to sit for 10 minutes.
3. In a large bowl, whisk together flour, baking powder, and salt. In a separate bowl, whisk together soymilk mixture, olive oil, sugar, and egg replacement. Add wet ingredients to flour mixture.
4. Place dough on a lightly floured surface and quickly roll out to an 8" × 10" rectangle, about 1½" thick. Using a biscuit cutter or the rim of a drinking glass, cut the dough into rounds and place on an ungreased baking sheet 1" apart.
5. Refrigerate scones for 15 minutes. Remove from the refrigerator and brush tops with additional soymilk, if desired.
6. Place the baking sheet in the oven and reduce the temperature to 425°F. Bake 15–18 minutes. Cool on baking sheet for 10 minutes, then transfer to a cooling rack.

**PER SERVING** Calories: 169 | Fat: 7 g | Protein: 3 g | Sugar: 7 g | Fiber: 1 g | Carbohydrates: 24 g

# Dilled Herb Scones

*Dilled Herb Scones are a fresh twist to the classic plain scone. They are wonderful to serve with more savory breakfasts, or as an appetizer spread with vegan cream cheese.*

**INGREDIENTS | SERVES 12**

2 cups all-purpose flour

1 tablespoon sugar

3 teaspoons baking powder

½ teaspoon salt

¼ cup flat-leaf parsley, chopped

1 tablespoon fresh dill weed, chopped

⅓ cup vegan margarine, cold and cut into pieces

½ cup soymilk

Egg replacement equal to 1 egg

1. Preheat oven to 400°F.
2. In a large bowl, whisk flour, sugar, baking powder, salt, parsley, and dill weed. Cut margarine into the flour with a pastry cutter or large fork until mixture has a coarse crumb consistency. Stir in soymilk and egg replacement until just moistened.
3. Turn dough out onto a lightly floured surface and knead gently 8–10 times. Roll into a 6" round and cut into 8 equal wedges. Place wedges 1" apart on a lightly greased baking sheet.
4. Bake 15–18 minutes, or until golden brown.

**PER SERVING** Calories: 129 | Fat: 5 g | Protein: 2 g | Sugar: 1 g | Fiber: 1 g | Carbohydrates: 18 g

## Shelf Life of Your Spices

Are you wondering if that jar of marjoram sitting in the back of the cupboard for the better part of a decade is still good? In general, most spices have a shelf life of 2–5 years, with ground spices having the shortest shelf life and whole spices having the longest. Keep spices in airtight containers away from heat and humidity. Avoid opening jars over steaming pots and don't dip wet spoons into the jar. Jarred spices often have expiration dates, but the true test to tell if an older spice has potency is to give the jar a little shake, open it, and see if there is still a strong aroma. If the aroma has faded, it's time to replace that spice.

# Vegan Cheeze Biscuits

*These biscuits will remind you of the famous biscuits at a popular chain seafood restaurant!*

**INGREDIENTS | MAKES 20 BISCUITS**

2½ cups all-purpose flour

1 tablespoon baking powder

2 teaspoons sugar

½ teaspoon cream of tartar

¼ teaspoon salt

½ teaspoon ground cayenne pepper

1½ teaspoons garlic powder, divided use

½ cup vegan margarine, cold and cut into pieces

1¼ cups vegan Cheddar cheese, grated

½ cup vegan sour cream

1¼ cups soymilk

6 tablespoons vegan margarine, melted

¼ teaspoon cracked black pepper

1. Preheat oven to 450°F.
2. In a large bowl, whisk together flour, baking powder, sugar, cream of tartar, salt, cayenne pepper, and ½ teaspoon garlic powder. Using a pastry cutter or large fork, cut margarine into flour mixture until it resembles coarse crumbs. Stir in vegan cheese, sour cream, and soymilk until just mixed.
3. Drop dough 1" apart by tablespoonful onto a greased baking sheet. Combine melted margarine, 1 teaspoon garlic powder, and cracked pepper in a small bowl. Brush margarine mixture over the tops of the biscuits. Reserve leftover margarine mixture.
4. Bake 23–25 minutes, or until golden brown. Brush tops with remaining margarine mixture. Cool on baking sheet for 10 minutes, then transfer to cooling racks.

**PER SERVING** Calories: 174 | Fat: 11 g | Protein: 3 g | Sugar: 1 g | Fiber: 1 g | Carbohydrates: 17 g

# Vegan Bacon Herb Biscuits

*Veggie bacon is every bit as addictive as the real thing!*
*Make a few extra slices for snacking while you make your scones.*

### INGREDIENTS | SERVES 8

2 cups all-purpose flour

1 tablespoon baking powder

½ teaspoon salt

1 teaspoon dry mustard

4 tablespoons vegan margarine, cold and cut into pieces

2 tablespoons flat-leaf parsley, chopped

2 tablespoons chives, chopped

4 slices vegan bacon, cooked crisp, finely chopped

⅔ cup soymilk, plus more as desired

1. Preheat oven to 425°F. In a large bowl, whisk flour, baking powder, salt, and dry mustard. With a pastry cutter or large fork, cut margarine into flour until mixture resembles coarse crumbs. Stir in parsley, chives, and bacon. Stir in ⅔ cup soymilk until just mixed.
2. Turn dough out onto a lightly floured surface and knead 8–10 times. Roll dough out to ¾" thick. Using a biscuit cutter or the rim of a drinking glass, cut dough into rounds and place on an ungreased baking sheet 1" apart. Brush tops with additional soymilk.
3. Bake 12–15 minutes, or until golden brown.

**PER SERVING** Calories: 183 | Fat: 7 g | Protein: 5 g | Sugar: 1 g | Fiber: 1 g | Carbohydrates: 25 g

# Currant-Cream Scones

*A classic scone! If you don't have access to currants,*
*small raisins will work just fine.*

### INGREDIENTS | MAKES 10 SCONES

2 cups all-purpose flour

2 teaspoons baking powder

¼ cup sugar

Pinch salt

⅓ cup vegan margarine, cold, cut into pieces

Egg replacement equal to 1 egg

1 teaspoon vanilla extract

½ cup soy creamer

1 cup currants

2–3 tablespoons soymilk

1. Preheat oven to 375°F.
2. Whisk together flour, baking powder, sugar, and salt in a large bowl. Using a pastry cutter or large fork, cut the cold margarine into the flour mixture until the margarine is in pea-sized bits. In a separate bowl, whisk together the egg replacement, vanilla extract, soy creamer, and currants. Add the wet ingredients to the flour mixture, stirring until just combined.
3. Place dough on lightly floured surface and shape into a 7" disk. Cut into 10 wedges and place 1"–2" apart on a lightly greased baking sheet. Brush with soymilk.
4. Bake 15–18 minutes until lightly browned.

**PER SERVING** Calories: 220 | Fat: 7 g | Protein: 3 g | Sugar: 15 g | Fiber: 2 g | Carbohydrates: 36 g

# Pumpkin Scones

*The pumpkin in this recipe gives the scones beautiful color and a rich, earthy flavor.*

**INGREDIENTS | MAKES 10 SCONES**

1 cup mashed, cooked pumpkin

3 tablespoons vegan margarine, melted, divided use

1 cup all-purpose flour

2 teaspoons baking powder

½ teaspoon salt

1 teaspoon sugar

1. Preheat oven to 375°F.
2. In a large bowl, combine pumpkin with 1½ tablespoons melted margarine. Set aside. In a separate bowl, whisk together flour, baking powder, salt, and sugar. Add flour mixture to pumpkin and mix until you have a soft dough.
3. Turn dough onto a floured surface and roll out to ½" thick. Using a biscuit cutter or the rim of a drinking glass, cut dough into rounds. Place 1" apart on an ungreased baking sheet and brush tops with remaining 1½ tablespoons melted margarine.
4. Bake 15–18 minutes, until tops are lightly browned.

**PER SERVING** Calories: 86 | Fat: 3 g | Protein: 2 g | Sugar: 1 g | Fiber: 1 g | Carbohydrates: 12 g

# Sour Cream Biscuits

*Sour cream adds moisture and richness to these simple biscuits.*
*It's a wonderful accompaniment to soups and stews!*

**INGREDIENTS | MAKES 10 BISCUITS**

1¼ cups all-purpose flour

2 tablespoons baking powder

½ teaspoon salt

4 tablespoons vegetable shortening

¾ cup vegan sour cream

1. Preheat oven to 450°F.
2. In a large bowl, whisk flour, baking powder, and salt together. With a pastry cutter or large fork, cut shortening into flour mixture until it resembles coarse crumbs. Stir in sour cream until well-blended.
3. Transfer to a floured surface and roll out dough to ⅛" thick. Using a biscuit cutter or the rim of a drinking glass, cut out rounds of dough and place on an ungreased baking sheet.
4. Bake 10–12 minutes, or until lightly browned. Transfer to wire racks to cool.

**PER SERVING** Calories: 205 | Fat: 11 g | Protein: 3 g | Sugar: 2 g | Fiber: 0 g | Carbohydrates: 23 g

# Jam and Cream Cheeze Biscuits

*These biscuits are almost a dessert! Sweet and tender, your family won't be able to resist them.*

### INGREDIENTS | MAKES 20 BISCUITS

2⅔ cups all-purpose flour

1½ tablespoons baking powder

½ teaspoon salt

3 tablespoons vegan margarine, cold and cut into small pieces

2 teaspoons orange zest, minced

¾ cup orange juice

3 ounces vegan cream cheese, softened

2 tablespoons strawberry preserves

3 tablespoons turbinado sugar

## Resting

Double-acting baking powder works in two stages; once when it is moistened, and again when it is heated. To get the full benefit (and the fluffiest biscuits), allow the dough to rest for a short time before baking.

1. Preheat oven to 450°F.
2. In a large bowl, whisk together flour, baking powder, and salt. Cut cold margarine into small pieces. Using a pastry cutter or large fork, cut the margarine into the flour until the mixture resembles coarse crumbs. Stir the orange zest and orange juice into the flour mixture until well blended.
3. Place dough on a floured surface and shape into a ball. Knead 10 times. Roll dough out ½" thick. Using a biscuit cutter or the rim of a drinking glass, cut dough into rounds and place on an ungreased cookie sheet.
4. In a small bowl, blend together cream cheese and strawberry preserves. Spoon 1 teaspoon of preserve mixture onto the center of each dough round. Sprinkle with turbinado sugar.
5. Bake 8–10 minutes, or until biscuits are golden brown. Serve warm.

**PER SERVING** Calories: 93 | Fat: 2 g | Protein: 2 g | Sugar: 3 g | Fiber: 0 g | Carbohydrates: 17 g

# Olive Oil Drop Biscuits

*Fruity olive oil is a healthful substitution for shortening or margarine in this yummy biscuit!*

### INGREDIENTS | MAKES 12 BISCUITS

2 cups all-purpose flour

1 tablespoon baking powder

2 teaspoons sugar

1 teaspoon salt

½ cup extra-virgin olive oil

1 cup soymilk

1. Preheat oven to 450°F.
2. Whisk flour, baking powder, sugar, and salt together in a large bowl. Stir in oil and soymilk until just mixed. Drop batter by the tablespoonful onto an ungreased baking sheet. Bake for 10–12 minutes, or until golden brown.
3. Remove from baking sheet and serve warm.

**PER SERVING** Calories: 166 | Fat: 9 g | Protein: 3 g | Sugar: 1 g | Fiber: 1 g | Carbohydrates: 17 g

# Rosemary-Thyme Scones

*The classic combination of rosemary and thyme add a delicious layer of flavor to these biscuits. Enjoy them warm, straight from the oven.*

### INGREDIENTS | MAKES 8 SCONES

2 cups all-purpose flour

1 tablespoon sugar

3 teaspoons baking powder

½ teaspoon salt

3 tablespoons fresh thyme leaves, chopped

1 tablespoon fresh rosemary leaves, chopped

⅓ cup vegan margarine, cold and cut into pieces

½ cup soymilk

Egg replacement equal to 1 egg

1. Preheat oven to 400°F.
2. In a large bowl, whisk flour, sugar, baking powder, salt, thyme, and rosemary. Cut margarine into the flour with a pastry cutter or large fork until mixture has a coarse crumb consistency. Stir in soymilk and egg replacement until just moistened.
3. Turn dough out onto a lightly floured surface and knead gently 8–10 times. Roll into a 6" round and cut into 8 equal wedges. Place wedges 1" apart on a lightly greased baking sheet.
4. Bake 13–15 minutes, until lightly browned.

**PER SERVING** Calories: 194 | Fat: 8 g | Protein: 4 g | Sugar: 2 g | Fiber: 1 g | Carbohydrates: 27 g

# Whole-Wheat Cracked Pepper Biscuits

*The aroma and flavor of freshly cracked black pepper takes this biscuit to another level!*

**INGREDIENTS | MAKES 8–10 BISCUITS**

1 cup all-purpose flour

1 cup whole-wheat flour

2½ teaspoons baking powder

1¼ teaspoons cracked black pepper

½ teaspoon salt

4 tablespoons vegan margarine, cold, cut into pieces

¾ cup soymilk

1 tablespoon vegan margarine, melted

## Pepper

Pepper is always a bit spicy, but when it's freshly ground, the amount of heat it adds to a recipe is more substantial. In this recipe, the heat adds a burst of flavor and contrast to the other mild ingredients.

1. Preheat oven to 400°F.
2. In a large bowl, whisk together all-purpose flour, whole-wheat flour, baking powder, pepper, and salt. Using a pastry cutter or large fork, cut the cold margarine into the flour mixture until it resembles coarse crumbs. Stir in the soymilk until well blended.
3. Turn dough out onto a floured surface and shape into a ball. Knead 10 times. Roll out dough to ½" thick. With a biscuit cutter or the rim of a drinking glass, cut dough into rounds and place on an ungreased cookie sheet 1" apart.
4. Brush tops with melted margarine. Bake 8–10 minutes, or until lightly browned.

**PER SERVING** Calories: 180 | Fat: 8 g | Protein: 4 g | Sugar: 1 g | Fiber: 2 g | Carbohydrates: 24 g

# Cocoa Scones

*With both cocoa and chocolate chips, these scones are a doubly good!*

### INGREDIENTS | MAKES 12 SCONES

2 cups all-purpose flour

½ cup sugar

⅓ cup unsweetened cocoa powder

1 tablespoon baking powder

¼ teaspoon salt

⅓ cup vegan margarine, cold and cut into small pieces

Egg replacement equal to 1 egg

½ cup soy creamer

1 teaspoon vanilla extract

¾ cup vegan chocolate chips, coarsely chopped

3 tablespoons soymilk

3 tablespoons turbinado sugar

1. Preheat oven to 400°F.
2. In a large bowl, whisk together flour, sugar, cocoa powder, baking powder, and salt. With a pastry cutter or large fork, cut margarine into flour mixture. In a separate bowl, mix egg replacement, soy creamer, and vanilla extract until blended. Add wet ingredients to flour mixture, stirring until just mixed. Stir in chocolate chips.
3. Turn dough out onto a lightly-floured surface and knead 10 times. Roll dough to 1" thick. Using a biscuit cutter or the rim of a drinking glass, cut dough into rounds and place 1" apart on an ungreased baking sheet.
4. Brush tops with soymilk and sprinkle with turbinado sugar. Bake 9–11 minutes, or until lightly browned on the bottom. Serve warm.

**PER SERVING** Calories: 174 | Fat: 6 g | Protein: 3 g | Sugar: 12 g | Fiber: 1 g | Carbohydrates: 30 g

# Curried Potato Biscuits

*This is an interesting and different biscuit that will surprise your friends and family!*

**INGREDIENTS | MAKES 12 BISCUITS**

2 cups all-purpose flour

1 tablespoon baking powder

½ teaspoon salt

2 tablespoons curry powder

¼ cup vegan margarine, cold and cut into pieces

1 cup potatoes, cooked and mashed

3–4 tablespoons soymilk

## Curry

If you'd like to make your own curry powder, combine the following ingredients in a coffee grinder or mortar: ¼ cup each coriander seed, cumin seed, and brown mustard seed; 3 tablespoons each turmeric, fenugreek, and black peppercorns; 2 tablespoons each ground ginger and cardamom seeds; 1 tablespoon dried chiles; and 2 cinnamon sticks.

1. Preheat oven to 450°F.
2. In a large bowl, whisk together flour, baking powder, salt, and curry powder. Using a pastry cutter or large fork, cut margarine and mashed potatoes into flour until the mixture resembles coarse crumbs. Add soymilk, stirring until just moistened.
3. Turn dough out onto a floured surface. Knead 10 times, then roll out to ½" thick. With a biscuit cutter or the rim of a drinking glass, cut dough into rounds and place on an ungreased baking sheet 1" apart.
4. Bake 12–15 minutes, or until tops are golden brown. Serve warm.

**PER SERVING** Calories: 126 | Fat: 4 g | Protein: 3 g | Sugar: 0 g | Fiber: 1 g | Carbohydrates: 20 g

# Pizza Scones

*Vegan pepperoni? Yes! If you can't find vegan pepperoni, try vegan Canadian bacon as an alternative.*

**INGREDIENTS | MAKES 8 SCONES**

¾ cup soymilk

2½ teaspoons lemon juice

2 cups all-purpose flour

½ cup whole-wheat flour

1 tablespoon baking powder

1 teaspoon dried basil

¼ teaspoon dried oregano

¼ teaspoon salt

½ cup vegan margarine, cold and cut into pieces

Egg replacement equal to 2 eggs

½ cup sun-dried tomatoes (in oil), drained and diced

1 cup vegan mozzarella-style cheese, shredded

⅓ cup vegan pepperoni, finely chopped

## Sun-Dried Tomatoes

If you're using dehydrated tomatoes, rehydrate them first by covering in water for at least 10 minutes. If you're using tomatoes packed in oil, make sure they're well-drained before adding to the mix.

1. Preheat oven to 375°F.
2. Combine soymilk and lemon juice in a cup and allow to stand for 10 minutes. In a large bowl, whisk together all-purpose flour, whole-wheat flour, baking powder, basil, oregano, and salt. Using a pastry cutter or large fork, cut margarine into flour until the mixture resembles coarse crumbs.
3. In a separate bowl, whisk together the soymilk mixture, egg replacement, sun-dried tomatoes, mozzarella-style cheese, and vegan pepperoni. Add to the dry ingredients and stir until a sticky dough is formed. Turn dough out onto a floured surface and knead 5 times. Divide dough in half, flattening each piece into a 1" thick disk.
4. Cut each disk into 4 wedges. Place wedges 1" apart on a lightly greased baking sheet. Bake 15–20 minutes, or until golden brown. Serve warm.

**PER SERVING** Calories: 283 | Fat: 12 g | Protein: 7 g | Sugar: 1 g | Fiber: 3 g | Carbohydrates: 37 g

# Spinach-Garlic Scones

*These scones are an elegant addition to your breakfast table.*
*Your guests will love them for special occasions, but they're great for snacking too.*

**INGREDIENTS | MAKES 12 SCONES**

¾ cup soymilk

2½ teaspoons lemon juice

2 tablespoons olive oil

3 cloves garlic, minced

2 cups fresh spinach, chopped

2 cups all-purpose flour

½ cup whole-wheat flour

1 tablespoon baking powder

¼ teaspoon salt

¼ teaspoon black pepper

½ cup vegan margarine, cold and cut into pieces

Egg replacement equal to 2 eggs

½ cup vegan feta cheese, crumbled (optional)

## It's Easy Being Green!

Learn to love your leafy greens! Pound for pound and calorie for calorie, dark, leafy green vegetables are the most nutritious food on the planet! Try a variety of greens: bok choy, collard greens, spinach, kale, mustard greens, Swiss chard, or watercress. When you find one or two that you like, sneak it into as many breads and meals as you can!

1. Preheat oven to 375°F.
2. Combine soymilk and lemon juice in a cup and allow to stand for 10 minutes.
3. Heat olive oil in a skillet over medium heat. Add garlic and sauté 2–3 minutes until garlic begins to brown. Add spinach and cook for another 2–3 minutes, stirring often. Set aside to cool.
4. In a large bowl, whisk together all-purpose flour, whole-wheat flour, baking powder, salt, and pepper. Using a pastry cutter or large fork, cut margarine into the flour until the mixture resembles coarse crumbs.
5. In a separate bowl, whisk together the soymilk mixture, egg replacement, spinach sauté, and if desired, vegan feta cheese. Add to the dry ingredients and stir until a dough is formed. Turn dough out onto a floured surface and knead 5 times. Divide dough in half, flattening each piece into a 1"-thick disk.
6. Cut each disk into 6 wedges. Place wedges 1" apart on a lightly greased baking sheet. Bake 15–20 minutes, or until golden brown. Serve warm.

**PER SERVING** Calories: 157 | Fat: 6 g | Protein: 3 g | Sugar: 0 g | Fiber: 1 g | Carbohydrates: 21 g

# CHAPTER 4

# Quick Breads and Muffins

# Banana–Chocolate Chip Muffins

*Little bits of chocolate make these banana muffins taste heavenly!*

**INGREDIENTS | YIELDS 18 MUFFINS**

½ cup soymilk
1 teaspoon lemon juice
¾ cup brown sugar
½ cup vegan margarine, softened
3 medium bananas, mashed
1 teaspoon vanilla extract
2¼ cups all-purpose flour
1 cup whole-wheat flour
½ teaspoon baking powder
½ teaspoon baking soda
¼ teaspoon salt
1 cup vegan chocolate chips, coarsely chopped
½ cup walnuts, chopped (optional)

1. Preheat oven to 350°F.
2. Stir soymilk and lemon juice together in a small bowl and allow to sit for 10 minutes. Cream brown sugar and margarine together in a large bowl until fluffy. Stir in bananas, vanilla extract, and soymilk mixture until blended.
3. In a separate bowl, whisk together flours, baking powder, baking soda, and salt. Add flour mixture to wet ingredients, stirring until just mixed. Fold in chocolate chips and optional walnuts. Fill greased or paper-lined muffin tins with batter up to ⅔ full.
4. Bake muffins for 20–25 minutes or until a toothpick comes out clean when inserted into the center of a muffin. Cool in the pan for 10 minutes, then transfer to wire racks. Cool completely.

**PER SERVING** Calories: 197 | Fat: 7 g | Protein: 3 g | Sugar: 15 g | Fiber: 2 g | Carbohydrates: 35 g

# Irish Soda Bread

*This is a traditional recipe that replaces buttermilk with the vegan alternative: soymilk and lemon juice! Enjoy this bread hot with a slather of vegan margarine.*

**INGREDIENTS | SERVES 12**

1¾ cups soymilk
5 teaspoons lemon juice
4 cups all-purpose flour
1 teaspoon baking soda
1 teaspoon salt

1. Preheat oven to 425°F.
2. In a small bowl stir together soymilk and lemon juice and allow to sit for 10 minutes. Whisk flour, baking soda, and salt together in a large bowl. Gradually stir in soymilk mixture, beating just until the dough forms a ball. Place dough on a lightly floured surface and shape into a flat, 8" round loaf.
3. Place loaf on a lightly greased baking sheet and bake 45–50 minutes, or until golden brown.

**PER SERVING** Calories: 166 | Fat: 1 g | Protein: 5 g | Sugar: 1 g | Fiber: 1 g | Carbohydrates: 33 g

# Spiced Apple Muffins

*Leaving peels on the apples gives these muffins rustic appeal and provides extra nutrition and fiber!*

**INGREDIENTS | MAKES 16 MUFFINS**

1 cup soymilk
4 tablespoons vegan margarine
Egg replacement equal to 1 egg
1 teaspoon vanilla extract
2 cups all-purpose flour
½ cup sugar
4 teaspoons baking powder
½ teaspoon salt
¾ teaspoon cinnamon
¼ teaspoon nutmeg
1 cup apples, diced
Additional sugar and cinnamon for topping, if desired

1. Preheat oven to 425°F.
2. Whisk soymilk, margarine, egg replacement, and vanilla extract in a large bowl. In a separate bowl, whisk together flour, sugar, baking powder, salt, cinnamon, and nutmeg. Gradually combine flour mixture with wet ingredients, stirring until well mixed. Fold in apples.
3. Spoon batter into greased or paper-lined muffin tins until ⅔ full. Sprinkle with additional cinnamon and sugar, if desired.
4. Bake for 15–18 minutes or until a toothpick comes out clean when inserted into the center of the muffins.

**PER SERVING** Calories: 118 | Fat: 3 g | Protein: 2 g | Sugar: 8 g | Fiber: 1 g | Carbohydrates: 20 g

# Cranberry-Orange Muffins

*Use frozen cranberries when fresh cranberries are out of season.*

**INGREDIENTS | MAKES ABOUT 20 MUFFINS**

⅓ cup canola oil

⅔ cup orange juice

Egg replacement equal to 1 egg

⅓ cup soymilk

½ teaspoon vanilla extract

2 cups all-purpose flour

½ cup sugar

½ cup brown sugar

2 teaspoons baking powder

2 tablespoons orange zest

1 cup fresh cranberries, coarsely chopped

1. Preheat oven to 375°F.
2. In a large bowl, whisk together oil, orange juice, egg replacement, soymilk, and vanilla extract. In a separate bowl stir together flour, sugar, brown sugar, and baking powder. Add flour mixture to wet ingredients, stirring until just mixed.
3. Gently fold in orange zest and cranberries. Pour batter ⅔ full into greased or paper-lined muffin tins.
4. Bake 20–22 minutes or until a toothpick comes out clean when inserted into the center of the muffins.

**PER SERVING** Calories: 126 | Fat: 4 g | Protein: 1 g | Sugar: 11 g | Fiber: 1 g | Carbohydrates: 22 g

# Apricot-Walnut Bread

*Try this bread toasted with a smear of vegan cream cheese for a simple breakfast.*

**INGREDIENTS | SERVES 12**

1 cup dried apricots, chopped

⅓ cup orange juice

¼ cup brown sugar

¼ cup canola oil

¾ cup soymilk

1 teaspoon vanilla extract

2 cups all-purpose flour

1 tablespoon baking powder

½ teaspoon baking soda

½ teaspoon salt

1 cup walnuts, chopped

1. Preheat oven to 350°F.
2. Combine apricots and orange juice in a small saucepan over medium-low heat and simmer 5–10 minutes until apricots are soft. Remove from heat and allow to cool. Drain apricots, reserving juice.
3. In a large bowl, whisk reserved juice, brown sugar, oil, soymilk, and vanilla extract. In a medium bowl, whisk flour, baking powder, baking soda, and salt. Add to wet ingredients, stirring until just mixed. Fold in apricots and walnuts. Pour batter into a greased 9" × 5" loaf pan.
4. Bake 45–55 minutes until golden brown and a toothpick comes out clean when inserted into the loaf.

**PER SERVING** Calories: 233 | Fat: 11 g | Protein: 5 g | Sugar: 11 g | Fiber: 2 g | Carbohydrates: 30 g

# Zucchini Bread

*Making this bread is a delicious way to use up the summer's bounty of these prolific squashes.*

## INGREDIENTS | SERVES 12

1½ cups all-purpose flour

1 teaspoon baking powder

1 teaspoon baking soda

½ teaspoon salt

2 teaspoons cinnamon

½ teaspoon nutmeg

1 cup sugar

½ cup canola oil

Egg replacement equal to 2 eggs

1 teaspoon vanilla extract

1 cup grated zucchini

1. Preheat oven to 350°F.
2. Whisk together flour, baking powder, baking soda, salt, cinnamon, and nutmeg in a large bowl. In a separate bowl, stir together sugar, oil, egg replacement, and vanilla extract. Add wet ingredients to flour mixture, stirring until just mixed. Fold in grated zucchini.
3. Pour batter into a greased loaf pan and bake 50–60 minutes until golden brown. A toothpick should come out clean when inserted into the center of the loaf. Cool in the pan.

**PER SERVING** Calories: 208 | Fat: 9 g | Protein: 2 g | Sugar: 17 g | Fiber: 1 g | Carbohydrates: 30 g

## Veggie Breads

Like most recipes, zucchini bread can be embellished with additional ingredients. Dried fruits and nuts are nice, and add a touch of sweetness and a pleasant crunch. This bread also stands up well to a variety of vegetable additions. Try grating in a mixture of carrots, yellow squash, and red bell peppers, for a bread that looks like a slice of confetti. You can add up to an additional 1½ cups of extra ingredients.

# Corn Bread

*Use this wonderful bread as an accompaniment to your favorite vegan chili or as the base for a cornbread stuffing.*

**INGREDIENTS | SERVES 12**

1 cup all-purpose flour

1 cup yellow cornmeal

¾ cup sugar

2½ teaspoons baking powder

1 teaspoon salt

Egg replacement equal to 2 eggs

1 cup soymilk

½ cup canola oil

1. Preheat oven to 400°F.
2. Combine flour, cornmeal, sugar, baking powder, and salt in a large bowl. In a separate bowl, mix egg replacement, soymilk, and oil. Add wet ingredients to flour mixture, stirring until just mixed. Pour batter into a greased 8" × 8" pan.
3. Bake 20–25 minutes, or until a toothpick comes out clean when inserted into the center of the bread and the top is golden brown.

**PER SERVING** Calories: 226 | Fat: 10 g | Protein: 3 g | Sugar: 13 g | Fiber: 1 g | Carbohydrates: 32 g

# Maple-Oat Muffins

*These muffins have the rich sweetness of maple and the heartiness of oats!*

**INGREDIENTS | SERVES 14**

⅔ cup cooked oatmeal, cold

Egg replacement equal to 1 egg

2 tablespoons canola oil

¼ cup Grade B maple syrup

¾ cup soymilk

2 cups all-purpose flour

3 teaspoons baking powder

2 tablespoons sugar

½ teaspoon salt

1. Preheat oven to 425°F.
2. Stir together oatmeal, egg replacement, oil, maple syrup, and soymilk in a large bowl until blended. In a separate bowl, whisk together flour, baking powder, sugar, and salt. Combine flour mixture with wet ingredients, stirring until just mixed.
3. Pour batter into greased or paper-lined muffin tins until ⅔ full. Bake 20–25 minutes or until a toothpick inserted into the center comes out clean.

**PER SERVING** Calories: 118 | Fat: 2 g | Protein: 2 g | Sugar: 6 g | Fiber: 1 g | Carbohydrates: 21 g

# Pumpkin Muffins

*You will smell autumn in the air as you bake these aromatic treats.*

INGREDIENTS | MAKES ABOUT 20 MUFFINS

1½ cups all-purpose flour

1 cup whole-wheat flour

¾ cup sugar

1 tablespoon baking powder

½ teaspoon baking soda

½ teaspoon salt

1 teaspoon cinnamon

½ teaspoon nutmeg

¼ teaspoon ground ginger

¼ teaspoon allspice

1 (15-ounce) can pumpkin purée

¼ cup canola oil

¼ cup soymilk

Egg replacement equal to 1 egg

½ teaspoon lemon zest, minced

½ cup raisins

1. Preheat oven to 375°F.
2. In a large bowl, combine all-purpose flour, whole-wheat flour, sugar, baking powder, baking soda, salt, cinnamon, nutmeg, ginger, and allspice. In a separate bowl, mix pumpkin purée, oil, soymilk, egg replacement, and lemon zest. Add to flour mixture, stirring until just mixed. Fold in raisins.
3. Pour batter into greased or paper-lined muffin tins until ⅔ full.
4. Bake 25–35 minutes or until a toothpick inserted into the center of the muffins comes out clean. Remove from pan to cool.

**PER 1 MUFFIN** Calories: 130 | Fat: 3 g | Protein: 2 g | Sugar: 11 g | Fiber: 2 g | Carbohydrates: 25 g

## Ditch the Can

If you've got the time, there's nothing like fresh roasted pumpkin! Make your own purée to substitute for canned. Carefully chop your pumpkin in half, remove the seeds (save and toast those later!), and place cut-side down in a large baking dish. Pour ¼" water into the bottom of the dish and roast for 45 minutes to 1 hour in a 375°F oven. Cool, then peel off and discard the skin. Mash or purée the flesh until smooth. Whatever you don't use will keep in the freezer for next time.

# Boston Brown Bread

*Traditionally made in tin cans, this bread is dark, dense, and satisfying.*

**INGREDIENTS | SERVES 18**

2 cups soymilk, less 2 tablespoons
2 tablespoons apple cider vinegar
1 cup all-purpose flour
2 cups whole-wheat flour
2 teaspoons baking soda
⅔ cup brown sugar, packed
¼ cup molasses
½ cup raisins

1. Preheat oven to 350°F.
2. Combine soymilk and vinegar in a small bowl; allow to sit for 10 minutes.
3. In a large bowl, combine all-purpose flour, whole-wheat flour, baking soda, and brown sugar. Stir in molasses and soymilk mixture until just combined. Fold in raisins.
4. Pour batter into a greased and floured 9" × 5" loaf pan and bake for 55–60 minutes. Remove from pan to cool.

**PER SERVING** Calories: 133 | Fat: 0 g | Protein: 3 g | Sugar: 14 g | Fiber: 2 g | Carbohydrates: 30 g

# Blueberry Crumb Muffins

*An abundance of fruit and a tender, cake-like texture make blueberry one of the most popular types of muffins!*

**INGREDIENTS | MAKES 18 MUFFINS**

2¾ cups all-purpose flour, divided use
1½ cups sugar, divided use
1 tablespoon baking powder
½ teaspoon salt
¼ cup vegan margarine, softened
½ cup unsweetened applesauce
½ cup soymilk
1 teaspoon vanilla extract
1½ cups frozen blueberries
⅓ cup vegan margarine, cold and cut into small pieces

1. Preheat oven to 350°F.
2. Combine 2 cups flour, 1 cup sugar, baking powder, and salt in a large bowl. In a separate bowl, mix softened margarine, applesauce, soymilk, and vanilla extract until blended. Fold in frozen blueberries. Pour batter into greased or paper-lined muffin tins until ¾ full.
3. In a small bowl, combine remaining ¾ cup flour, and ½ cup sugar. Cut cold margarine into flour and sugar until mixture is crumbly. Sprinkle mixture over the top of muffin batter.
4. Bake 30–35 minutes or until a toothpick comes out clean when inserted into center of the muffins.

**PER SERVING** Calories: 198 | Fat: 6 g | Protein: 2 g | Sugar: 19 g | Fiber: 1 g | Carbohydrates: 34 g

# Banana Bread

*Use brown, spotted bananas for this recipe to get the best banana flavor.*

**INGREDIENTS | SERVES 12**

3 ripe bananas, mashed

½ cup sugar

¼ cup brown sugar, packed

Egg replacement equal to 2 eggs

1 teaspoon vanilla extract

1½ cups all-purpose flour

½ cup whole-wheat flour

1 teaspoon baking soda

1 teaspoon salt

½ cup chopped walnuts, optional

## Baking with Bananas

The best bananas for baking are overripe and black. Their starch has completely converted to sugar, which makes them awful to eat fresh, but perfectly moist and sweet for baking. If your bananas are headed in that direction but you don't have time to bake, remove them from their skin, place them in a plastic zipper bag, mash them up a little, and store in the freezer. They'll be ready at a moment's notice for your next banana bake-off.

1. Preheat oven to 350°F.
2. In a large bowl, stir together mashed bananas, sugar, brown sugar, egg replacement, and vanilla extract until well blended. In a separate bowl, combine the flours, baking soda, and salt. Add flour mixture to wet ingredients, stirring until just mixed. Fold in walnuts, if desired.
3. Pour batter into a greased 9" × 5" loaf pan and bake for 1 hour, or until top is golden brown and a toothpick comes out clean when inserted into the center of the loaf. Cool in the pan.

**PER SERVING** Calories: 168 | Fat: 3 g | Protein: 3 g | Sugar: 14 g | Fiber: 2 g | Carbohydrates: 32 g

# Date-Nut Loaf

*This bread is sweet and chewy with a nutty crunch!*

**INGREDIENTS | SERVES 16**

½ cup brown sugar, packed

½ cup vegan margarine, softened

1 cup water

1 teaspoon vanilla extract

2 cups all-purpose flour

2 teaspoons baking powder

1 teaspoon baking soda

¼ teaspoon salt

1 cup pitted dates, chopped

½ cup walnuts, chopped

1. Preheat oven to 400°F.
2. In a large bowl, cream brown sugar and margarine together until fluffy. Mix in water and vanilla extract. In a separate bowl, whisk together flour, baking powder, baking soda, and salt. Add flour mixture to margarine mixture, stirring until just blended. Fold in chopped dates and nuts.
3. Pour batter into a greased 9" × 5" loaf pan. Bake for 40–45 minutes, or until golden brown and a toothpick comes out clean when inserted into the center of the loaf. Cool in the pan.

**PER SERVING** Calories: 189 | Fat: 8 g | Protein: 2 g | Sugar: 7 g | Fiber: 2 g | Carbohydrates: 28 g

# Beer Bread

*This is a hearty, savory bread, and is so simple to make.*
*Explore using different varieties of beer to transform the flavor!*

**INGREDIENTS | SERVES 16**

2 cups all-purpose flour

1 cup whole-wheat flour

1 tablespoon baking powder

¼ cup sugar

1½ teaspoons salt

12 ounces beer

3 tablespoons vegan margarine, melted

1. Preheat oven to 375°F.
2. In a large bowl, whisk together all-purpose flour, whole-wheat flour, baking powder, sugar, and salt. Stir in beer until just mixed. Spread dough in a greased 9" × 5" loaf pan. Brush top of dough with melted margarine.
3. Bake 40–45 minutes, or until a toothpick comes out clean when inserted into the center of the loaf and the top is golden brown.

**PER SERVING** Calories: 123 | Fat: 2 g | Protein: 2 g | Sugar: 3 g | Fiber: 1 g | Carbohydrates: 22 g

# Lemon Bread

*Delight your guests with this sweet, tangy quick bread; it's bursting with the bright flavor of fresh lemons.*

**INGREDIENTS | SERVES 16**

2 cups all-purpose flour

2 teaspoons baking powder

¼ teaspoon salt

½ cup vegetable shortening

1 cup sugar

2 tablespoons lemon juice

2 tablespoons lemon zest, minced

Egg replacement equal to 2 eggs

1 teaspoon vanilla extract

½ cup soymilk

½ batch Lemon Glaze (see Chapter 14)

## Quick Baking

Quick breads are so named because they are leavened with baking powder and/or baking soda, which do not require the prolonged fermentation time that yeast does. However, quick breads are not necessarily quick to bake. Batters baked in a loaf pan require time to allow heat to penetrate to the center. Regardless of the indicated baking time, the toothpick test is the only true measure of doneness. When inserted, it must come out clean.

1. Preheat oven to 350°F.
2. In a medium bowl, whisk together the flour, baking powder, and salt. Set aside. In a large bowl, cream the shortening and sugar until fluffy. Add the lemon juice, lemon zest, egg replacement, and vanilla extract, whisking until well blended.
3. Add the flour mixture to the wet ingredients alternating with the soymilk, stirring until just mixed. Pour batter into a greased 8" × 4" loaf pan and bake 45–50 minutes or until a toothpick comes out clean when inserted into the center.
4. Remove bread from pan and while still warm, drizzle with lemon glaze.

**PER SERVING** Calories: 201 | Fat: 7 g | Protein: 2 g | Sugar: 20 g | Fiber: 0 g | Carbohydrates: 33 g

# Southwest Green Chile Corn Muffins

*These muffins feature the bold flavors of the Southwest! If you can take the heat, replace the green chiles with an equal amount of canned jalapeños.*

**INGREDIENTS | MAKES 16 MUFFINS**

¼ cup vegetable shortening

¼ cup sugar

1 cup soymilk

Egg replacement equal to 1 egg

½ cup cream-style corn

1 (4-ounce) can diced green chiles, drained

1 cup cornmeal

1 cup all-purpose flour

4 teaspoons baking powder

½ teaspoon salt

1. Preheat oven to 375°F.
2. In a large bowl, cream shortening and sugar until fluffy. Add soymilk, egg replacement, cream-style corn, and green chiles. Stir to combine. In a separate bowl, whisk together cornmeal, flour, baking powder, and salt. Add flour mixture to wet ingredients, stirring until just mixed.
3. Pour batter into greased or paper-lined muffin tins until ⅔ full. Bake 15–20 minutes, or until a toothpick comes out clean when inserted into the center of the muffins and the tops are lightly browned.

**PER SERVING** Calories: 119 | Fat: 4 g | Protein: 2 g | Sugar: 4 g | Fiber: 1 g | Carbohydrates: 20 g

# Peach Muffins

*Try using spiced peaches as a yummy alternative to regular peaches.*

**INGREDIENTS | SERVES 12**

1¾ cups all-purpose flour

1 tablespoon baking powder

¼ teaspoon salt

½ cup sugar

½ cup soymilk

1 teaspoon vanilla extract

2 tablespoons vegan margarine, melted

1½ tablespoons apple cider vinegar

1 cup canned peaches, drained and diced

1. Preheat oven to 400°F.
2. In a large bowl, whisk together flour, baking powder, salt, and sugar. In a separate bowl, combine soymilk, vanilla extract, melted margarine, and vinegar. Quickly combine soymilk mixture with dry ingredients, stirring until just mixed. Fold in peaches. Pour batter into greased or paper-lined muffin tins until ⅔ full.
3. Bake 15–20 minutes, or until a toothpick comes out clean when inserted into the center of the muffins and the tops are golden brown.

**PER SERVING** Calories: 132 | Fat: 2 g | Protein: 2 g | Sugar: 11 g | Fiber: 1 g | Carbohydrates: 26 g

# Carrot-Raisin Muffins

*A classic combination of carrots, raisins, and spices makes this muffin a delight to eat!*

## INGREDIENTS | MAKES 16 MUFFINS

2 cups all-purpose flour

¼ teaspoon salt

1 teaspoon baking powder

¼ teaspoon baking soda

1 teaspoon cinnamon

½ cup canola oil

½ cup sugar

¼ cup brown sugar

1 tablespoon soy yogurt, plain

1 teaspoon vanilla extract

1 cup carrots, grated

1 cup raisins

½ cup walnuts, chopped

1. Preheat oven to 375°F.
2. In a large bowl, whisk together the flour, salt, baking powder, baking soda, and cinnamon. In a separate bowl, whisk oil, sugar, brown sugar, yogurt, and vanilla extract until well blended. Add wet ingredients to the flour mixture, stirring until just mixed. Fold in carrots, raisins, and walnuts.
3. Pour batter into greased or paper-lined muffin tins until ⅔ full. Bake 20–25 minutes, or until a toothpick comes out clean when inserted into the center of the muffins and the tops are golden brown. Allow to cool 15 minutes in pans, then transfer to wire racks.

**PER SERVING** Calories: 214 | Fat: 9 g | Protein: 3 g | Sugar: 16 g | Fiber: 1 g | Carbohydrates: 31 g

## Self-Rising Flour

Because it already contains leaveners, self-rising flour is perfect for quick bread baking. You can also make your own self-rising flour by combining 3 cups flour with 4½ teaspoons baking powder and 1½ teaspoons kosher salt. Blend this mixture well before measuring. Self-rising flour is not a substitute for yeast.

# CHAPTER 5

# Yeast Breads

# Italian Loaf

*This is a delicious bread with a beautiful crust! For dipping, pour some fruity, extra-virgin olive oil on a plate, drizzle on some balsamic vinegar, and top with freshly cracked black pepper.*

**INGREDIENTS | SERVES 18**

2¼ teaspoons active dry yeast

1¼ cups water, warm (105°–115°)

3 cups all-purpose flour

2 teaspoons sugar

1 teaspoon salt

1 tablespoon olive oil

Cornmeal, as needed

## Bread Shapes of Italy

Italy encompasses many regions, and each has its own specialty breads. Often, the name of the dough is reflective of its shape. The same dough recipe can be formed into a number of different shapes, including rolls (panini), flatbreads (focaccia, fougasse, or ciabatta), breadsticks (gris-sino), or crackers (salatini).

1. Dissolve yeast in ¼ cup warm water in a medium-sized bowl. Allow to sit 3–5 minutes until bubbly. Stir in the rest of the water. In a large bowl, whisk together flour, sugar, and salt until well mixed. Add oil, stirring until blended.

2. Turn the dough out onto a floured surface. Knead dough 5–8 minutes, or until smooth, then continue to knead for an additional 6–7 minutes. Place dough in an oiled bowl, turning once to coat entire surface with oil. Lay plastic wrap over the exposed surface of the dough, set in a warm place, and allow to rise 1½–2 hours until doubled in bulk. Punch down dough a few times and turn out onto a floured surface. Divide dough into 2 equal pieces, and gently form each piece into a loaf shape.

3. Sprinkle cornmeal over a wooden cutting board and place loaves on top. Cover with plastic wrap. Allow to rise a second time for another 35–40 minutes. With a very sharp knife, make a ¼" deep, lengthwise slice down the center of each loaf.

4. Place a rimless, ungreased baking sheet on the lower rack of the oven and preheat to 425°F. Carefully transfer loaves to baking sheet and bake for 10 minutes. Reduce heat to 400°F and bake for an additional 25–30 minutes.

**PER SERVING** Calories: 85 | Fat: 1 g | Protein: 2 g | Sugar: 1 g | Fiber: 1 g | Carbohydrates: 16 g

# Potato Rolls

*Savory, fluffy, and golden—potato rolls are a culinary classic, and are perfect for holiday feasts.*

**INGREDIENTS | SERVES 12**

3 cups all-purpose flour

1 tablespoon sugar

2 teaspoons dried minced onion

1 envelope or 2¼ teaspoons Rapid Rise yeast

1 teaspoon salt

¾ cup soymilk

½ cup potatoes, cooked and mashed

2 tablespoons olive oil

1. In a large bowl, whisk together flour, sugar, onion, yeast, and salt. Heat soymilk, mashed potatoes, and oil in a saucepan to 120°–130°F. Remove from heat and stir into flour mixture, adding additional flour as needed to make a soft dough.

2. Turn dough out onto a floured surface and knead 8–10 minutes until smooth and elastic. Cover with a clean kitchen towel and allow to rise 10 minutes. Cut dough into 12 equal pieces. Roll each piece into a 9" rope. Form each rope into a "6" shape. Push the long end of the "6" underneath and through the loop to create a knot. Place rolls 2" apart on a lightly greased baking sheet. Cover and allow to rise in a warm place until doubled in size, about 30–40 minutes.

3. Preheat oven to 375°F. Bake 15–20 minutes, until golden brown. Transfer to wire racks to cool.

**PER SERVING** Calories: 152 | Fat: 3 g | Protein: 4 g | Sugar: 2 g | Fiber: 1 g | Carbohydrates: 27 g

# Whole-Wheat Rolls

*Hearty, good-for-you whole wheat gives these rolls a bit of fiber and extra nutrients!*
*The all-purpose flour helps to keep them light and tender.*

**INGREDIENTS | MAKES 12 ROLLS**

5½ teaspoons active dry yeast (2 packets)

¼ cup water, warm (110°F–115°F)

1 cup soymilk

3½ tablespoons vegan margarine, divided use

3 tablespoons rapadura or sugar

1 teaspoon salt

1½ cups all-purpose flour

1½ cups whole-wheat flour

1. In a small bowl, dissolve yeast in water. Let stand until bubbly, about 10 minutes. Warm soymilk in a small saucepan until it begins to simmer. Remove from heat and stir in 1½ tablespoons vegan margarine, rapadura, and salt. Cool.

2. Pour the cooled yeast mixture into a large bowl. Stir in the milk mixture and flours. Mix until dough comes together. Turn dough out onto a floured surface. Knead 8–10 minutes until dough is smooth and elastic. Place dough in a lightly oiled bowl, turning once to coat. Place plastic wrap over exposed surface of dough and place bowl in a warm area. Allow dough to rise for about 45 minutes, until doubled in size.

3. Punch dough down a few times and turn out onto a floured surface. Divide into 12 equal pieces. Form each piece into a roll shape and place on a lightly greased baking sheet. Melt remaining 2 tablespoons margarine and brush on the tops of the rolls. Cover and let rise for another 40 minutes, until doubled in size.

4. Preheat oven to 375°F. Bake for 13–15 minutes, or until golden brown.

**PER SERVING** Calories: 159 | Fat: 4 g | Protein: 5 g | Sugar: 4 g | Fiber: 2 g | Carbohydrates: 27 g

# French Bread

*French Bread is great for sandwiches and recipes that use bread as an ingredient, such as a Panzanella Bread Salad (see Chapter 17).*

**INGREDIENTS | MAKES 2 LOAVES
(APPROX. 32 SLICES)**

2 cups soymilk, warmed (110°F–115°F)

2¼ teaspoons active dry yeast

¾ cup vegan margarine, melted

1 teaspoon salt

6 cups all-purpose flour

## The Perfect Vegan French Toast

Creating an eggless French toast is a true art. Is your French toast too dry? Thickly sliced bread lightly toasted will be more absorbent. Too mushy, or the mixture doesn't want to stick? Try spooning it onto your bread, rather than dipping.

1. Pour soymilk into a large bowl, add yeast, and stir to dissolve. Stir in margarine and salt. Add flour to the yeast mixture, stirring until a dough is formed. Cover exposed surface of dough with plastic wrap. Place bowl in a warm area and allow to rise until dough is doubled in size.

2. Turn dough out onto a floured surface and knead until smooth and elastic, 8–10 minutes. Divide dough in half and place on a large ungreased baking sheet. Shape each piece into an oblong loaf. Cover and allow to rise until doubled in size, about 40 minutes.

3. Preheat oven to 350°F. Bake loaves for 20 minutes, or until golden brown.

**PER SERVING** Calories: 129 | Fat: 5 g | Protein: 3 g | Sugar: 0 g | Fiber: 1 g | Carbohydrates: 18 g

# Dinner Rolls

*Yeasted dinner rolls take a little extra time and effort but the end result is so worthwhile!*

**INGREDIENTS | MAKES 12 ROLLS**

2¼ teaspoons active dry yeast

1 cup water, warm (110°F–115°F), divided use

2 tablespoons sugar, divided use

2¼ cups all-purpose flour, divided use

1 teaspoon salt

Egg replacement equal to 1 egg

2 tablespoons vegan margarine, softened

1. Dissolve yeast in ¼ cup warm water in a small bowl. Stir in 1 teaspoon sugar and let sit for 10 minutes.
2. In a large bowl, whisk together 1¼ cups flour, remaining sugar, and salt. Stir in the yeast mixture and then add the remaining ¾ cup warm water, egg replacement, and margarine. Gradually add the remaining 1 cup flour and mix until dough is smooth. Cover, place in a warm area, and allow to rise for 1–2 hours until doubled in bulk.
3. Knead dough for 1–2 minutes, then cut into 12 equal pieces. Shape each piece into a ball and place 1" apart on a greased baking sheet. Cover and allow to rise for another 30 minutes.
4. Preheat oven to 400°F. Bake rolls for 15–18 minutes until golden brown. Transfer to wire racks to cool.

**PER SERVING** Calories: 113 | Fat: 2 g | Protein: 3 g | Sugar: 2 g | Fiber: 1 g | Carbohydrates: 20 g

# Raisin-Cinnamon Bread

*This bread makes the most amazing raisin toast!*
*Try using thick slices to make a yummy French toast breakfast.*

**INGREDIENTS | SERVES 28**

1 cup raisins

2 cups water, the hottest you can get from the tap

1⅓ cups soymilk, divided use

2¼ teaspoons active dry yeast (1 packet)

½ cup plus 2 tablespoons sugar, divided use

Egg replacement equal to 1 egg

¼ teaspoon salt

½ cup vegan margarine, melted

4 cups all-purpose flour

2 tablespoons cinnamon

1. Soak raisins in hot water until plump; drain. Set aside. Heat ⅓ cup soymilk to 110°–115°F. Dissolve yeast in warm soymilk and allow to sit for 5–10 minutes.

2. In a large bowl, stir together remaining 1 cup soymilk, ½ cup sugar, egg replacement, salt, and margarine. Stir in yeast. Gradually add flour, stirring until a soft dough is formed.

3. Turn dough out onto a lightly floured surface. Knead for 8–10 minutes or until dough is smooth and elastic. Place in a lightly greased bowl, turning once to coat. Cover and place in a warm area and allow to rise until doubled in size, about 1 hour. Punch dough down and place on a lightly floured surface.

4. Roll dough out into a 14" × 12" rectangle. Mix remaining 2 tablespoons sugar with cinnamon in a small bowl. Spread cinnamon mixture evenly over dough and roll up jellyroll-style into loaf. Place seam-side down on a greased baking sheet. Cover and allow to rise for another 30–40 minutes.

5. Preheat oven to 350°F. Bake 35–40 minutes. Transfer to wire rack to cool.

**PER SERVING** Calories: 135 | Fat: 4 g | Protein: 2 g | Sugar: 8 g | Fiber: 1 g | Carbohydrates: 24 g

# English Muffins

*Top a split English Muffin half with diced bell peppers and shredded vegan cheese and then heat in the toaster oven until the cheese is melty. These make great mini-pizzas, too!*

### INGREDIENTS | MAKES ABOUT 18 MUFFINS

1 cup soymilk, warm (110°–115°F)
1 cup water, warm (110°–115°F)
3 tablespoons sugar
2¼ teaspoons active dry yeast (1 packet)
4 tablespoons vegan margarine, melted but not hot
5–6 cups unbleached, all-purpose flour
¾ teaspoon salt
Cornmeal, for dusting

1. Combine soymilk and water in a large bowl. Add sugar and yeast, stirring to dissolve. Let stand 5–10 minutes. Stir in the margarine.
2. In a separate bowl, whisk together 5 cups of flour and salt. Gradually add flour mixture to the wet ingredients until a soft dough is formed, adding the remaining 1 cup of flour as needed so that dough is not sticky.
3. Turn dough out onto a floured surface and knead just until dough becomes smooth and elastic. Place in a lightly oiled bowl, turning once to coat. Cover and allow to rise 1–1½ hours, or until doubled in size. Punch dough down a couple of times, then gently roll out to 1" thick.
4. With a lightly floured biscuit cutter, cut dough into rounds. Place rounds on a baking sheet that has been generously dusted with cornmeal. Cover with a towel and let rise for another 30–40 minutes.
5. Preheat a lightly oiled griddle to 300°F. Place muffins on griddle and cook for 10 minutes. Flip and cook muffins for an additional 10 minutes, or until lightly browned. Cool on wire racks.

**PER SERVING** Calories: 163 | Fat: 3 g | Protein: 4 g | Sugar: 2 g | Fiber: 1 g | Carbohydrates: 29 g

# Onion-Dill Bread

*Onion-Dill Bread is an unusual sandwich bread!*
*It's perfect for vegan bologna or a grilled cheese.*

**INGREDIENTS | MAKES 2 LOAVES**
**(16 SLICES)**

2¼ teaspoons active dry yeast

¼ cup water, warm (110°–115°F)

¾ cup firm tofu, drained

3 tablespoons nutritional yeast

¼ teaspoon garlic powder

Egg replacement equal to 2 eggs

¼ cup onion, minced

1 tablespoon vegan margarine

1 tablespoon sugar

2 tablespoons fresh dill, chopped

3½ cups bread flour

1¼ teaspoons salt

1. In a small bowl, dissolve active dry yeast in warm water. Allow to sit for 5 minutes. In a large bowl, mash tofu, nutritional yeast, and garlic powder to a cottage cheese consistency. Beat in egg replacement, onion, margarine, sugar, and dill. Add active yeast mixture and 1½ cups flour, beating 2 minutes until smooth.
2. Stir in salt and gradually add remaining flour until dough becomes stiff. Knead for 8–10 minutes until dough is smooth and elastic. Shape dough into a ball and place in an oiled bowl, turning once to coat. Cover bowl and let rise in a warm area for 1–1½ hours until doubled in size. Punch down dough and allow to rest for 10 minutes.
3. Divide dough in half, shaping each piece into a round loaf shape. Place on a greased baking sheet, cover loosely, and allow to rise another 45–60 minutes until almost doubled in size.
4. Cut 2 or 3 ¼"-deep slices into the top of each loaf. Preheat oven to 400°F. Bake for 25–30 minutes, or until golden brown. Loaves will sound hollow when tapped.

**PER 1 SLICE** Calories: 133 | Fat: 2 g | Protein: 5 g | Sugar: 1 g | Fiber: 1 g | Carbohydrates: 25 g

# White Bread

*Making bread from scratch is so satisfying, even this basic sandwich bread will feel like a reward for all the hard work!*

**INGREDIENTS | SERVES 16**

1½ tablespoons sugar

2¼ teaspoons active dry yeast (1 packet)

1¼ cups water, warm (110°–115°F)

1½ tablespoons vegetable shortening, melted but not hot

1½ teaspoons salt

3¼ cups bread flour

1. In a large bowl, dissolve sugar and yeast in warm water. Stir in shortening, salt, and 1 cup of flour. Beat in remaining flour, ½ cup at a time. Turn dough out onto a lightly floured surface and knead 8–10 minutes.
2. Place dough in an oiled bowl, turning once to coat. Cover with plastic wrap and place in a warm area. Allow dough to rise for 1½ hours until doubled. Punch down, turn onto a lightly floured surface, and shape to fit a 9" × 5" loaf pan. Place loaf in greased loaf pan. Cover and allow to rise another 30–40 minutes, until doubled in size.
3. Preheat oven to 375°F. Bake for 25–30 minutes.

**PER SERVING** Calories: 124 | Fat: 2 g | Protein: 4 g | Sugar: 1 g | Fiber: 1 g | Carbohydrates: 23 g

# High-Protein Bread

*The extra protein in this bread comes from the soymilk powder. Be sure to use soymilk powder and not soy protein isolate.*

**INGREDIENTS | MAKES 2 LOAVES (32 SLICES)**

2¼ teaspoons active dry yeast (1 packet)

¼ cup water, warm (110F°–115°F)

2 cups water, hot from the tap

3 cups dry soymilk powder

2 tablespoons vegetable shortening

2 tablespoons sugar

2 teaspoons salt

6½ cups all-purpose flour

1. Dissolve yeast in warm water in a small bowl. Combine hot water, dry soymilk, shortening, sugar, and salt in a large bowl. Mix in yeast mixture and begin adding flour, 2 cups at a time, mixing well. Turn onto a floured surface and knead 8–10 minutes until smooth and elastic.
2. Place in an oiled bowl, turning once to coat, cover, and allow to rise for 1½ hours until doubled. Punch dough down a few times, cover, and allow to rise until doubled in size. Divide in half and shape into loaves. Place loaves on a large baking sheet and allow to rise until doubled.
3. Preheat oven to 400°F. Bake for 45 minutes. Transfer to wire racks to cool.

**PER 1 SLICE** Calories: 139 | Fat: 3 g | Protein: 6 g | Sugar: 1 g | Fiber: 2 g | Carbohydrates: 23 g

# Potato Bread

*This bread is so gorgeous and has such an amazing texture
that your loved ones will be certain you purchased it from a bakery!*

### INGREDIENTS | SERVES 20

2¼ teaspoons active dry yeast (1 packet)

¼ cup water, warm (110°–115°F)

½ cup soymilk, warm (110°–115°F)

½ cup potatoes, cooked and mashed

2 tablespoons vegan margarine, melted

3 tablespoons sugar

Egg replacement equal to 1 egg

3 cups bread flour

1 teaspoon salt

Additional flour for dusting

1. In a small bowl, dissolve yeast in the warm water. Set aside.

2. In a large bowl, combine warm soymilk, mashed potatoes, margarine, sugar, and egg replacement. Add 1½ cups flour and mix well. Stir in salt and yeast mixture. Cover and allow to rise in a warm area for 1½ hours. Mix in remaining 1½ cups flour.

3. Turn dough out onto a lightly floured surface and knead for 10 minutes. Place dough in an oiled bowl, cover with a kitchen towel, and allow to rise until doubled in bulk. Punch down dough a few times and shape into a slightly oblong loaf. Place loaf on a lightly greased baking sheet. Cover and allow to rise again until doubled in size.

4. Preheat oven to 350°F. Cut a ¼" deep slice down the length of the loaf. Lightly dust the top with flour and bake for 30–40 minutes. Transfer to wire rack to cool.

**PER 1 SLICE** Calories: 95 | Fat: 2 g | Protein: 3 g | Sugar: 2 g | Fiber: 1 g | Carbohydrates: 17 g

# Rye Bread

*This artisan-style bread will impress! Try making vegan Reuben sandwiches with corned beef tempeh, sauerkraut, vegan Swiss cheese, and lots of whole-grain mustard.*

**INGREDIENTS | MAKES 2 LOAVES (24 SLICES)**

2¼ teaspoons active dry yeast (1 packet)

¼ cup water, warm (110°F–115°F)

2 cups soymilk, warm (110°F–115°F)

2 tablespoons olive oil, plus more if desired

1 tablespoon caraway seeds

1 tablespoon salt

2 tablespoons molasses

2 cups rye flour

1 cup whole-wheat flour

½–1 cup all-purpose flour

½ cup vital wheat gluten

½ cup wheat germ

1 cup wheat bran

Cornmeal for dusting

1. Combine yeast with warm water in a large bowl. Allow to sit for 5–10 minutes. Stir the warm soymilk, olive oil, caraway seeds, salt, and molasses into the yeast mixture. Mix in rye flour, whole-wheat flour, and ½ cup all-purpose flour. Then add gluten, wheat germ, and wheat bran.

2. Turn dough out onto a floured surface. Knead for 8–10 minutes, adding in remaining all-purpose flour, 1 tablespoon at a time, until dough is no longer sticky. Shape into a ball, cover with a towel, and allow to rise in a warm place for 1½–2 hours. Divide dough in half and shape each piece into a round loaf.

3. Place loaves on a baking sheet dusted with cornmeal, cover, and allow to rise for 1 hour.

4. Preheat oven to 375°F. Cut an "X" into the top of each loaf. Brush tops with olive oil, if desired. Bake 45–50 minutes. Transfer to wire racks to cool.

**PER SERVING** Calories: 116 | Fat: 2 g | Protein: 5 g | Sugar: 2 g | Fiber: 4 g | Carbohydrates: 21 g

# Rosemary Focaccia

*This bread is airy, bubbly, and full of flavor! Serve it warm to your guests as a predinner appetizer.*

**INGREDIENTS | SERVES 24**

2¼ teaspoons active dry yeast (1 packet)

2 cups water, warm (110°F–115°F)

4½ cups all-purpose flour

2 teaspoons salt

1 tablespoon sugar

1 tablespoon fresh rosemary, chopped

½ cup vegan margarine, melted

½ cup vegan Parmesan cheese (optional)

## Crunchy Croutons

Slice your favorite vegan artisan bread, focaccia, or whatever you've got into 1" cubes. Toss them in a large bowl with a generous coating of olive oil or a flavored oil, a bit of salt, and some Italian seasonings, garlic powder, a dash of cayenne, or whatever you prefer, then transfer to a baking sheet and bake 15–20 minutes at 275°F, tossing once or twice.

1. Dissolve yeast in ¼ cup warm water in a small bowl. Allow to sit for 5–10 minutes. In a large bowl, combine remaining 1¾ cups warm water, flour, salt, sugar, and dissolved yeast, stirring until well mixed. Add in rosemary.

2. Cover bowl with plastic wrap and allow to rise in a warm place until doubled in size, about 1 hour. Put dough into a greased 9" × 13" pan. With greased or oiled hands, press dough out to the edges of the pan. Dough will be sticky. Cover and allow dough to rise for another 20 minutes.

3. Preheat oven to 400°F. Press rows of indentations with your fingers across the dough. Drizzle melted margarine over the top. Sprinkle with vegan Parmesan, if desired. Bake 20 minutes. Cool for 10 minutes, then transfer to cutting board. Cut into squares to serve.

**PER SERVING** Calories: 122 | Fat: 4 g | Protein: 3 g | Sugar: 1 g | Fiber: 1 g | Carbohydrates: 19 g

# Pizza Dough

*Use a baking stone if you have one! A baking stone is a great addition to your kitchen arsenal, giving pizza and other baked goods a wonderful bottom crust.*

### INGREDIENTS | MAKES TWO ROUND 14" PIZZAS

2¼ teaspoons active dry yeast (1 packet)

1 cup water, warm (110°F–115°F), divided use

3 cups all-purpose flour

1 teaspoon sea salt

1 tablespoon agave syrup

2 tablespoons olive oil, plus additional oil for the baking sheet

## Pizza Stones

A stone is not a necessity, but it makes the best pizza. A preheated cookie sheet will work, but a better substitute is an outdoor grill. Preheat the grill on high, brush it lightly with olive oil, and cook the dough on one side until golden and marked by the grill (about 5 minutes). Flip dough over, add sauce and toppings, then close the grill cover and cook until bubbly, about 2–5 more minutes.

1. Dissolve yeast in ¼ cup warm water in a medium bowl. Allow to sit for 10–15 minutes.
2. In a large bowl, whisk together the flour and sea salt. Combine the agave syrup, 2 tablespoons olive oil, and remaining ¾ cup warm water with the yeast mixture, stirring to blend. Add the wet ingredients to the flour mixture and mix until the dough comes together. Knead for 8–10 minutes until the dough is soft and smooth.
3. Place dough in a lightly oiled bowl, turning once to coat, and allow to rise for 1½ hours, or until dough is very puffed up. Divide dough in half. Stretch each piece into a 14" circle, being careful not to flatten dough too much. Cover with a piece of lightly oiled plastic wrap and allow to rest for 15 minutes. Use additional olive oil to grease the pizza pan. Place dough in the pizza pan, stretching it to meet the edges of the pan. Cover and allow to rise for another 1½ hours.
4. Preheat oven to 450°F. To make a pizza, arrange sauce and toppings and bake 20–25 minutes, or until bottom and top of crust are browned and toppings are cooked.

**PER ⅛ PIZZA (8 SLICES PER PIZZA)** Calories: 105 | Fat: 2 g | Protein: 3 g | Sugar: 0 g | Fiber: 1 g | Carbohydrates: 18 g

# Multi-Grain Bread

*Full of vitamins, minerals, and fiber, this bread is chock-full of flavor too!*

**INGREDIENTS | MAKES 2 LOAVES (24 SLICES)**

2 cups whole-wheat flour

1 cup bread flour

½ cup spelt flour

½ cup millet flour

¼ cup sunflower seeds

2 teaspoons millet

2 teaspoons flaxseeds

2¼ teaspoons active dry yeast (1 packet)

2 cups water, warm (110°F–115°F)

2 tablespoons agave syrup

¾ teaspoon sea salt

2 tablespoons vegan margarine, melted

1. Combine whole-wheat flour, bread flour, spelt flour, and millet flour in a large bowl. Mix in sunflower seeds, millet, and flaxseeds.
2. Dissolve yeast with ¼ cup warm water in a small bowl. Allow to sit for 5–10 minutes to get bubbly. Add agave syrup, salt, melted margarine and the remaining 1¾ cups warm water to the yeast mixture. Stir to blend.
3. Add wet ingredients to flour mixture, mixing until the dough begins to come together. Turn dough out onto a floured surface and knead for 8–10 minutes, adding additional all-purpose flour as needed, until dough is smooth and elastic. Place dough in an oiled bowl, turning once to coat, cover, and allow to rise in a warm area for 1–1½ hours, or until doubled in bulk.
4. Punch dough down a few times and knead 1 minute. Cover and allow to rise for an additional 1–1½ hours. Punch dough down again. Divide dough into half and shape into loaves. Place on an oiled baking sheet and allow to rise a third time for 1–1½ hours.
5. Preheat oven to 400°F. Bake for 20–35 minutes until browned. When tapped, the bread should make a hollow sound. Transfer to wire racks to cool.

**PER 1 SLICE** Calories: 89 | Fat: 1 g | Protein: 3 g | Sugar: 0 g | Fiber: 2 g | Carbohydrates: 15 g

# Whole-Wheat Pizza Dough

*Whole-wheat flour gives this pizza dough lots of whole-grain flavor and a rustic appearance.*

**INGREDIENTS | MAKES 2 ROUND 14" PIZZAS**

2¼ teaspoons active dry yeast (1 packet)

1 cup water, warm (110°F–115°F), divided use

1½ cups whole-wheat flour

1½ cups all-purpose flour

1 teaspoon sea salt

1 tablespoon agave syrup

2 tablespoons olive oil, plus additional oil for the baking sheet

## Vegan Pizza

More and more pizzerias are offering vegan cheese, but cheeseless pizza is more delicious than you might think. When ordering out, fill your pizza with tons of extra toppings, and sprinkle it with nutritional yeast if you want that cheesy flavor, or make some dairy-free dressing to dip it in.

1. Dissolve yeast in ¼ cup warm water in a medium bowl. Allow to sit for 10–15 minutes. In a large bowl, whisk together the whole-wheat flour, all-purpose flour, and sea salt.
2. Combine the agave syrup, olive oil, and remaining ¾ cup warm water with the yeast mixture, stirring to blend. Add the wet ingredients to the flour mixture and mix until the dough comes together. Knead for 7–8 minutes until the dough is soft and smooth.
3. Place dough in a lightly oiled bowl, turning once to coat, and allow to rise for 1½ hours, or until dough is very puffed up. Divide dough in half. Stretch each piece into a 14" circle, being careful not to flatten dough too much. Cover with a piece of lightly oiled plastic wrap and allow to rest for 15 minutes. Use additional olive oil to grease the pizza pan. Place dough in the pizza pan, and stretch it to meet the edges of the pan. Cover and allow to rise for another 1½ hours.
4. Preheat oven to 450°F. Arrange sauce and toppings and bake 20–25 minutes, or until bottom and top of crust are browned and toppings are cooked.

**PER ⅛ PIZZA (8 SLICES PER PIZZA)** Calories: 101 | Fat: 2 g | Protein: 3 g | Sugar: 0 g | Fiber: 3 g | Carbohydrates: 17 g

# Olive and Artichoke Fougasse

*Fougasse is a pretty, rustic bread from France. It's known for having a pattern of slashes cut into the dough to make the bread resemble a tree or an ear of wheat.*

**INGREDIENTS | MAKES 5 BREADS (10 SERVINGS)**

1½ teaspoons active dry yeast

1 teaspoon sugar

1⅔ cups water, warm (110°–115°F)

4 tablespoons olive oil, divided use

4½ cups unbleached all-purpose flour

1¼ teaspoons sea salt

¼ cup pitted kalamata olives, quartered

¼ cup pitted green olives, quartered

½ cup marinated artichoke hearts, coarsely chopped

2 tablespoons flat-leaf parsley, coarsely chopped

2 tablespoons fresh thyme leaves

2 teaspoons lemon zest, coarsely chopped

Cornmeal or flour for dusting baking sheets

1 tablespoon fresh rosemary, minced

Coarse sea salt for sprinkling

Cracked black pepper for sprinkling

1. In a large bowl, dissolve yeast and sugar in 1 cup water. Allow to sit for 10 minutes to get bubbly. Add the remaining ⅔ cup water and 3 tablespoons olive oil. In a separate bowl, whisk flour and salt together. Add the flour mixture to the wet ingredients and mix until dough begins to come together, about 10 minutes.

2. Mix in kalamata olives, green olives, artichoke hearts, parsley, thyme, and lemon zest. Place dough in a lightly oiled bowl. Brush top of dough with additional oil, if needed, to cover entire surface. Cover with oiled plastic wrap and allow to rise 1½ hours, until doubled in bulk. Punch dough down a few times, cover with oiled plastic, and refrigerate 8 hours.

3. Punch dough down several times and divide into 5 equal pieces. Working with one piece at a time, transfer to a floured surface and roll out to a rectangle measuring approximately 8" × 5", adding flour as needed to prevent sticking.

4. Place rolled-out dough on a baking sheet that has been dusted with cornmeal or flour. Cut 5–8 slashes all the way through each piece of dough in the pattern of a tree or ear of wheat. Stretch dough out a bit so that the slashes are open about ½" wide. Brush with oil and sprinkle with rosemary, coarse sea salt, and cracked black pepper. Cover and allow dough to rest for 20–30 minutes.

5. Preheat oven to 450°F. Bake for 15 minutes, or until golden brown.

**PER ½ BREAD** Calories: 265 | Fat: 7 g | Protein: 6 g | Sugar: 1 g | Fiber: 2 g | Carbohydrates: 44 g

# Seed Bread

*The variety of seeds in this recipe provides super nutrition by way of protein, vitamins, and essential fatty acids. Satisfyingly crunchy and delicious!*

## INGREDIENTS | SERVES 24

2¼ teaspoons active dry yeast (1 packet)

1½ cups water, warm (110°F–115°F), divided use

¼ cup agave syrup

¼ cup soymilk

¼ cup sunflower seeds

¼ cup pumpkin seeds, shelled

2 tablespoons millet

1 tablespoon flaxseeds

3 cups bread flour

1 cup whole-wheat flour

2 teaspoons salt

## For the Birds?

In the United States, millet is most frequently spotted being used as a bird-friendly rice alternative at weddings and as a filler in bird feeders. But it's also a healthy whole grain used in one form or another across much of Africa. With a longer cooking time and harder texture than other grains, it tends to be less popular than other whole-grain options, but this recipe uses it well.

1. Dissolve yeast in ¼ cup warm water in a medium bowl. Allow to sit 10–15 minutes to get bubbly. Add agave syrup, soymilk, and remaining 1¼ cups warm water, stirring to blend. Mix in sunflower seeds, pumpkin seeds, millet, and flaxseeds.

2. In a large bowl, whisk together bread flour, whole-wheat flour, and salt. Add wet ingredients to flour mixture, mixing until dough begins to come together. Turn dough out onto a floured surface and knead until dough is smooth and elastic, adding additional bread flour as needed, for about 10 minutes. Place dough in a lightly oiled bowl, turning once to coat. Cover, and allow to rise in a warm area for 1½ hours, or until doubled in size.

3. Punch dough down and divide in half. Form each piece into a round loaf shape and place on a lightly oiled baking sheet. Cover and allow to rise for an additional 40–50 minutes, or until dough has doubled in size.

4. Preheat oven to 400°F. Bake for 25–30 minutes until loaf is browned and sounds hollow when tapped on the bottom. Transfer to wire racks to cool.

**PER SERVING** Calories: 113 | Fat: 2 g | Protein: 4 g | Sugar: 0 g | Fiber: 1 g | Carbohydrates: 18 g

# Pita Bread

*Dip this bread in hummus, or stuff it with the cumin-infused chickpea dish called falafel.*

**INGREDIENTS | SERVES 24**

2¼ teaspoons active dry yeast (1 packet)
1 tablespoon sugar
2½ cups soymilk, warm (110°–115°F)
¼ cup olive oil
6 cups bread flour
1½ teaspoons salt

1. Dissolve yeast and sugar in warm soymilk in a medium bowl. Allow to sit for 10 minutes to get bubbly. Stir in oil.
2. In a large bowl, whisk together flour and salt. Add wet ingredients to flour mixture, stirring until dough begins to come together. Turn dough out onto a floured surface and knead until dough is smooth and elastic, about 10 minutes.
3. Place dough in a lightly oiled bowl, turning once to coat. Cover, and allow to rise 1–1½ hours until doubled in size. Turn dough out onto a lightly floured surface. Divide dough into 24 equal pieces. Roll each piece into a ball, then roll out to a 6" circle with a rolling pin, adding a small amount of additional bread flour as needed to prevent sticking. Cover and allow to rise another 30 minutes.
4. Adjust rack to lower position and preheat oven to 500°F. Place dough rounds on an ungreased baking sheet. Bake 4–5 minutes until pita breads are puffed up and lightly browned. Remove from oven and cover with a slightly damp kitchen towel to cool and soften.

**PER SERVING** Calories: 156 | Fat: 3 g | Protein: 5 g | Sugar: 1 g | Fiber: 1 g | Carbohydrates: 26 g

# Baguettes

*Baguettes are long and slender French breads that are great for grinders or submarine sandwiches.*

**INGREDIENTS | SERVES 12**

2¼ teaspoons active dry yeast (1 packet)

1¼ cups water, warm (110°F–115°F)

2¾–3 cups bread flour

1½ teaspoons salt

Cornmeal, for dusting

1 tablespoon olive oil, for brushing

## Greasing Your Baking Pans

Have you ever tried to turn a cake out of a pan only to have it fall out in pieces because parts of it stuck to the pan? Greasing pans is necessary for many baked goods, such as cakes, to help them release from the pan. This can be done with a cooking spray or by dipping a folded paper towel in shortening, margarine, or oil and rubbing evenly over the sides and bottom of the pan.

1. Dissolve yeast in warm water in a small bowl. Allow to sit for 5–10 minutes to get bubbly. In a large bowl, whisk together 2¾ cups flour and salt. Stir yeast mixture into dry ingredients, mixing until a soft dough is formed. Cover and allow to rest for 15 minutes.

2. Turn dough out onto a lightly floured surface. Knead dough 8–10 minutes until smooth and elastic, adding additional flour as needed so dough is not too sticky. Place dough in a lightly oiled bowl, turning once to coat the surface of the dough. Allow to rise 40–50 minutes, or until doubled in bulk. Punch dough down a few times and divide in half.

3. Place dough halves on a lightly floured surface. Roll each piece into a 12" rope-shaped loaf. Place dough on a baking sheet that has been sprinkled with cornmeal. Brush dough lightly with olive oil, cover, and allow to rise an additional 20 minutes, or until doubled.

4. Preheat oven to 450°F. Cut a long, ¼"-deep slice across the length of each loaf. Bake for 20 minutes, or until the bottoms are browned and loaves produce a hollow sound when tapped. Transfer to wire racks to cool.

**PER SERVING** Calories: 125 | Fat: 2 g | Protein: 4 g | Sugar: 0 g | Fiber: 1 g | Carbohydrates: 23 g

# Garlic Breadsticks

*Try these soft, garlicky breadsticks as a complement to your favorite pasta dish,
or use them to dunk in hot homemade soup!*

**INGREDIENTS | SERVES 16**

2¼ teaspoons active dry yeast (1 packet)
½ teaspoon sugar
1 cup soymilk, warm (110°F–115°F)
¼ cup vegan margarine, melted
1 teaspoon salt
2¾ cups bread flour
6 cloves garlic, pressed
⅓ cup olive oil

1. In a large bowl, dissolve yeast and sugar in ½ cup warm soymilk. Let stand 5–10 minutes to get bubbly. Mix in margarine, salt, and remaining ½ cup soymilk. Gradually add flour until a soft dough is formed. Turn dough out onto a floured surface and knead 8–10 minutes, or until dough is smooth and elastic. Place dough in an oiled bowl, turning once to coat. Cover bowl and allow to rise in a warm area for 1½ hours, or until doubled in bulk.

2. Punch dough down a few times. Turn out onto a floured surface and knead for 3–4 minutes. Divide dough in half. Gently roll each piece into a 10" × 5" rectangle. Cut in half lengthwise and again crosswise. You should have 4 sections. Cut each section lengthwise, into 4 breadsticks, for a total of 16 breadsticks.

3. Place breadsticks on greased baking sheets, 2" apart. Cover and allow to rise 25–30 minutes or until doubled in size. Preheat oven to 375°F. Combine garlic and olive oil in a small bowl. Brush breadsticks with oil mixture. Bake for 10–15 minutes, or until golden brown. Serve warm.

**PER SERVING** Calories: 158 | Fat: 8 g | Protein: 3 g | Sugar: 1 g | Fiber: 1 g | Carbohydrates: 18 g

# Whole-Wheat Veggie Burger Buns

*These buns are very filling, so have a healthful, green salad alongside your burger instead of a starchy side dish!*

**INGREDIENTS | SERVES 16–18**

3 cups whole-wheat flour

1¾ cups water, warm (110°F–115°F), divided use

4½ teaspoons active dry yeast (2 packets)

2 tablespoons agave syrup

½ cup soymilk, warm (110°F–115°F)

2 tablespoons vegan margarine, melted

2 teaspoons salt

2 cups all-purpose flour

1. Place whole-wheat flour in a large bowl and stir in 1½ cups warm water. Set aside and allow to rest for 30 minutes.
2. In a medium bowl, combine remaining ¼ cup water with yeast and agave syrup, stirring to mix. Allow yeast mixture to sit for 10 minutes to get bubbly. Add warm soymilk, melted margarine, and salt to the yeast mixture.
3. Stir the soymilk mixture into the whole-wheat flour mixture; mix well. Gradually stir in the all-purpose flour. Add additional all-purpose flour, 1 tablespoon at a time, if dough is too sticky. Turn dough out onto a lightly floured surface and knead until smooth and elastic, 8–10 minutes. Place dough in lightly oiled bowl, turning once to coat. Cover, and allow to rise until doubled in bulk, about 1½ hours.
4. Turn dough out onto a lightly floured surface and knead for 2–3 minutes. Roll dough out to ¾" thickness. Using a hamburger ring, an English muffin ring, or a large-rimmed drinking glass, cut dough into rounds and place 1" apart on a well-oiled baking pan. Allow to rise for 25–30 minutes.
5. Preheat oven to 350°F. Bake for 20–25 minutes. Transfer to wire racks to cool.

**PER SERVING** Calories: 159 | Fat: 2 g | Protein: 5 g | Sugar: 0 g | Fiber: 3 g | Carbohydrates: 29 g

# Maple-Oat Bread

*This is a hearty, aromatic bread that tastes great toasted and slathered with peanut butter!*

---

**INGREDIENTS | MAKES 2 LOAVES (28–32 SLICES)**

2 tablespoons active dry yeast

1¼ cups water, warm (110°F–115°F)

⅓ cup Grade B maple syrup, divided use

1 cup soymilk, warm (110°F–115°F)

2 tablespoons canola oil

2 teaspoons salt

2 cups whole-wheat flour

4½ cups bread flour

1 cup rolled oats

---

## Making Nut Butters

Nut butters can be very expensive to purchase, but are so easy to make at home! Try making almond, walnut, or macadamia nut butter for a delicious alternative to store-bought peanut butter. Roasted nuts work best, so heat them in the oven at 400°F for 6–8 minutes or toast them on the stove top in a dry skillet for a few minutes. Then toss them in the food processor fitted with the "S" blade and process them until you have nut butter! If the nut butter is too thick for the blade to turn well, add a few drops of a bland oil, such as canola, to help it along. Store nut butters in the refrigerator in an airtight container.

1. In a large bowl, dissolve yeast in ½ cup warm water. Add 1 teaspoon maple syrup. Allow to sit for 5–10 minutes to get bubbly.
2. Mix in remaining ¾ cup warm water, maple syrup, warm soymilk, canola oil, and salt. Stir in whole-wheat flour and 2½ cups bread flour. Add 1 more cup of bread flour and the oats; mix well. Turn dough out onto a floured surface and knead for 10–15 minutes, adding additional bread flour as needed, until dough is smooth and elastic.
3. Shape dough into a ball and place in an oiled bowl, turning to coat entire surface of dough. Cover bowl with a towel and allow to rise in a warm place for 1½ hours, or until doubled in bulk. Punch dough down and divide in half. Shape each half into a smooth round loaf and place on a lightly oiled baking sheet. Cover and allow to rise again until doubled in bulk, about 30–40 minutes.
4. Preheat oven to 350°F. Bake 30–40 minutes until lightly browned. Loaves should sound hollow when tapped. Transfer to wire racks to cool.

**PER SERVING** Calories: 144 | Fat: 2 g | Protein: 5 g | Sugar: 3 g | Fiber: 2 g | Carbohydrates: 27 g

# Sun-Dried Tomato Pesto Focaccia

*The aroma of the sun-dried tomato, basil, and pine nuts is incredible in this wonderful bread!*

**INGREDIENTS | SERVES 24**

2¼ teaspoons active dry yeast

4½ cups all-purpose flour

1½ teaspoons salt

4 tablespoons extra-virgin olive oil, divided use

2 cups water, warm (110°F–115°F)

5 sun-dried tomatoes, oil-packed, drained

¼ cup fresh basil leaves

2 tablespoons pine nuts

1 clove garlic, peeled

½ teaspoon lemon zest, minced

## Types of Basil

Sweet·Italian basil may be the most common basil, but other varieties can add a layer of sensually enticing flavor. Lemon basil is identifiable by its lighter green color and fresh citrusy scent. Look for Thai holy basil with a purplish stem and jagged leaf edge for a delightfully scorching flavor.

1. Combine yeast, 4¼ cups flour, and salt in a large bowl, stirring with a fork to mix well. Mix in 2 tablespoons olive oil and the warm water with your hands, adding water ¼ cup at a time until all the water is incorporated. Add the remaining ¼ cup flour as needed if dough is too sticky to knead. Scrape the dough out onto a floured surface and knead for 5–7 minutes, continuing to add flour as needed.

2. Return dough to bowl, cover with plastic wrap or a towel, and allow to rise until doubled in bulk, about 1 hour. Spread dough somewhat evenly in an oiled 9" × 13" baking pan. Cover with plastic wrap or a towel and allow to rise for another 30 minutes. Preheat oven to 425°F.

3. While oven preheats, prepare pesto by placing remaining 2 tablespoons olive oil, 3 sun-dried tomatoes, basil, pine nuts, and garlic in a blender. Purée, and then stir in lemon zest. Poke finger holes across the top of the dough, then spread evenly with pesto. Coarsely chop the remaining 2 sun-dried tomatoes and sprinkle over the top.

4. Bake 25–30 minutes or until the top is lightly browned. Serve warm with additional olive oil for dipping, if desired.

**PER SERVING** Calories: 112 | Fat: 3 g | Protein: 3 g | Sugar: 0 g | Fiber: 1 g | Carbohydrates: 18 g

# Sweet Potato Braid

*This richly flavored bread will add homespun beauty to your holiday table.*

**INGREDIENTS | MAKES 2 LOAVES (APPROX. 24 SLICES)**

2¼ teaspoons active yeast (1 packet)

¼ cup water, warm (110°–115°F)

3 tablespoons maple syrup or agave syrup

¼ cup olive oil

1½ cups sweet potatoes, baked, peeled, and mashed

1 cup soymilk

2 cups whole-wheat flour

2–2½ cups unbleached all-purpose flour

1½ teaspoons salt

Additional soymilk, for brushing

1. In a medium bowl, dissolve yeast in warm water and allow to sit for 5–10 minutes to get bubbly. Stir in maple syrup, oil, sweet potatoes, and soymilk. In a large bowl, whisk together the whole-wheat flour, unbleached flour, and salt. Gradually add wet ingredients to flour mixture, stirring until well incorporated.

2. Turn dough out onto a floured surface and knead until dough is smooth and elastic, adding all-purpose flour as needed. Place dough in a lightly oiled bowl, turning once to coat. Cover, and allow to rise in a warm place until doubled, about 1½ hours. Punch dough down and turn out onto a floured surface. Divide dough into 6 equal pieces.

3. Shape each piece of dough into a 1" thick rope. To make each loaf, place 3 dough ropes on a lightly greased baking sheet. Braid ropes together with no loose gaps between them, but not too tightly. Pinch the ends together and tuck underneath the loaf. Brush with soymilk.

4. Preheat oven to 350°F. Bake 40–50 minutes, until golden brown and a hollow sound is produced when loaves are tapped.

**PER SERVING** Calories: 128 | Fat: 3 g | Protein: 3 g | Sugar: 3 g | Fiber: 2 g | Carbohydrates: 23 g

# Onion Rolls

*Caramelized onion takes these rolls from good to fantastic!*
*Try caramelizing a few cloves of garlic with the onions for a garlic enhancement.*

**INGREDIENTS | SERVES 16**

1 tablespoon olive oil

2 tablespoons vegan margarine, divided use

2 cups onion, diced

1¾ teaspoons salt, divided use

3½ cups bread flour

2 teaspoons sugar

2¼ teaspoons active dry yeast (1 packet)

1¼ cups soymilk, warm (110°F–115°F)

1. Heat olive oil and 1 tablespoon margarine in a medium skillet over low heat. Add onion and ¼ teaspoon salt. Cook, stirring often, until onions are caramelized, about 25–30 minutes. Remove from heat and allow to cool.

2. In a large bowl, whisk together flour, sugar, remaining salt, and yeast. Add onion mixture, 1 cup warm soymilk, and remaining 1 tablespoon margarine. Mix until a soft dough begins to come together. Knead for 8–10 minutes, adding the remaining ¼ cup soymilk or flour as needed.

3. Cover bowl with plastic wrap or a towel and allow to rise in a warm area until doubled in bulk, about 1 hour. Turn dough out onto a floured surface and divide into 4 equal pieces. Divide each piece into 4 more pieces, for a total of 16 pieces.

4. Shape each piece into a ball and place 1" apart on an ungreased baking sheet. Cover and allow to rise again for 30 minutes. Preheat oven to 325°F. Bake for 25–30 minutes, until golden brown. Transfer to wire racks to cool.

**PER SERVING** Calories: 146 | Fat: 3 g | Protein: 5 g | Sugar: 2 g | Fiber: 1 g | Carbohydrates: 25 g

# Mustard Bread

*This bread is an upgrade from the mustard sandwiches that you ate as a kid!*

**INGREDIENTS | SERVES 16**

1 cup water, warm (110°–115°F)

2 tablespoons whole-grain mustard

2 tablespoons olive oil

3½ cups all-purpose flour

2¼ teaspoons active dry yeast (1 packet)

1 tablespoon dry mustard powder

½ teaspoon turmeric

½ teaspoon sea salt

Soymilk for brushing

1. In a large bowl, stir water, mustard, and oil. In a separate bowl, whisk flour, yeast, mustard powder, turmeric, and salt. Add dry ingredients into the water mixture, stirring until combined. Knead until you have a smooth dough, 8–10 minutes. Cover with plastic wrap and allow to rise in a warm place 1½ hours, until doubled.
2. Punch down a few times and knead for another 4–5 minutes. Shape into a round loaf and transfer onto an oiled baking sheet. Cover, allow to rest for 1 hour.
3. Preheat oven to 400°F. Cut a few long, ¼"-deep slices across the top of the loaf. Brush top with soymilk and bake for 25–30 minutes until golden brown.

**PER SERVING** Calories: 118 | Fat: 2 g | Protein: 3 g | Sugar: 0 g | Fiber: 1 g | Carbohydrates: 21 g

# Anadama Bread

*Anadama is a homey, farm-style bread popular on the northern east coast of the United States.*

**INGREDIENTS | SERVES 18**

1½ cups water

1 teaspoon salt

1½ tablespoons vegetable shortening

⅓ cup molasses

⅓ cup cornmeal

2¼ teaspoons active dry yeast (1 packet)

¼ cup water, warm (110°F–115°F)

4¼ cups bread flour

1. In a medium saucepan, combine water and salt and bring to a boil. Remove from heat and stir in shortening, molasses, and cornmeal. Transfer into a large bowl and allow to cool until lukewarm.
2. In a small bowl, dissolve yeast in warm water. Add to cornmeal mixture. Gradually add flour, stirring until dough is stiff. Knead 8–10 minutes. Cover and allow to rise in a warm area until doubled, about 1½ hours. Punch down and place in a lightly greased 9" × 5" loaf pan. Cover and allow to rise for 45 minutes, until doubled.
3. Preheat oven to 375°F. Bake for 40–45 minutes.

**PER SERVING** Calories: 156 | Fat: 2 g | Protein: 4 g | Sugar: 4 g | Fiber: 1 g | Carbohydrates: 31 g

# Naan

*Fresh, hot Indian naan bread is one of the best treats on the planet! Try brushing the dough with melted margarine, chopped garlic, and cilantro before it goes in the oven.*

## INGREDIENTS | SERVES 12

2¼ teaspoons active dry yeast (1 packet)

2 teaspoons sugar

1⅓ cups water, warm (110°–115°F)

4 cups all-purpose flour

2 teaspoons salt

¼ cup plain soy yogurt

½ cup vegan margarine, melted, divided use

1. Dissolve the yeast and sugar in the water in a small bowl. Set aside for 10 minutes to let it get bubbly. Whisk flour and salt together vigorously in a large bowl. Stir in the yeast mixture, the soy yogurt, and ¼ cup of the melted margarine. Continue to stir until a soft dough is formed.
2. Transfer dough to a floured surface and knead until dough is smooth and elastic, about 5–7 minutes. Place dough in lightly oiled bowl, turning once to coat. Cover bowl and allow to rise in a warm area until doubled in bulk, about 1½ hours.
3. Place a baking or pizza stone on the bottom rack of the oven and preheat to 450°F. Punch dough down. Knead for another 4–5 minutes. Divide dough into 12 equal pieces and place naan on a foil-lined and oiled baking pan. Cover and allow to rise another 45–60 minutes, until doubled in bulk.
4. Place 2 naan on the preheated baking stone and bake for 2–3 minutes until golden brown. Remove from the oven and brush lightly with the remaining melted margarine. Wait for a few minutes for the baking stone to heat up again and repeat with the rest of the naan.

**PER SERVING** Calories: 226 | Fat: 8 g | Protein: 5 g | Sugar: 1 g | Fiber: 1 g | Carbohydrates: 33 g

# Pan Micha

*This French-style loaf from Panama is soft and delicious
with nothing more than a smear of vegan margarine.*

**INGREDIENTS | SERVES 24**

2¼ teaspoons active dry yeast (1 packet)

3 tablespoons sugar, divided use

¼ cup water, warm (110°F–115°F)

2 tablespoons vegan margarine, melted

1½ teaspoons salt

2 cups soymilk, warm (110°F–115°F)

6 cups unbleached all-purpose flour

Additional soymilk for brushing

1. In a large bowl, dissolve yeast and 1 tablespoon sugar in warm water. Allow to sit for 5–10 minutes to let it get bubbly. Stir in the margarine, salt, remaining 2 tablespoons sugar, and the soymilk. Gradually add flour, 2 cups at a time, stirring until dough comes together. Transfer to a floured surface and knead for 8–10 minutes until dough is smooth and elastic. Shape dough into a ball and place in an oiled bowl, turning to coat dough with oil. Cover with plastic wrap and allow to rise in a warm area for about 2 hours, or until doubled in bulk.

2. Punch dough down, cover, and allow to rise again for about 30 minutes, until doubled in bulk again. Divide dough in half and shape into loaves. Place in lightly greased 9" × 5" loaf pans and cut a ¼"-deep diagonal slash across the top of each loaf. Brush tops with soymilk.

3. Preheat oven to 350°F. Bake for 35–40 minutes, until golden brown and bread sounds hollow when tapped on the bottom.

**PER SERVING** Calories: 136 | Fat: 1 g | Protein: 4 g | Sugar: 2 g | Fiber: 1 g | Carbohydrates: 26 g

# CHAPTER 6

# Flatbreads

# Moroccan Harsha with Thyme

*Harsha (a.k.a. harcha) is a savory pancake traditionally made with semolina flour and wild thyme (za'atar). Regular thyme or oregano may be substituted! The word "za'atar" is also used in reference to a mixture of spices including sumac and green herbs.*

**INGREDIENTS | SERVES 8**

2 cups fine semolina flour

2 teaspoons baking powder

2 tablespoons sugar

½ teaspoon sea salt

½ cup olive oil

2 tablespoons fresh thyme

¾ cup soymilk

1. In a large bowl, whisk together semolina flour, baking powder, sugar, and salt. Work the olive oil into the semolina mixture with your hands. Add thyme and soymilk, continuing to mix until mixture forms a dough with a wet sand consistency. Add more soymilk or water, if needed.
2. Shape dough into 8 balls and allow to rest for 5–10 minutes. While dough is resting, preheat ungreased griddle over medium-low heat.
3. Flatten balls into ¼" thick pancakes, place on heated griddle, and cook on one side until browned, about 8–10 minutes. Flip over and cook the other side for an additional 8–10 minutes. Serve warm with vegan margarine.

**PER SERVING** Calories: 281 | Fat: 14 g | Protein: 6 g | Sugar: 5 g | Fiber: 1 g | Carbohydrates: 34 g

# Puri (Poori)

*Puri is an Indian deep-fried puff bread that is traditionally served with vegetable side dishes like potato masala. If it is available to you, use an equal amount of chapati flour in place of the whole-wheat and all-purpose flours for an authentic puri.*

**INGREDIENTS | MAKES APPROX. 14 PURIS 6" IN DIAMETER**

1 cup whole-wheat flour

1 cup all-purpose flour

½ teaspoon sea salt

1½ teaspoons olive oil

1 cup water

Canola oil for deep frying

## Indian Vegan Options

In India, many vegetarians forswear eggs as well as onions and garlic for religious purposes, making Indian food an excellent choice for vegans. When eating at Indian restaurants, be sure to ask about ghee, clarified butter, which is a traditional ingredient, but easily and frequently substituted with oil.

1. Whisk whole-wheat flour, all-purpose flour, and salt together in a large bowl. Gradually add oil and water while mixing by hand until dough comes together. Knead dough until it is smooth. Shape dough into 12–16 small round balls. Cover and allow to rest for 30–60 minutes.
2. Roll each ball into a 4"-diameter circle, with the thickness of a dime. Preheat canola oil in a large skillet or deep fryer to 350°F. Cook one puri at a time, browning on both sides.
3. Drain on paper towels. Serve warm.

**PER SERVING** Calories: 106 | Fat: 5 g | Protein: 2 g | Sugar: 0 g | Fiber: 1 g | Carbohydrates: 13 g

# Lavash (Armenian Cracker Bread)

*This is a thin, crispy bread that goes well with hummus and is also a good base for a quick pizza.*

**INGREDIENTS | MAKES 10 LAVASH**

2½ cups all-purpose flour

1 teaspoon sugar

1 teaspoon sea salt

⅔ cup water

Egg replacement equal to 1 egg

2 tablespoons vegan margarine, melted

2 tablespoons sesame seeds

1. Preheat oven to 400°F.
2. Whisk together flour, sugar, and salt in a large bowl. Add water, egg replacement, and melted margarine, stirring until dough is stiff. Knead for about 5 minutes until dough is smooth. Cut dough into 10 even pieces; shape into balls.
3. Roll out each ball on a lightly floured surface until very thin. Place on an ungreased cookie sheet and sprinkle with sesame seeds, pressing lightly to make them stick.
4. Bake 10–12 minutes, until browned.

**PER ½ LAVASH** Calories: 74 | Fat: 2 g | Protein: 2 g | Sugar: 0 g | Fiber: 1 g | Carbohydrates: 13 g

# Corn Tortillas

*Corn tortillas are so easy to make with masa harina! Masa harina is a type of instant corn flour available at Latin markets and many grocers. Some stores even sell prepared corn tortilla dough.*

**INGREDIENTS | MAKES 16–18 TORTILLAS**

2 cups masa harina
¼ teaspoon baking soda (optional)
1⅓–2 cups water, warm

1. In a large bowl, combine masa harina, baking soda, and 1⅓ cups water. Mix well until you have a soft dough, and allow to rest for 5 minutes. Preheat an ungreased griddle over medium flame.
2. Divide dough into 12–14 ball-shaped pieces. Line the bottom of a tortilla press with plastic wrap. Place a ball in the center of the press, cover with another section of plastic, and close the top part of the press down on the dough. Open press and peel back top piece of plastic. Remove the tortilla from the press by lifting the plastic, and turning it out onto your hand.
3. Slide the tortilla onto the hot griddle and cook for 45 seconds. Flip over and cook for 1 minute. Flip one last time and cook 15 seconds longer, then transfer to a tortilla warmer or a bowl lined with a clean kitchen towel. Cover to keep warm while cooking the rest of the tortillas.

**PER 1 TORTILLA** Calories: 50 | Fat: 0 g | Protein: 2 g | Sugar: 0 g | Fiber: 1 g | Carbohydrates: 10 g

# Cabbage Pierogi

*These Polish stuffed dumplings are also popular when filled with potatoes or sauerkraut, and are sometimes served as a dessert with a filling of dried plums! Pierogi are a Polish Christmas holiday tradition.*

**INGREDIENTS | SERVES 8**

2½ cups all-purpose flour

½ teaspoon salt

1 cup water, boiling

1 small head cabbage, shredded

3 tablespoons vegan margarine

1 medium onion, diced

¼ teaspoon caraway seeds

Additional salt and black pepper, as desired

1. Whisk flour and salt together in a large bowl. Gradually stir in the boiling water until a dough forms. Transfer dough to a floured surface and knead for 15–20 minutes until dough is elastic and smooth. Shape dough into a ball and place in a bowl. Cover with plastic wrap and allow to sit for 1 hour.
2. While dough is resting, prepare filling by adding shredded cabbage to a pot of boiling water. Cook for 3 minutes, reduce heat, and simmer for 15–20 minutes. Drain.
3. Melt margarine in a large skillet over medium heat and cook onions until tender. Add cabbage, caraway seeds, salt, and pepper; cover and continue cooking until cabbage is tender. Remove lid and simmer for a few more minutes to evaporate excess moisture. Chop cabbage into small pieces.
4. To make pierogi, take ⅓ of the dough, leaving the rest covered, and roll out very thin. Using a biscuit-cutter or the rim of drinking glass, cut rounds out of the dough. Place a heaping tablespoon of cabbage mixture onto one half of the circle, leaving a small border around the edge. Fold the other half over the filling and pinch the edges together tightly. Repeat with remaining dough.
5. Boil a large pot of water. Add salt to the water if desired. Slide a few pierogi at a time into the boiling water. Return to a slow boil and cook pierogi for about 10 minutes. Drain. Serve hot or let them cool for a few minutes, then brown in a skillet with vegan margarine. Try serving these with vegan sour cream and caramelized onions!

**PER SERVING** Calories: 208 | Fat: 5 g | Protein: 5 g | Sugar: 4 g | Fiber: 4 g | Carbohydrates: 36 g

# Roti

*Indian Roti is a basic daily bread that is so simple to make that many families make fresh roti for each meal! Give your fork a rest and use torn bits of roti to scoop up your food.*

**INGREDIENTS | SERVES 16**

1½ cups whole-wheat flour

½ teaspoon sea salt

1 cup water

1. In a large bowl, whisk together the flour and salt. Make a well in the center and gradually mix in the water by hand until you have a soft dough. Knead for 7–8 minutes; cover and allow to rest for 15–20 minutes. Divide into 16 equal pieces, and shape into balls. On a floured surface, roll each ball into a 6"–8" circle.
2. Preheat a large, heavy skillet over high heat. Once hot, reduce heat to medium. Cook roti in skillet, flipping over when dough begins to bubble up. Gently press down on the roti with a spatula, flip over again, then remove from pan. Cover to keep warm while others are cooking.
3. Serve warm, as is, or with melted vegan margarine.

**PER SERVING** Calories: 38 | Fat: 0 g | Protein: 2 g | Sugar: 0 g | Fiber: 1 g | Carbohydrates: 8 g

# Rieska

*This is a quick rye flatbread from Finland that is sometimes made with oats or potatoes. Rieska is a nice accompaniment to a bowl of hot soup!*

**INGREDIENTS | SERVES 8**

½ cup soymilk powder

1 cup water

2 cups rye flour

¾ teaspoon salt

2 teaspoons sugar

2 teaspoons baking powder

2 tablespoons vegan margarine, melted

Coarse sea salt for sprinkling, optional

1. Preheat oven to 450°F.
2. Mix soymilk powder with water until well blended. This is meant to substitute for evaporated milk, so it will be thicker than regular soymilk. Set aside.
3. In a large bowl, whisk together the flour, salt, sugar, and baking powder. Stir in soymilk mixture and melted margarine until smooth. Turn onto a greased cookie sheet and pat to a 14" circle, about ½" thick.
4. Sprinkle with sea salt to taste, if desired. Bake until lightly browned, about 10 minutes. Cut into wedges and serve hot with vegan margarine.

**PER SERVING** Calories: 140 | Fat: 4 g | Protein: 4 g | Sugar: 1 g | Fiber: 4 g | Carbohydrates: 22 g

# Flour Tortillas

*Flour tortillas are a classic Mexican flatbread and a perfect wrap for your favorite burrito fillings. For that little something extra, try reheating cooked tortillas over an open flame until charred in spots.*

**INGREDIENTS | SERVES 10**

2 cups all-purpose flour

1 teaspoon baking powder

½ teaspoon sea salt

2 tablespoons vegetable shortening

¾ cup water

## Breakfast Tortillas

Sure, tortillas are great for burritos, tacos, and fajitas, but why not use them for breakfast? Fill them with your favorite tofu scramble recipe, perhaps topped with some salsa or beans. Your tofu will taste even better wrapped in a warm, freshly made tortilla.

1. In a large bowl, whisk together flour, baking powder, and salt. Mix in shortening by hand until mixture resembles crumbs. Gradually add water, mixing by hand, until dough can be gathered together in a ball. Add additional water 1 tablespoon at a time as needed if dough is too dry.

2. Knead dough 4–5 minutes on a floured surface, until dough becomes smooth and elastic. Cover and allow dough to rest for 1 hour. Divide dough into 10 equal pieces, each shaped into a ball. Roll out each ball into an ⅛" thick circle, on a lightly floured surface. Preheat an ungreased skillet over medium-high heat. Cook tortillas for 1–2 minutes on each side. Keep prepared tortillas warm while others are being cooked.

**PER SERVING** Calories: 114 | Fat: 3 g | Protein: 3 g | Sugar: 0 g | Fiber: 1 g | Carbohydrates: 19 g

# Whole-Wheat Pita Bread

*Whole-wheat pita bread is hearty and delicious!*
*This bread makes a great base for hummus or super-fast pizzas.*

**INGREDIENTS | MAKES 6 PITA BREADS**

1 tablespoon agave syrup

1¼ cups water, warm (110F°–115°F), divided use

2¼ teaspoons active dry yeast (1 packet)

2 tablespoons olive oil

1½ cups whole-wheat flour

1½ cups all-purpose flour

2 teaspoons sea salt

1. In a large bowl, combine agave syrup, ½ cup of the water, and the yeast. Stir well and allow to sit for 10 minutes to get bubbly. Stir in 2 tablespoons olive oil and ½ cup water.
2. Whisk together the whole-wheat flour, all-purpose flour, and salt in a separate bowl. Gradually combine flour mixture with wet ingredients, adding more water as needed. Knead dough for 8–10 minutes. Dough should be smooth and elastic.
3. Shape into a ball and place in a lightly oiled bowl, turning to coat surface of dough with oil. Cover the bowl with plastic wrap and allow dough to rise in a warm place for 1 hour, until doubled in bulk. Punch dough down and allow to rest for 15–20 minutes.
4. Turn dough out onto a floured surface and divide into 12 equal pieces. Shape dough pieces into balls. Cover with plastic wrap to keep them from drying out while you roll them out one at a time. Roll each piece into a circle 7"–8" across and about ⅛" thick. Arrange pitas so they are not touching, on a baking sheet that has been dusted with cornmeal. Cover with a damp towel and allow to rise for 1 hour.
5. Place oven rack in the bottom third of the oven and preheat to 500°F. Bake for 5 minutes, or until lightly browned and puffed up. Wrap pitas in kitchen towels to keep warm while the rest are baking.

**PER ½ PITA BREAD** Calories: 134 | Fat: 3 g | Protein: 4 g | Sugar: 0 g | Fiber: 2 g | Carbohydrates: 23 g

# Chinese Scallion Pancakes

*Serve these savory treats as snacks or appetizers with a variety of Asian-inspired dipping sauces.*

**INGREDIENTS | MAKES 4 PANCAKES**

2 cups all-purpose flour

1 cup water, boiling

1 tablespoon toasted sesame seed oil

1 cup scallions, thinly sliced

1 teaspoon sea salt

Canola oil, for frying

Black pepper, to taste

1. Place flour in a large bowl. Gradually add boiling water, stirring until dough begins to come together. Turn dough out onto a floured surface and knead until smooth, about 5 minutes. Place in a bowl, cover, and allow to sit for 30 minutes in a warm place.

2. Divide dough into 4 equal pieces and roll into balls. Cover to keep from drying out. Roll one ball into an 8" circle on a lightly floured surface. Spread a thin layer of sesame oil over the surface of the dough. Sprinkle evenly with ¼ cup scallions and ¼ teaspoon sea salt. Roll up circle into a cigar shape, then shape into a spiral like a cinnamon roll. Tuck the outside end underneath the roll. Using the palm of your hand, gently flatten the spiral, then roll out into a 7" circle. Repeat with the rest of the dough.

3. Heat ¼" of canola oil in a heavy 8" cast-iron or nonstick skillet over medium-high heat. Cook pancakes about 2 minutes on each side, until golden brown. Drain on paper towels. Season with black pepper and additional sea salt, if desired. Serve as is, or with dipping sauce.

**PER ½ PANCAKE SERVING** Calories: 148 | Fat: 4 g | Protein: 3 g | Sugar: 0 g | Fiber: 1 g | Carbohydrates: 25 g

# Socca

*Popular in France, socca is a savory, gluten-free chickpea flour "pancake" that is cooked over high heat, giving it crispy edges. Serve socca as an appetizer with a good wine.*

**INGREDIENTS | MAKES 3 BREADS**

1 cup chickpea (garbanzo) flour

¾ teaspoon sea salt

½ teaspoon cracked black pepper

½ tablespoon fresh rosemary leaves, minced

1 cup warm water

2½ tablespoons olive oil, divided use

½ medium onion, thinly sliced

1. Place a 9" cast-iron skillet in the oven and preheat to 450°F. In a large bowl, whisk together chickpea flour, sea salt, and pepper. Stir in minced rosemary. Add water and 1½ tablespoons olive oil. Whisk batter until well blended. Cover bowl and allow batter to rest at room temperature for at least 2 hours while batter thickens. Stir in sliced onions.

2. Remove the skillet from the oven and add the remaining 1 tablespoon oil. Pour approximately ⅓ of the batter into the hot skillet. Set skillet back in the oven and bake 12–15 minutes or until edges are crispy and batter has become firm. Place skillet under broiler and heat for a few minutes, until socca begins to burn in spots.

3. Transfer socca onto a wooden cutting board and cut into pieces. Repeat process two more times with remaining batter. Serve with additional sea salt and olive oil, as desired.

**PER SERVING** Calories: 227 | Fat: 13 g | Protein: 7 g | Sugar: 4 g | Fiber: 4 g | Carbohydrates: 20 g

# Whole-Wheat Tortillas

*These tortillas have a wholesome, nutty flavor! Use just like regular flour tortillas.*

**INGREDIENTS | SERVES 10**

2 cups whole-wheat flour

1 teaspoon baking powder

½ teaspoon sea salt

2 tablespoons olive or canola oil

½ cup water, warm

## Baked Tortilla Chips

Why not make your own tortilla chips? Slice whole-wheat tortillas into strips or triangles, and arrange in a single layer on a baking sheet. Drizzle with olive oil for a crispier chip, and season with a bit of salt and garlic powder if you want, or just bake them plain. It'll take about 5–6 minutes on each side in a 300°F oven.

1. In a large bowl, whisk together whole-wheat flour, baking powder, and salt. Mix in olive oil. Gradually add water, mixing by hand, until dough comes together as a ball. Add additional water, 1 tablespoon at a time as needed, if dough is too dry.
2. Knead dough 20 times on a floured surface. Cover and allow dough to rest for 15 minutes. Divide dough into 10 equal pieces and shape into balls. Roll out each ball into an 8"–10" circle on a lightly floured surface.
3. Preheat an ungreased skillet over medium-high heat. Cook tortillas 30 seconds on each side, or until they puff up. These are doubly delicious when reheated over the direct flame of the burner!

**PER SERVING** Calories: 105 | Fat: 3 g | Protein: 3 g | Sugar: 0 g | Fiber: 3 g | Carbohydrates: 18 g

# Chapati

*Chapati is a simple Indian flatbread that pairs well with vegetable stews and bean dishes.*

**INGREDIENTS | SERVES 10**

1 cup all-purpose flour

1 cup whole-wheat flour

1 teaspoon salt

2 tablespoons olive oil

¾ cup water, hot from the tap, plus more if needed

1. Whisk together all-purpose flour, whole-wheat flour, and salt. Mix in olive oil. Gradually add water, stirring until mixture comes together as a soft dough. Turn onto a floured surface and knead until smooth.
2. Cut dough into 10 pieces and roll each into a ball. Cover and allow to rest for 5 minutes. Roll dough out into thin, 8"–10" circles on a lightly floured surface.
3. Heat a heavy skillet over medium heat. Once pan is hot, oil lightly, and cook chapatis for about 30 seconds on each side. Keep warm while others are cooked.

**PER SERVING** Calories: 110 | Fat: 3 g | Protein: 3 g | Sugar: 0 g | Fiber: 2 g | Carbohydrates: 18 g

# Potato Bolani

*Similar to a savory turnover, this special occasion bread originates from Afghanistan where it is usually found stuffed with potatoes, spinach, lentils, or pumpkin.*

## INGREDIENTS | MAKES 6 BOLANI

3½ cups all-purpose flour

2½ teaspoons sea salt, divided use

1 cup water

¼ cup plus 1 teaspoon olive oil, divided use

1 pound russet potatoes, boiled, drained

½ cup cilantro, finely chopped

2 tablespoons vegan margarine, melted

1 teaspoon cracked black pepper

1. Whisk flour and 1 teaspoon sea salt together in a large bowl. Gradually add 1 cup water and 1 teaspoon olive oil, mixing by hand until dough begins to come together. Add more water 1 tablespoon at a time as needed, if dough is too dry. Turn dough out on a lightly floured board and knead for 10 minutes. Return dough to the bowl, cover, and allow to rest for 1 hour.

2. While dough rests, slip skins off of cooked potatoes. Mash potatoes with cilantro, margarine, 1½ teaspoons sea salt, and black pepper.

3. Divide dough into 6 equal pieces. Roll each piece into a smooth ball. Roll each dough ball into a 10"–12" circle on a lightly floured surface. Dough will be very thin. Spread ¼ cup of the potatoes evenly over half of the circle, leaving a small border around the edge to seal the turnover. Fold the other half over the potato mixture and pinch the two edges together to form a seal.

4. Heat ¼ cup olive oil in a heavy skillet over medium-high heat. Brown 3–4 minutes per side or until golden. Drain on paper towels. Serve warm with vegan sour cream or plain soy yogurt.

**PER ½ BOLANI** Calories: 226 | Fat: 7 g | Protein: 5 g | Sugar: 0 g | Fiber: 2 g | Carbohydrates: 36 g

# Gordita

*"Gorda" means "fat" in Spanish and "–ita" refers to something small.*
*So Gorditas are the little, fat relative of corn tortillas!*

**INGREDIENTS | SERVES 5**

2 cups masa harina (instant corn flour)

1⅓ cups water, warm

1 tablespoon baking powder

¼ cup vegetable shortening, slightly warmed

Canola oil for frying

1. Combine masa harina with the warm water and baking powder, stirring until a soft dough is formed. Using your hand, mix in the shortening. Add more water or masa harina, as needed, so that dough is not too dry or too wet. Transfer dough into a plastic zip-top bag, seal top, and and allow to rest for 10 minutes.

2. Heat a dry cast-iron skillet over medium heat. Pinch off enough dough to make a 2" ball. By hand or with a tortilla press, shape ball into a 4" circle about ¼" thick. Place in skillet and cook for 1 minute on each side. Repeat with the rest of the dough.

3. Heat 3" of canola oil to 350°–375°F in a cast-iron pot or deep skillet. Slide prebrowned gorditas into the hot oil, a few at a time, and fry for 30 seconds. Carefully turn gorditas over and continue to cook until golden brown. Gorditas should puff slightly.

4. Cool for a few minutes, then split in half and fill as desired. Try a layer of Mexican-style beans topped with potatoes that have been stewed with tomatoes, onions, garlic, chiles, and cilantro.

**PER SERVING** Calories: 83 | Fat: 7 g | Protein: 1 g | Sugar: 0 g | Fiber: 0 g | Carbohydrates: 4 g

# Arepa

*A popular South American bread, arepas are fried and baked corn cakes. This recipe calls for arepa flour, which is precooked corn flour, also known as* masa al instante. *Find this flour at Latin food stores.*

**INGREDIENTS | SERVES 12**

2¾ cups water, hot from the tap

1 teaspoon sea salt

2½ cups arepa flour (precooked corn flour)

2 tablespoons vegan margarine, melted

Olive oil, for frying

1. Preheat oven to 350°F.
2. Pour hot water into a large bowl and add salt. Stir to dissolve. Gradually mix in arepa flour by hand until incorporated. Add melted margarine and mix well. Cover bowl with plastic wrap and allow to rest for 15 minutes.
3. Divide dough into 12 equal pieces. Shape each piece into a 3" round disk with a thickness of about 1", smoothing any cracks that occur on the edges. Place arepas on a baking sheet and cover with plastic wrap as you finish them. Heat a cast-iron skillet over medium heat and add ½ tablespoon olive oil. Place arepas in the skillet and brown for 4–5 minutes per side. Add more oil as needed to brown all the arepas.
4. To finish, remove plastic wrap and place cookie sheet in the preheated oven. Bake for 15 minutes. Arepas should sound hollow when they are done. To serve, split arepas open like a sandwich and smear with vegan margarine, salsa, or your favorite fixings! Serve warm.

**PER SERVING** Calories: 130 | Fat: 6 g | Protein: 1 g | Sugar: 0 g | Fiber: 0 g | Carbohydrates: 16 g

# Spinach Paratha (Palak Paratha)

*Parathas are a very versatile flatbread that can be stuffed or made plain with a variety of vegetables and spices incorporated into the dough. The process of folding the dough is very important to the development of the tender layers, so don't be tempted to skip it!*

**INGREDIENTS | SERVES 6**

1½ cups whole-wheat flour

¼ cup plus 1 tablespoon olive oil, divided use

½ cup cooked spinach, drain excess moisture

¼ cup plain soy yogurt

2 cloves garlic

1 teaspoon salt

¼ teaspoon ground cumin

¼ teaspoon turmeric

Pinch ground cayenne pepper

Water, as needed, lukewarm

1. Combine flour and 1 tablespoon olive oil in a medium bowl, mixing until well combined. Set aside. Place spinach, soy yogurt, garlic, salt, cumin, turmeric, and cayenne in a blender and blend into a paste. Add spinach mixture to flour. Mix, adding water as needed, until dough is somewhat firm. Shape dough into a ball and place in an oiled bowl, turning to coat dough with oil. Cover and allow to rest for 15–20 minutes.

2. Knead dough for 10 seconds and divide into 6 pieces. Roll each piece into a smooth ball, then use your hands to flatten them. Roll dough out into a 5"–6" circle, on a lightly floured surface. Spread ½ teaspoon olive oil across one half of the circle, sprinkle with a bit of flour, and then fold in half to make a semicircle. Spread ½ teaspoon olive oil on one half of the semi-circle, sprinkle with a bit more flour, and fold into a triangle shape. Sprinkle with flour. Repeat the procedure with the rest of the dough. Roll each piece into a triangle or a circle, a little less than ¼" thick.

3. Heat a dry griddle or heavy skillet over medium heat. Place paratha on the hot skillet and cook until bubbles appear. Turn paratha over and cook for about 30 seconds. Spread ½ teaspoon of olive oil over the top of the paratha and turn over again. Use the spatula to lightly press down on the paratha. Spread ½ teaspoon olive oil on this side of the paratha and turn over again. Press with spatula until paratha appears completely cooked.

4. Place finished parathas in kitchen towels to keep warm while the rest are being cooked. Serve parathas hot with your favorite curried vegetable dish and Indian pickles.

**PER SERVING** Calories: 213 | Fat: 12 g | Protein: 5 g | Sugar: 1 g | Fiber: 4 g | Carbohydrates: 24 g

# Navajo Fry Bread

*This puffy and wonderfully satisfying bread is a traditional food,
steeped in the history of the Navajo people. Top with beans, vegan taco meat,
lettuce, tomato, and vegan Cheddar cheese for delicious Navajo tacos!*

**INGREDIENTS | SERVES 8**

2 cups unbleached all-purpose flour

2 teaspoons soymilk powder

2 teaspoons baking powder

½ teaspoon salt

1 cup water

Canola oil for frying

## Vegan Burritos

Brown some vegetarian chorizo or mock sausage crumbles and wrap in tortillas or fry bread, perhaps topped with some shredded vegan cheese to make vegan burritos. Or, combine with TVP taco meat for a "meaty" Mexican main.

1. In a large bowl, whisk together the flour, soymilk powder, baking powder, and salt. Add all of the water and stir until the dough just begins to come together. Dust hands with flour and mix dough well by hand to incorporate all the flour, without actually kneading the dough. Dough will be somewhat sticky. Shape into a ball.
2. Divide dough into 8 equal pieces. Flour hands and stretch and shape each piece of dough into a 5"–7" circle. Don't worry about making them perfectly round.
3. Heat 1" of canola oil in a fryer or deep skillet to 350°F. Carefully slide dough into hot oil and cook 3–4 minutes until brown, gently pressing dough down so that it is submerged in the oil. Then turn over and cook the other side for another 3–4 minutes. Remove from oil and drain on paper towels. Serve hot.

**PER SERVING** Calories: 196 | Fat: 9 g | Protein: 3 g | Sugar: 0 g | Fiber: 1 g | Carbohydrates: 24 g

# Sope

*Sopes are little boats made from corn flour (masa harina); they can be filled with almost anything!*

**INGREDIENTS | MAKES 8 SOPES**

1 cup masa harina
⅛ teaspoon baking powder
¼ teaspoon salt
¾ cup water
Canola oil for frying

1. Combine masa harina, baking powder, salt, and water in medium bowl. Use your hands to mix dough until a smooth ball is formed. Add more water if needed. Divide dough into eight equal pieces and shape into balls. To shape sopes, place a dough ball between two pieces of plastic wrap. Use a flat-bottomed pot to flatten ball into a 2½" circle, about ¼" thick. Fold up the sides of the circle to make a ½" wall all the way around the edge.

2. Heat a dry skillet over high heat and brown the sopes on the flat side only, for about 1 minute. In a small pot, heat ½" of oil to 350°F. Use a fork to prick the inside of the sopes 3 or 4 times, being careful not to poke all the way through the bottom.

3. Cook one sope at a time in the hot oil for 1–2 minutes, until browned. Drain sopes upside down on paper towels. Fill sopes with your favorite taco fixings!

**PER SERVING** Calories: 110 | Fat: 7 g | Protein: 2 g | Sugar: 0 g | Fiber: 1 g | Carbohydrates: 11 g

# Papadum

*Papadum is a very thin, crispy flatbread that tastes great with sweet chutney. After they're dried they can be stored in an airtight container for later use. Simply fry them up when you want them!*

**INGREDIENTS | SERVES 15**

8 cups lentil flour (black gram flour)

1½ teaspoons cracked black pepper

½ teaspoon cumin seeds

½ teaspoon sea salt

¼ cup water

## Salt in Vegan Baking

The trick to successful vegan baking using non-vegan recipes is in the conversion! Salt is a great example. If a recipe calls for unsalted butter, a common vegan substitution is vegan margarine. However, using vegan margarine may add more salt to the recipe than is called for, making the end result too salty! To avoid this, simply use less salt, or for recipes where a "buttery" flavor is not needed, use vegetable shortening in place of the unsalted butter.

1. Preheat oven to 200°F.
2. In a large bowl, combine lentil flour, black pepper, cumin, and salt. Using your hand, mix in water and knead until you have a smooth dough, about 8–10 minutes. Use additional water, if needed.
3. Divide dough into 15 even pieces, shaping each piece into a ball. Place dough balls in an airtight container to keep them from drying out. Working with one ball at a time, roll out to very thin circle, about ⅛" thick on a lightly oiled surface. Place papadums on a baking sheet and dry in the oven for 1 hour. Place dried papadums in an airtight container.
4. To prepare papadums, toast over open flame on the stove top, turning them constantly with tongs, until they are crisp and very lightly browned in spots. This will take approximately 30 seconds total. Serve as an appetizer or snack with chutney or your favorite Indian dipping sauces.

**PER SERVING** Calories: 192 | Fat: 3 g | Protein: 11 g | Sugar: 5 g | Fiber: 5 g | Carbohydrates: 29 g

# CHAPTER 7

# Sourdough and Fermented Breads

# Sourdough Starter

*This is a basic sourdough starter made with yeast.*
*Be sure to use bottled or other nonchlorinated water.*

### INGREDIENTS | MAKES 2–3 CUPS STARTER

2 cups all-purpose or bread flour

2¼ teaspoons active dry yeast (1 packet)

2 cups pure water, warm (110°F–115°F)

## The Sponge Method

The sponge method extends the fermentation time, which creates a more complex flavor in the finished bread. Any recipe can be made into a sponge recipe, simply by prefermenting part of the ingredients. A small amount of water, yeast, and flour is all it takes, plus 8–12 hours for the sponge to sit and bubble.

1. Sterilize all equipment first by boiling in water for 5 minutes. This includes the container for the starter and all measuring cups and utensils. Combine the flour and yeast in the sterile 2-quart glass or glazed ceramic bowl or container. Gradually stir in the water to form a thick, pasty mixture. Cover with a clean dish towel and set container on a baking sheet to catch any overflow that may occur. Place in a warm area, ideally 70°–80°F, and allow to sit for 3–4 days, stirring once each day.

2. When the starter is ready it will be bubbly and will have a sour but pleasant aroma. (If starter smells bad or develops a pink or orange tint, throw it out and start over.) The starter is ready to use and can be covered with a tight-fitting lid and stored in the refrigerator at this point.

3. The starter will need to be fed once every other week. To feed the refrigerated starter, bring starter to room temperature then add 1 cup warm water and 1 cup flour. Let sit at room temperature for 8 hours and return to the refrigerator. Sometimes a brown liquid byproduct of fermentation called "hooch" will appear on the starter. This is harmless and can be stirred back into the starter.

4. Any amount of starter that is removed for use in a recipe should be replaced with equal amounts of both water and flour, using the same procedure as for feeding. To replace ¼ cup starter, add ¼ cup water and ¼ cup flour.

# Sourdough Bread

*Sourdough Bread is chewy and full of beautiful holes!*
*The tangy flavor tastes great with creamy chowders, as toast, or in sandwiches.*

**INGREDIENTS** | MAKES 2 LOAVES
(24 SLICES)

2¼ teaspoons active dry yeast (1 packet)

1¼ cups soymilk, warm (110°F–115°F)

1 tablespoon sugar

1 cup sourdough starter, room temperature

1 tablespoon olive oil

2 teaspoons sea salt

5–6 cups unbleached all-purpose flour

Cornmeal for sprinkling

1. Stir together yeast, soymilk, and sugar in a large bowl. Allow to sit for 5–10 minutes to get bubbly. Mix in the sourdough starter and allow to sit for 1–2 hours. Stir in olive oil, salt, and 3 cups flour. Gradually add the rest of the flour, ½ cup at a time, until dough is smooth and not too sticky.

2. Turn dough out onto a floured surface and knead 10–12 minutes until elastic. Shape into a ball and place in a large oiled bowl, turning to coat surface of dough with oil. Cover with a kitchen towel and set in a warm place to rise until doubled in bulk, about 1 hour. Punch dough down, divide in half, and shape into two round loaves. Sprinkle cornmeal on 2 lightly greased baking sheets. Place loaves on baking sheets and allow to rise again until doubled in bulk.

3. Preheat oven to 375°F. Bake for 30–40 minutes until tapping on the bottom of the loaves produces a hollow sound. Transfer to wire racks to cool.

**PER SERVING** Calories: 126 | Fat: 1 g | Protein: 4 g | Sugar: 1 g | Fiber: 1 g | Carbohydrates: 25 g

# Sourdough-Buckwheat Pancakes

*Try making a sweet, homemade blackberry topping
to complement the wonderful sour flavor of the pancakes.*

**INGREDIENTS | SERVES 8**

1½ cups sourdough starter

1¼ cups soymilk

½ cup all-purpose flour

½ cup buckwheat flour

⅓ cup canola oil

2 tablespoons sugar

1 teaspoon baking powder

½ teaspoon salt

½ teaspoon baking soda

1. Combine sourdough starter with soymilk, all-purpose flour, buckwheat flour, oil, sugar, baking powder, and salt, stirring until well mixed. Allow to rest for 3–5 minutes. Sprinkle batter with baking soda and stir gently.
2. Heat an oiled griddle to 375°F. Pour ⅓ cup batter on griddle and cook until bubbles form across the top and the bottom is browned. Flip and cook on the other side until browned.
3. Repeat until all pancakes are cooked, as batter does not keep well. Serve with maple syrup, fruit topping, fruit compote, or preserves.

**PER SERVING** Calories: 244 | Fat: 10 g | Protein: 5 g | Sugar: 4 g | Fiber: 2 g | Carbohydrates: 33 g

# Whole-Wheat Sourdough

*The fermentation process reduces the amount of kneading required for this hearty bread.*

**INGREDIENTS | MAKES 2 LOAVES
(24 SLICES)**

1 cup sourdough starter

¾ cup plus 1⅓ cups water, divided use

4 cups unbleached all-purpose flour, divided use

2 tablespoons agave syrup

2 cups whole-wheat flour

2 teaspoons salt

## An Amish Tradition

Sourdough is a common starter made by the Amish. Before yeast was readily available, the creation of a starter was the only way bread could be made; starters were often shared among families. Continue the tradition and share sourdough with your friends!

1. Refresh the sourdough starter by combining the starter with ¾ cup water and 1 cup unbleached all-purpose flour in a large bowl. Mix well and allow to sit for 4 hours.

2. Stir in the remaining 1⅓ cups water and the agave syrup. In a separate bowl, whisk together the remaining unbleached all-purpose flour, whole-wheat flour, and salt. Gradually add the flour to the sourdough mixture, adding only a small amount of additional water if needed. Stir until flour is incorporated. Dough will be stiff. Cover with a kitchen towel and allow to rise in a warm place (70°–85°F) for 6–8 hours.

3. Transfer dough to a lightly floured surface and knead for 5 minutes. Allow dough to rest for 10 minutes, and then knead again for 5 minutes. Allow dough to rest for 10 more minutes. Divide dough in half and form each piece into a firm ball. Place dough balls on a nonstick baking sheet that has been dusted with cornmeal. Cover with a kitchen towel and allow to rise for another 2–4 hours.

4. Preheat oven to 375°F and bake for 55–60 minutes, or until browned. The loaves will sound hollow when tapped on the bottom. Transfer to wire racks to cool.

**PER 1 SLICE** Calories: 134 | Fat: 0 g | Protein: 4 g | Sugar: 0 g | Fiber: 2 g | Carbohydrates: 27 g

# Rosemary–Roasted Garlic Bread

*This recipe employs a lengthy fermentation as the key to an exciting "no-knead" method, made famous by a New York baker named Jim Lahey.*

**INGREDIENTS | MAKES 1 LOAF
(16 SLICES)**

1 head garlic, about 16 good-sized cloves

1 tablespoon olive oil

⅛ teaspoon salt

⅛ teaspoon cracked black pepper

¼ teaspoon active dry yeast

3 cups bread flour

1¼ teaspoons sea salt

½ tablespoon fresh rosemary, chopped

1½ cups plus 2 tablespoons water

Olive oil for brushing

1. To roast garlic, preheat oven to 400°F. Cut the top off the head of garlic so that cloves are slightly exposed. Place on a piece of foil large enough to enclose the head. Drizzle with olive oil and sprinkle with salt and pepper. Place foil-wrapped garlic in the cup of a muffin tin and roast for 35–40 minutes until soft. When cool, pop cloves out of the paper skin with a fork. Cut cloves in half and place in a large bowl.

2. Add the yeast, flour, sea salt, and rosemary, stirring until combined. Mix in the water until well-blended. The dough will still be sticky. Scoop into a lightly oiled bowl, brush a small amount of oil over the surface, and cover with plastic wrap. Place in a warm area and allow to rise for 16–18 hours.

3. When the surface is bubbly, turn onto a lightly floured surface. Sprinkle with a small amount of flour and fold the dough over on itself a few times. Lightly cover with plastic wrap and allow to rest for 15 minutes.

4. Lightly flour hands and quickly shape dough into a ball. Place seam-side down on a floured tea towel. Dust the top of the dough with flour and cover with a second tea towel. Allow to rise for about 2 hours.

5. One half hour before dough is ready, place a covered 6–8 quart cast-iron or enameled iron pot in the oven and preheat oven to 450°F. To bake, carefully remove the pot from the oven. Carefully remove lid. Use the towel the dough is resting on to pick it up and turn it into the pot. The seam side will now be up.

6. Replace lid and bake for 30 minutes. Remove lid and bake for 15–30 minutes. Use a probe to ensure the internal temperature reached 200°F. Transfer to a wire rack to cool.

**PER 1 SLICE** Calories: 174 | Fat: 2 g | Protein: 5 g | Sugar: 0 g | Fiber: 1 g | Carbohydrates: 32 g

# Dosa

*Visit an Indian market to find the split black gram lentils (urad ki dhuli dal),
chana dal, and fenugreek (methi) seeds needed to make these delicious, fermented flatbreads!
Dosas may be served plain or with a filling such as chutney or masala.*

**INGREDIENTS | SERVES 12**

2 cups long grain white rice

1 tablespoon fenugreek seeds

1 cup split black gram lentils

¼ cup chana dal or yellow split peas

1 teaspoon salt

Olive oil, as needed

1. Place rice and fenugreek seeds in one bowl and lentils and chana dal in another bowl. Add enough water to both bowls so that everything will remain covered with water for the duration of the soaking step. Soak for 6–8 hours. Drain most of the water from each bowl, reserving drained water in a separate bowl.

2. Place rice and fenugreek seeds in a strong blender with a small amount of the reserved water. Blend until smooth, adding small amounts of water as needed. Pour into a large pot with a lid. Repeat this process with the lentils and chana dal, blending until smooth. Combine the blended lentils with the rice mixture. The consistency should be that of a very thin pancake batter. Cover pot with lid, and allow to ferment in a warm place for 12 hours.

3. After batter has fermented, mix in salt. Heat an ungreased griddle or large skillet over medium-high heat. Turn heat down to medium and ladle ¼ cup batter onto the griddle. Using the back of the ladle, spread the batter in a circle using a spiral motion, similar to the method for spreading tomato sauce on pizza dough. Batter should be spread so thinly that the pan shows through in places.

4. Cook dosa for 1–2 minutes. If desired, turn over and cook on the other side. Alternatively, dosa is now ready to be filled with ¼–½ cup of your favorite filling and rolled like a crepe.

**PER SERVING** Calories: 189 | Fat: 1 g | Protein: 8 g | Sugar: 1 g | Fiber: 4 g | Carbohydrates: 37 g

# Sourdough Dinner Rolls

*The beauty of these rolls is their simplicity. The pleasant tang of sourdough is even better when served warm from the oven.*

**INGREDIENTS | SERVES 14**

1 tablespoon active dry yeast

2 tablespoons sugar

1 cup water, warm (110°F–115°F)

½ cup soymilk, warm (110°F–115°F)

1 cup sourdough starter

2 tablespoons olive oil

3½–4 cups unbleached all-purpose flour

1 tablespoon sea salt

3 tablespoons vegan margarine, melted

1. In a large bowl, dissolve yeast and sugar in water. Allow to sit for 5 minutes to get bubbly. Stir in soymilk, sourdough starter, and oil until well mixed. In a separate bowl, whisk together flour and salt. Gradually add 3½ cups flour mixture to wet ingredients. Add more flour as needed, mixing until dough comes together.

2. Turn dough out onto a floured surface and knead 10–12 minutes until dough is smooth and elastic. Place dough in a lightly oiled bowl, turning to coat. Cover with a kitchen towel and allow to rise in a warm place until doubled in bulk, about 1 hour. Punch dough down and divide into 14 equal pieces.

3. Shape pieces of dough into rolls and place, just touching, on a lightly oiled 9" × 13" pan. Cover and allow to rise again until doubled. Preheat oven to 375°F. Bake rolls for 20–25 minutes until golden brown. Brush rolls with melted margarine during the last 5 minutes of baking. Serve warm.

**PER SERVING** Calories: 197 | Fat: 5 g | Protein: 5 g | Sugar: 2 g | Fiber: 1 g | Carbohydrates: 33 g

# Injera

*Injera is a fermented Ethiopian bread which has a spongy texture and a somewhat sour flavor that is loved!*

**INGREDIENTS | SERVES 10**

2 cups teff flour

2 cups unbleached all-purpose flour

½ teaspoon salt

5 cups water, lukewarm

## Ethiopian Injera

Injera is an essential part of Ethiopian cuisine. Meals are typically served communally with several types of stew or "wat" and salads all ladled atop one large injera which acts as a sponge, soaking up the juices to be enjoyed at the end of the meal. Additional injera is torn into pieces and used to scoop up the food.

1. In a large bowl, whisk together the teff flour, all-purpose flour, and salt. Add the water and stir until well mixed. Cover with a tea towel and allow to sit for 8–10 hours, or overnight. After 8–10 hours there should already be some liquid risen to the top and bubbles appearing. Stir gently with a wooden spoon. Replace tea towel and allow mixture to continue to sit at room temperature for 2–3 more days, stirring once a day with the wooden spoon.

2. When the batter is ready it will be quite bubbly and will have a sour aroma. Stir the batter well to mix in any liquid that may have separated. The consistency of the batter should be thin enough to run off your fingers quickly but still leave a thin coating.

3. Heat a nonstick or lightly oiled, 10"–12" heavy skillet over medium-high heat. Pour ⅓–½ cup batter into the pan and immediately swirl the pan so a thin layer of batter coats the entire flat cooking area of the pan. Cook one side only, until the edges of the injera pull away from the pan and the surface is covered with bubbles. Remove from pan without cooking the other side. Wipe out pan with a paper towel between each injera and re-oil pan if not nonstick. Allow injera to cool completely. Place foil between injeras as they are stacked to prevent them from sticking together.

**PER SERVING** Calories: 206 | Fat: 4 g | Protein: 6 g | Sugar: 0 g | Fiber: 4 g | Carbohydrates: 37 g

# CHAPTER 8

# Tarts and Pastries

# Tart Crust for Sweet Fillings

*This tart is crispy and with a hint of sugar to complement a fruity filling!*

**INGREDIENTS | MAKES 1 (9") TART CRUST**

1¼ cups unbleached all-purpose flour

½ teaspoon sugar

¼ teaspoon salt

6 tablespoons vegan margarine, very cold, cut into small pieces

2½ tablespoons vegetable shortening, cold

Ice water, as needed

1. Preheat oven to 400°F.
2. Whisk together flour, sugar, and salt in a large bowl. Quickly cut margarine and shortening into the flour with a pastry cutter or large fork until mixture resembles crumbs. Sprinkle 2 tablespoons ice water over the surface. Stir the dough with a wooden spoon, adding ice water 1 tablespoon at a time as needed, to bring dough together.
3. Shape dough into a ball and then wrap in plastic wrap. Using the palm of your hand, press dough into a disk shape inside the plastic wrap. Chill in the refrigerator for 30 minutes.
4. Roll chilled dough out to a thickness of ⅜". Fold dough in half or quarters, gently lift it up, and lay dough in a 9" tart pan. Unfold dough across the rest of the pan. Lift outer edges of dough with one hand while pressing dough down into the pan and into the fluted edges. Pinch off any excess dough. Save extra bits of dough for another use, if desired. Chill for 30 minutes. Dock with the tines of a fork.
5. For a recipe calling for a partially baked crust, lay a sheet of foil over the crust, fill with dry beans to keep the crust from puffing up, and bake for 10 minutes. Remove the foil along with the beans and continue baking for another 5 minutes. For a completely baked crust, follow the same procedure, but bake the crust for 15–18 minutes after the foil and beans have been removed.

**PER SERVING** Calories: 182 | Fat: 12 g | Protein: 2 g | Sugar: 0 g | Fiber: 1 g | Carbohydrates: 15 g

# Tart Crust for Savory Fillings

*A delicious, flaky pastry that is well-suited to vegetable and herb fillings.*

**INGREDIENTS | MAKES 1 (9") TART CRUST**

1¼ cups unbleached all-purpose flour

¼ teaspoon salt

6 tablespoons vegan margarine, very cold, cut into small pieces

1 tablespoon vegetable shortening, cold

Ice water, as needed

1. Preheat oven to 400°F.
2. Whisk together flour and salt in a large bowl. Quickly cut margarine and shortening into the flour with a pastry cutter or large fork until mixture resembles crumbs. Sprinkle 2 tablespoons ice water over the surface. Stir the dough with a wooden spoon, adding ice water 1 tablespoon at a time as needed, to bring dough together.
3. Shape dough into a ball and then wrap with plastic wrap. Using the palm of your hand, press dough into a disk shape inside the plastic wrap. Chill in the refrigerator for 30 minutes.
4. Roll chilled dough out to a thickness of ¼". Fold dough in half or quarters, gently lift it up, and lay dough in a 9" tart pan. Unfold dough across the rest of the pan. Lift outer edges of dough with one hand while pressing dough down into the pan and into the fluted edges. Pinch off any excess dough. Save extra bits of dough for another use, if desired. Chill for 30 minutes. Dock with the tines of a fork.
5. For a recipe calling for a partially baked crust, lay a sheet of foil over the crust, fill with dry beans to keep the crust from puffing up, and bake for 10 minutes. Remove the foil along with the beans and continue baking for another 5–10 minutes. For a completely baked crust, follow the same procedure, but bake the crust for 15 minutes after the foil and beans have been removed.

**PER SERVING** Calories: 160 | Fat: 10 g | Protein: 2 g | Sugar: 0 g | Fiber: 1 g | Carbohydrates: 15 g

# Whole-Wheat Tart Crust

*A slightly healthier tart crust! Try adding a half teaspoon of sugar to the dough when using a sweet filling.*

**INGREDIENTS | MAKES 1 (9") TART CRUST**

1 cup unbleached all-purpose flour

¼ cup whole-wheat flour

¼ teaspoon salt

6 tablespoons vegan margarine, very cold, cut into small pieces

1 tablespoon vegetable shortening, cold

Ice water, as needed

1. Preheat oven to 400°F.
2. Whisk together all-purpose flour, whole-wheat flour, and salt in a large bowl. Quickly cut margarine and shortening into the flour with a pastry cutter or large fork until mixture resembles crumbs. Sprinkle 2 tablespoons ice water over the surface. Stir the dough with a wooden spoon, adding ice water 1 tablespoon at a time as needed, to bring dough together.
3. Shape dough into a ball and then wrap with plastic wrap. Using the palm of your hand, press dough into a disk shape inside the plastic wrap. Chill in the refrigerator for 30 minutes.
4. Roll chilled dough out to a thickness of ¼". Fold dough in half or quarters, gently lift it up, and lay dough in a 9" tart pan. Unfold dough across the rest of the pan. Lift outer edges of dough with one hand while pressing dough down into the pan and into the fluted edges. Pinch off any excess dough. Save extra bits of dough for another use, if desired. Chill for 30 minutes. Dock with the tines of a fork.
5. For a recipe calling for a partially baked crust, lay a sheet of foil over the crust, fill with dry beans to keep the crust from puffing up, and bake for 10 minutes. Remove the foil along with the beans and continue baking for another 5–10 minutes. For a completely baked crust, follow the same procedure, but bake the crust for 15 minutes after the foil and beans have been removed.

**PER SERVING** Calories: 159 | Fat: 10 g | Protein: 2 g | Sugar: 0 g | Fiber: 1 g | Carbohydrates: 15 g

# Vegan Puff Pastry

*Commercially packaged puff pastry dough is often vegan,*
*but here's a recipe for inspired cooks who simply must make their own!*

### INGREDIENTS | SERVES 12

2 cups unbleached all-purpose flour, divided use

16 tablespoons vegan margarine, cold, divided use

2 tablespoons vegetable shortening, cold

⅔ cup ice water

1. Make a margarine dough by combining ¼ cup flour with 14 tablespoons margarine and the shortening with a pastry cutter until smooth. Shape into a ½"-thick square, wrap in plastic wrap, and refrigerate for 30 minutes.
2. In a medium bowl, make a flour dough by combining the ice water, remaining 2 tablespoons margarine, and the remaining 1¾ cups flour. After dough comes together, knead for 1 minute. Wrap in plastic wrap and refrigerate for 30 minutes. Place chilled flour dough on a lightly floured surface and roll out to ⅜"-thick square. Place the margarine dough on top of the flour dough in such a way that the corners of the margarine dough fall in the midline area of the straight edges of the flour dough.
3. Fold the corners of the flour dough up and over the straight edges of the margarine dough to surround it like a postal envelope. Roll dough out to ⅜" thick and fold into thirds like a letter. Roll out to ⅜" thick and fold in thirds a second time. Chill in the refrigerator for 30 minutes. Repeat process by rolling out and folding into thirds two more times. Refrigerate 30 minutes. Repeat process again, by rolling out and folding into thirds two more times, for a total of six times.
4. Wrap in plastic wrap and refrigerate for 30 minutes or until ready to use.

**PER SERVING** Calories: 228 | Fat: 17 g | Protein: 2 g | Sugar: 0 g | Fiber: 1 g | Carbohydrates: 16 g

# Rhubarb Tart

*Rhubarb has a pleasant sourness that adds a flavor dimension to sweet desserts!*

## INGREDIENTS | SERVES 8

1 unbaked 9" Tart Crust for Sweet Fillings, frozen for 15 minutes (see recipe in this chapter)

3 tablespoons apricot jam

⅓ cup water

1 cup sugar

2 long strips lemon zest

1 cinnamon stick, broken in 2 or 3 pieces

6 cups rhubarb stalks, cut into ½" chunks

## Making Marmalade

Marmalade is nothing more than citrus jam, and is easy to make. Combine the zest from 6–8 oranges or lemons with their juice and sugar to taste. (The amount of sugar will vary from ¼ cup to 3 or 4 cups depending on the fruit.) Boil, stirring, until the liquid is reduced and thick. (Be careful not to burn the jam.) Cool citrus jam completely, and store in the refrigerator. Now you can have a taste of sunshine whenever you want.

1. Preheat oven to 350°F. Fit a sheet of foil inside the crust and fill with dried beans to prevent crust from getting too puffy. Bake for 20 minutes. Remove foil and beans. Bake for 15 minutes, until golden brown. Spread crust evenly with apricot jam and bake for another 5 minutes. Cool crust in pan on a wire rack.

2. In a large pot over low heat, add water. Stir sugar into the water until dissolved. Add lemon zest, cinnamon stick, and rhubarb. Bring to a boil, then cover and simmer over medium-low heat for 5 minutes. Remove from heat and let sit, covered, for 15 minutes. Rhubarb should be tender. Uncover and allow mixture to cool completely. Separate the rhubarb from the cooking liquid and arrange in the tart crust in a circular pattern. Strain the cooking liquid to remove the cinnamon stick and lemon peel.

3. Return cooking liquid to the pot, bring to boil, and cook for 5 minutes, or until liquid has reduced to ¼ cup. Cool completely and spoon evenly over rhubarb. Cool at room temperature.

**PER SERVING** Calories: 316 | Fat: 13 g | Protein: 3 g | Sugar: 30 g | Fiber: 2 g | Carbohydrates: 49 g

# Mixed Berry Tart

*This berrylicious tart tastes great warm with a scoop of vegan vanilla ice cream!*

**INGREDIENTS | SERVES 8**

1 cup blackberries, divided use
1 cup blueberries, divided use
1 cup raspberries, divided use
¼ cup cornstarch
¼ cup sugar
1 partially baked 9" Tart Crust for Sweet Fillings (see recipe in this chapter)

1. Preheat oven to 350°F.
2. Mix ⅔ cup blackberries, ⅔ cup blueberries, and ⅔ cup raspberries together in a large bowl. Roughly mash about ⅓ of the berries. In a small bowl, whisk cornstarch and sugar together. Pour cornstarch mixture over berries and stir to combine.
3. Spread berry mixture in the tart crust. Spread remaining berries over the top.
4. Bake until bubbly, about 30 minutes. Serve warm.

**PER SERVING** Calories: 247 | Fat: 13 g | Protein: 3 g | Sugar: 10 g | Fiber: 3 g | Carbohydrates: 31 g

# Lemon Tart

*Decorate this luscious tart by using a stencil to create a beautiful pattern, and then accent with the berries.*

**INGREDIENTS | SERVES 10**

1 cup silken tofu, drained and patted dry
1¼ cups sugar
⅔ cup fresh lemon juice
4 tablespoons cornstarch
2 tablespoons all-purpose flour
Zest from 2 lemons, roughly chopped
1 partially baked 9" Tart Crust for Sweet Fillings (see recipe in this chapter)
⅓ cup powdered sugar
½ cup raspberries or blueberries for decoration

1. Preheat oven to 350°F.
2. Blend tofu in a food processor until smooth. Add 1¼ cups sugar, lemon juice, cornstarch, and flour. Continue to process until blended. Taste and adjust for sweetness by adding more sugar, if needed. Stir in the lemon zest. Pour mixture evenly over the crust.
3. Bake at 350°F for 35–40 minutes, until filling is set and lightly browned. Cool completely and sift powdered sugar over the top. Decorate with fresh berries.

**PER SERVING** Calories: 293 | Fat: 11 g | Protein: 3 g | Sugar: 30 g | Fiber: 1 g | Carbohydrates: 47 g

# Apple Tarte Tatin

*This is a fantastic, beautiful dessert when you take the time to arrange the apple slices in a pattern!*

**INGREDIENTS | SERVES 10**

1 batch dough for Tart Crust for Sweet Fillings, chilled (see recipe in this chapter)

7–9 medium Granny Smith or other firm apples, peeled and cored

8 tablespoons vegan margarine

1 cup sugar

1. Preheat oven to 375°F.
2. Roll tart dough out to a 10" or 11" circle, large enough to fit the pan that will be used to bake the tarte tatin. Fold circle in half, and then in half again. Wrap in plastic wrap and refrigerate. Slice each apple into 4 wedges. Set aside.
3. Melt margarine over medium heat in a 10"–11" cast-iron or heavy, ovenproof skillet. While still over the heat, sprinkle sugar evenly across the pan. Arrange apple wedges in the pan in a circular pattern, packing them tightly. Apples should be stacked about an inch higher than the rim of the pan. Increase flame to moderately high heat and cook for about 25 minutes until the color of the juices is deep amber.
4. Place folded dough over the apples with the point in the center of the pan. Unfold dough across the pan and tuck edges into the sides of the pan. Cut a couple of vent slashes into the dough. Bake for 25–30 minutes until crust is golden brown. Place pan on a wire rack and allow to cool for 30 minutes. Carefully invert onto a serving platter. If any apple pieces fall out of place, simply reset them.

**PER SERVING** Calories: 354 | Fat: 19 g | Protein: 2 g | Sugar: 31 g | Fiber: 2 g | Carbohydrates: 46 g

# Apple-Raisin Puffs

*Use either packaged or homemade puff pastry (see the*
*Vegan Puff Pastry recipe in this chapter) for this warm, homey dessert.*

**INGREDIENTS | SERVES 9**

¼ cup raisins, soaked in ¼ cup hot water for 20 minutes

2 cups apples, peeled, cored, and diced

1 teaspoon lemon juice

⅓ cup brown sugar, packed

2 tablespoons unbleached all-purpose flour

1 teaspoon cinnamon

¼ teaspoon nutmeg

2 (9" × 9") puff pastry dough sheets, thawed if frozen

Soymilk for brushing

White sugar and additional cinnamon for sprinkling, optional

1. Preheat oven to 350°F.
2. Drain raisins. In a medium bowl, toss together raisins, apples, lemon juice, brown sugar, flour, cinnamon, and nutmeg. Set aside.
3. Flour pastry dough lightly and cut each sheet into 9 (3" × 3") squares, for a total of 18 squares. Lay out 9 squares. Set aside the rest. Spoon ¼ cup of the apple-raisin mixture into the center of each square. Cover each filled square with another pastry square to form a pillow. Use your fingers to press the edges together, and crimp with a fork to seal. With the tip of a sharp knife, make 2 ½" cuts in the top center of each puff.
4. Place puffs on an ungreased baking sheet and brush lightly with soymilk. Sprinkle with sugar and cinnamon, if desired. Bake until golden brown, about 20 minutes. Cool for several minutes before serving as the filling will be hot!

**PER SERVING** Calories: 378 | Fat: 23 g | Protein: 3 g | Sugar: 15 g | Fiber: 2 g | Carbohydrates: 40 g

# Sweet Potato and Swiss Chard Tarte Tatin

*Serve this savory vegetable tart with a spring greens salad for a light lunch.*

**INGREDIENTS | SERVES 8**

2 medium sweet potatoes, peeled, cut into ¼" slices

1 small russet potato, cut into ¼" slices

1 medium onion, cut into ¼" slices

1 teaspoon fresh thyme, chopped

½ teaspoon fresh rosemary, chopped

2 tablespoons olive oil

½ teaspoon sea salt

¼ teaspoon cracked black pepper

1 batch dough for Tart Crust for Savory Fillings (see recipe in this chapter)

2 tablespoons vegan margarine

1 tablespoon apple cider vinegar

2 tablespoons brown sugar

1 cup Swiss chard, coarsely chopped

1. Preheat the oven to 400°F.
2. Place sweet potatoes, russet potato, onion, thyme, and rosemary in a large bowl and toss with olive oil. Spread evenly on a baking sheet and season with sea salt and cracked pepper. Place in oven and roast for 30 minutes, stirring once halfway through. Remove from oven and reduce temperature to 375°F.
3. On a floured surface, roll tart dough out in an 11"–12" circle, adding flour as needed to prevent sticking. Fold circle in half, and then fold in half again.
4. Melt margarine over medium heat in a 10"–12" cast-iron skillet. Stir in the vinegar and brown sugar and heat until bubbly. Remove from heat. Arrange layers of sweet potatoes, russet potatoes, onions, and then Swiss chard in the cast-iron skillet, taking care to make the bottom layer uniform and attractive, as this will be the presentation side of the dish once it's inverted. Repeat layers until all veggies are used.
5. Place the pastry dough on top of the veggies with the point in the center. Unfold dough across the rest of the pan. Tuck the edges between the veggies and the sides of the pan. Place skillet in the oven and bake until crust is golden brown, about 30 minutes. Cool at room temperature for 20 minutes. Loosen edges with a knife, and invert onto serving platter. Cut into wedges to serve.

**PER SERVING** Calories: 281 | Fat: 16 g | Protein: 3 g | Sugar: 6 g | Fiber: 2 g | Carbohydrates: 31 g

# Roasted Peach Tart

*Roasting the peaches gives them a deeper flavor, which is complemented by the cream cheese filling!*

**INGREDIENTS | SERVES 10**

6 medium peaches, peeled and quartered

2 tablespoons vegan margarine

4 tablespoons sugar, divided use

7 ounces vegan cream cheese, softened

¾ cup soy creamer

1 teaspoon vanilla extract

¼ cup vanilla soymilk

1 prebaked 10" Tart Crust for Sweet Fillings (see recipe in this chapter)

¼–½ cup apricot preserves for glaze, if needed

1. Preheat oven to 400°F.
2. Place peaches, margarine, and 2 tablespoons sugar in a baking dish just large enough to fit. Roast peaches for 15 minutes, stirring once. Remove from oven and set aside to cool.
3. To make the filling, whisk the cream cheese with creamer until smooth. Whisk in the remaining 2 tablespoons sugar and vanilla extract. Gradually add soymilk until the desired consistency is achieved. Fill the tart crust with the cream cheese mixture. Arrange peaches in a decorative pattern over the filling.
4. Place the pan juices from roasting the peaches in a small saucepan and reduce over medium-high heat to a thickened syrup. If there are not enough pan juices to make ½ cup syrup, add enough apricot preserves before cooking to make up the difference and proceed in the same manner. Drizzle over the peaches. Allow to cool.

**PER SERVING** Calories: 295 | Fat: 15 g | Protein: 3 g | Sugar: 16 g | Fiber: 1 g | Carbohydrates: 37 g

# Ratatouille Tarte Tatin

*Roasting the veggies reduces some of the moisture to help keep the pastry dry and flaky.*

### INGREDIENTS | SERVES 10

4 large Roma tomatoes, sliced into ¼" rounds

2 Japanese eggplants, sliced in ¼" rounds

1 medium zucchini, sliced in ¼" rounds

1 medium yellow summer squash, cut into ¼" rounds

1 medium red bell pepper, cut into ¼" strips

1 medium yellow bell pepper, cut into ¼" strips

1 medium onion, cut into ¼" slices

½ cup ripe olives, pitted and halved, optional

3 cloves garlic, thinly sliced

1½ teaspoons coarse sea salt

¼ teaspoon cracked black pepper

¼ teaspoon cayenne pepper flakes, or more to taste

3 tablespoons olive oil, plus additional oil for brushing

1 sheet Vegan Puff Pastry, chilled (see recipe in this chapter)

¼ cup fresh basil, cut into thin ribbons

1. Preheat oven to 425°F.
2. To make ratatouille, combine all of the vegetables, olives, garlic, sea salt, black pepper, and cayenne pepper together in a large bowl. Add 3 tablespoons olive oil and toss to coat. Turn out onto a large baking sheet and roast until vegetables are tender and beginning to brown, about 45 minutes. Stir occasionally.
3. Preheat a baking sheet. Roll out dough to approximately an 8" × 14" rectangle on a lightly floured surface. Transfer to preheated baking sheet. Dock surface of dough with the tines of a fork and bake until browned, about 20–25 minutes. Remove from oven.
4. Arrange ratatouille evenly over the pastry, leaving a 1" border all the way around. Brush the border edges with olive oil. Bake 10–12 minutes until pastry is golden brown. Sprinkle with basil ribbons.

**PER SERVING** Calories: 349 | Fat: 26 g | Protein: 4 g | Sugar: 3 g | Fiber: 3 g | Carbohydrates: 25 g

## Roasting Squash

Tossing squash in the oven couldn't be easier. A drizzle of olive oil and a dash of garlic powder, salt, nutritional yeast, and perhaps a touch of cayenne will also produce a satisfying roasted squash for a side dish you don't need to sweat over.

# Baklava

*Gooey, crispy, and crunchy! Keep phyllo sheets covered with a damp towel to prevent them from drying out while you assemble the dish.*

**INGREDIENTS | SERVES 16**

1⅓ cups water

1½ cups plus 2 tablespoons sugar, divided use

2 tablespoons agave syrup

2 tablespoons lemon juice

1 (2") strip orange peel

1 cinnamon stick

3 cardamom pods, crushed

1 teaspoon ground cinnamon

⅔ cup pistachios, chopped medium-fine

⅔ cup walnuts, chopped medium-fine

1 pound package vegan phyllo pastry

1 cup vegan margarine, melted

1. To make the syrup, combine water, 1½ cups sugar, agave syrup, lemon juice, orange peel, cinnamon stick, and cardamom pods in a medium saucepan. Bring to boil over medium-high heat and boil for 5–10 minutes. Discard solids. Chill syrup in the refrigerator.
2. Preheat oven to 350°F. Generously grease the bottom and sides of a 9" × 9" baking dish with margarine.
3. Toss ground cinnamon and 2 tablespoons sugar with chopped pistachios and walnuts in a small bowl. Trim phyllo sheets to fit baking dish. Begin layering phyllo, 1 sheet at a time, in the bottom of the dish, thoroughly brushing each sheet with melted margarine. When about ⅓ of the sheets have been positioned in the dish and brushed with margarine, spread half of the nut mixture evenly over the top. Cover with another ⅓ of the phyllo sheets, brushing each with margarine and spread the remaining nut mixture over the top. Finish with the last third of the phyllo sheets, brushing with margarine between each sheet. Brush the top with margarine.
4. Cut entire pan into diamonds by making diagonal, parallel cuts about 2" apart, all the way through to bottom of the dish. Bake for 30–35 minutes, until golden brown. Immediately pour half of the syrup over the baklava. Allow a few minutes for syrup to soak in, then pour the rest of the syrup over the top

**PER SERVING** Calories: 222 | Fat: 15 g | Protein: 3 g | Sugar: 1 g | Fiber: 1 g | Carbohydrates: 17 g

# Onion and Herb Tart

*The rich sweetness of slowly caramelized onions makes this tart something special!*

**INGREDIENTS | SERVES 8**

2 tablespoons vegan margarine

2 tablespoons olive oil

2 pounds onions, thinly sliced

½ teaspoon dried thyme

½ teaspoon sea salt, or to taste

¼ teaspoon cracked black pepper

1 batch dough for Tart Crust for Savory Fillings (see recipe in this chapter), chilled, unbaked

1. Melt margarine in a large skillet over medium-low heat. Add olive oil. When oil is hot, add onions, stirring to coat with oil. Spread onions evenly in the pan and sprinkle with thyme, sea salt, and pepper. Cook onions, stirring every few minutes, for at least 30 minutes, until onions are deep brown in color, but not burned. Transfer to a bowl to cool.

2. Preheat the oven to 375°F. Roll dough to form a 14" circle on a lightly floured surface. Place dough on a parchment-lined baking sheet and chill for 10 minutes in the refrigerator.

3. Leaving a 1½" border around the edge, fill the center of the dough with an even layer of the onion mixture. Fold the edges up and lay over the onion layer. Bake until crust is deep brown on the bottom, about 50 minutes. Transfer to a rack and cool completely.

**PER SERVING** Calories: 260 | Fat: 16 g | Protein: 3 g | Sugar: 5 g | Fiber: 2 g | Carbohydrates: 25 g

# Mushroom-Tofu Packets

*Tofu boosts the protein in this dish! Serve with a lightly dressed salad of mixed spring greens and grape tomatoes for a terrific lunch.*

**INGREDIENTS | SERVES 8**

3 tablespoons olive oil

2 tablespoons vegan margarine

2 tablespoons onion, diced small

1 clove garlic, minced

½ cup extra-firm tofu, drained and patted dry with paper towels

1 pound mixed fresh mushrooms, coarsely chopped

¼ cup frozen baby peas, thawed

1 tablespoon herbs de Provence

¼ teaspoon sea salt

¼ teaspoon cracked black pepper

1 tablespoon lemon juice

1 (8-ounce) package vegan cream cheese, diced

1 (17.3-ounce) package frozen vegan puff pastry, thawed

Soymilk, for brushing

1. Preheat oven to 450°F.
2. Combine olive oil and margarine in a large skillet and heat on medium-high. Add the onion and garlic and cook for 2 minutes. Cut tofu in ¼" cubes, add to the pan, and cook for 2–3 minutes. Add mushrooms, peas, herbs de Provence, sea salt, and black pepper. Continue to cook, stirring often, about 10 minutes or until the liquid has evaporated. Remove from the heat and stir in lemon juice and cream cheese.
3. Roll out one puff pastry sheet to an 11" × 11" square on a lightly floured surface. Cut in half lengthwise to create two rectangles. Repeat with the second puff pastry sheet. Spoon ¼ of the filling on one half of each rectangle. Leave a ½" border around the edges. Fold dough over filling and crimp with the tines of the fork to seal. Line a baking sheet with parchment paper. Transfer turnovers to baking sheet and brush tops and edges with soymilk.
4. Bake 18–20 minutes, or until golden and puffy. Cut in half diagonally to serve.

**PER SERVING** Calories: 540 | Fat: 37 g | Protein: 11 g | Sugar: 4 g | Fiber: 2 g | Carbohydrates: 31 g

# Chocolate-Pecan Tart

*An elegant dessert with a decadent flavor combination, this Chocolate-Pecan Tart is a showstopper served with fresh berries and an extra drizzle of Raspberry Sauce (see Chapter 14).*

**INGREDIENTS | SERVES 10**

¾ cup water

¾ cup soymilk

1¾ cups brown sugar, packed

2 teaspoons vanilla extract

4 tablespoons vegan margarine, melted

4 tablespoons cornstarch

2 tablespoons all-purpose flour

2 cups pecan pieces

1 unbaked Tart Crust for Sweet Fillings (see recipe in this chapter)

½ cup vegan chocolate chips

1 teaspoon vegetable shortening

1. Preheat oven to 400°F.
2. Whisk together water, soymilk, brown sugar, and vanilla extract. Add margarine, cornstarch, and flour, continuing to whisk until blended. Spread pecans evenly over the tart crust. Pour wet ingredients over pecans.
3. Bake tart for 50–55 minutes until filling has firmed up and pecans are golden brown. Allow tart to cool for 5–10 minutes, then remove from pan. Cool completely.
4. Melt chocolate chips and shortening together in a metal bowl over simmering water, stirring to blend. Drizzle chocolate over the tart.

**PER SERVING** Calories: 509 | Fat: 30 g | Protein: 4 g | Sugar: 41 g | Fiber: 2 g | Carbohydrates: 60 g

# Apricot Tart

*This dish explodes with a concentrated apricot flavor!*

**INGREDIENTS | SERVES 8**

6 ounces vegan cream cheese

3 tablespoons apricot preserves

1 partially baked 10" Tart Crust for Sweet Fillings (see recipe in this chapter)

8 apricots, halved and pitted

1½ tablespoons powdered sugar, for dusting

1. Preheat oven to 400°F.
2. Spread the cream cheese and then the apricot preserves inside the crust. Cut each apricot half into 6 slices and arrange on the crust.
3. Bake for 15–20 minutes until apricots are tender and the crust is golden brown. Cool completely and dust with powdered sugar.

**PER SERVING** Calories: 287 | Fat: 16 g | Protein: 3 g | Sugar: 10 g | Fiber: 1 g | Carbohydrates: 32 g

# Fresh Fruit Tart

*This versatile recipe can be changed and adapted to reflect the freshest fruits of the season.*
*Use your favorite fruits to make your own gorgeous creations!*

**INGREDIENTS | SERVES 8**

¼ cup cornstarch

2 tablespoons all-purpose flour

⅓ cup sugar

⅓ cup water

1⅓ cups soymilk

2 teaspoons vanilla extract

1 prebaked Tart Crust for Sweet Fillings (see recipe in this chapter)

2–3 cups fresh fruit (berries, mango, kiwi, peaches, etc.)

½ cup apricot jam

2 tablespoons water

## Be Gentle with Your Berries

Berries, such as strawberries, blueberries, blackberries, and especially raspberries, are very delicate fruits and should be handled carefully after you purchase them. Once you get them home, resist the urge to rinse them before you put them in the refrigerator. The water can make the berries go soggy and encourages the growth of molds which spoil the fruit. Instead, store berries as-is in the refrigerator until you're ready to use them. When you are ready, remove them from the refrigerator and give them a quick, gentle rinse.

1. With an electric mixer on high speed, beat together cornstarch, flour, sugar, and water in a medium bowl for 2 minutes, or until mixture is smooth and creamy. Set aside.
2. In a medium saucepan, warm soymilk over medium-low heat until it simmers. Take ⅓ cup of the warm soymilk and mix into the cornstarch mixture until blended. Add the contents of the bowl to the saucepan with the warm soymilk. Heat mixture over medium-low, whisking vigorously until mixture has the consistency of a pudding. Stir in vanilla extract and pour into the prebaked tart crust. Smooth the top. Cool.
3. Arrange fruit on top of the cooled tart. Combine apricot jam and water in a small saucepan and heat over medium-low. Strain through fine sieve. Cool slightly then brush evenly over fruit.

**PER SERVING** Calories: 321 | Fat: 13 g | Protein: 4 g | Sugar: 22 g | Fiber: 1 g | Carbohydrates: 47 g

# Bubble and Squeak Packets

*Bubble and Squeak is an English dish that is traditionally made from
the previous day's leftover vegetables, usually potatoes and cabbage or Brussels sprouts,
which are chopped up and fried together until brown and crisp.*

**INGREDIENTS | SERVES 8**

2½ cups red potatoes, boiled

1 tablespoon vegan margarine, melted

1 teaspoon sea salt

½ teaspoon cracked black pepper

3–4 tablespoons soymilk, as needed

1 cup Brussels sprouts, boiled until just tender

4 tablespoons olive oil

1 (17.3-ounce) package frozen vegan puff pastry, thawed

1. Preheat oven to 350°F.

2. Place potatoes in large bowl and coarsely mash with the vegan margarine, salt, and pepper, adding soymilk as needed to help mixture hold together. Thinly slice Brussels sprouts and stir into potato mixture. Heat olive oil in a large skillet over medium-high heat. Scoop potato mixture into pan and press to flatten into a large cake. Fry for 4–5 minutes, or until nicely browned on the bottom. Flip over, in batches if necessary, and cook for another 4–5 minutes until browned. Set aside to cool for 5 minutes.

3. Roll out one puff pastry sheet to an 11" × 11" square on a lightly floured surface. Cut in half lengthwise to create two rectangles. Repeat with the second puff pastry sheet. Spoon a quarter of the filling on one half of each rectangle. Leave a ½" border around the edges. Fold dough over filling and crimp with the tines of a fork to seal. Line a baking sheet with parchment paper. Transfer turnovers to baking sheet and brush tops and edges with soymilk.

4. Bake 18–20 minutes, or until golden and puffy. Cool slightly; cut into halves or quarters to serve.

**PER SERVING** Calories: 456 | Fat: 31 g | Protein: 6 g | Sugar: 1 g | Fiber: 2 g | Carbohydrates: 38 g

# Heirloom Tomato Puff Pastry

*Sweet, luscious heirloom tomatoes and caramelized onions are nestled in flaky puff pastry.*
*Use different types and colors of tomatoes for a striking presentation. It makes a great appetizer!*

**INGREDIENTS | SERVES 16**

1 recipe Vegan Puff Pastry (see recipe this chapter)

8 ounces vegan cream cheese

2 tablespoons soymilk

1 teaspoon sea salt, divided use

½ teaspoon cracked black pepper, divided use

3 tablespoons fresh basil, cut into thin ribbons

5 tablespoons olive oil, divided use

4 cups onion, thinly sliced

2 cloves garlic, minced

1½ pounds heirloom tomatoes, cherry tomatoes, or other varieties

## Pick a Pepper

Did you know that although black, green, and white peppercorns have different flavors, they all come from the same plant? Like black, green, and white teas, each color represents a different stage of maturity and has a specific manner of being processed. Pink peppercorns, which are often included in peppercorn blends, are not actually related to pepper!

1. Divide puff pastry dough in half. On a lightly oiled floured surface, roll each half of puff pastry dough to a 12" × 12" square. Cut 2 (6") circles from each square so that you have a total of 4 circles. Place the circles on parchment-lined baking sheets. With a sharp knife, make small score lines around each circle of dough, about ¼" from the edge to create a border. Dock the center area with the tines of a fork. Refrigerate until ready to fill.

2. In a medium bowl, combine cream cheese, soymilk, ¼ teaspoon salt, and ¼ teaspoon pepper. Mix until smooth. Stir in basil ribbons. Set aside.

3. Preheat oven to 425°F. Warm a large skillet over medium heat and add 3 tablespoons olive oil. When oil is hot, add the onions and the remaining salt and pepper. Sauté for 15 minutes; add garlic and sauté and additional 15 minutes, until onions are caramelized. Set aside.

4. Spread 3–4 tablespoons cream cheese mixture on each pastry puff circle, being careful to stay within the ¼" border. Divide the onion mixture evenly between the four circles. Slice cherry tomatoes in half, or larger tomatoes into ¼" slices. Arrange tomatoes on top of onion mixture. If using cherry tomatoes, place cut side up. Brush tomatoes and edges of dough with remaining 2 tablespoons olive oil. Sprinkle with additional sea salt and cracked pepper if desired.

5. Bake tarts until puff pastry is golden brown, about 20–25 minutes. Cool 10–15 minutes. Cut into quarters to serve.

**PER SERVING** Calories: 271 | Fat: 20 g | Protein: 3 g | Sugar: 3 g | Fiber: 1 g | Carbohydrates: 21 g

# Fresh Cherry Turnovers

*Fresh cherries make all the difference in these fantastic pastries.*
*The end result is well worth the time and effort that goes into pitting the fruit!*

**INGREDIENTS | SERVES 8**

1 package (2 sheets) vegan puff pastry, thawed

2 pounds fresh cherries, pitted

1 cup sugar

¼ cup orange juice

¼ cup cornstarch

2 tablespoons vegan margarine

¼ cup soymilk

1 tablespoon olive oil

⅓ cup turbinado raw sugar

1. Preheat oven to 400°F. On a lightly floured board, gently roll 1 sheet of puff pastry into a 10" × 10" square. Cut in half and then in half again, to make 4 equal squares. Repeat with the second pastry sheet. Refrigerate until ready to fill.
2. In a large saucepan, bring cherries, sugar, orange juice, and cornstarch to a boil over medium heat, stirring constantly. Turn heat to low and continue to cook until thickened, about 5 minutes. Stir in the margarine and remove from the heat. Cool for 15–20 minutes. Place about 2 tablespoons of filling into the center of each pastry square. Whisk soymilk and olive oil together until blended.
3. Brush the edges of each pastry with the soymilk mixture. Take one corner of each pastry and fold over to the opposite corner, forming a triangle. Crimp the edges together with the tines of a fork. Brush the top of each pastry with the soymilk mixture and sprinkle with 1–2 teaspoons of raw sugar on the top. Place on a parchment-lined baking sheet and bake until puffy and golden brown, about 20 minutes. Transfer to wire racks to cool. Serve warm or at room temperature.

**PER SERVING** Calories: 545 | Fat: 28 g | Protein: 5 g | Sugar: 38 g | Fiber: 2 g | Carbohydrates: 71 g

# Cheeze Danish

*Try spreading a few teaspoons of fruit preserves on the pastry
before adding the cheese for a fruit and cheese danish!*

## INGREDIENTS | SERVES 16

1 package (2 sheets) vegan puff pastry, defrosted

8 ounces vegan cream cheese, softened

⅓ cup sugar

2 tablespoons vegan sour cream

2 tablespoons silken tofu, well mashed

1 teaspoon vanilla extract

¼ teaspoon sea salt

¼ teaspoon lemon juice

1 tablespoon lemon zest, minced

3 tablespoons soymilk

1 teaspoon olive oil

## A Zesty Flavor Boost

As the word implies, using the zest of the lemon and other citrus fruits is a great way to add a fresh, intense citrus flavor to your foods. Use a handheld zester or a fine grater to remove only the colored portion of the citrus peel. This is where the natural, flavor-carrying oils are found. The white layer, or pith, just beneath the zest has a bitter flavor and should be avoided.

1. Preheat oven to 400°F. On a lightly floured board, gently roll 1 sheet of puff pastry into a 10" × 10" square. Cut in half and then in half again, to make 4 equal squares. Repeat with the second pastry sheet. Refrigerate until ready to fill.

2. Beat vegan cream cheese and sugar with an electric mixer on low speed, until smooth. Add the sour cream, mashed tofu, vanilla extract, salt, lemon juice, and lemon zest. Continue to mix on low speed until just blended. Pile a heaping tablespoon of filling into the center of each pastry square. Whisk soymilk and olive oil together until blended.

3. Brush the edges of each pastry with the soymilk mixture. For each pastry, take hold of 2 opposite corners and fold over the filling, and overlapping with each other as though giving the filling a hug. Pinch the two corners together to help them stick together. Brush the top of each pastry with the soymilk mixture, place on a parchment-lined baking sheet, and bake until puffy and golden brown, about 20 minutes.

**PER ½ TURNOVER** Calories: 353 | Fat: 28 g | Protein: 3 g | Sugar: 6 g | Fiber: 0 g | Carbohydrates: 23 g

# CHAPTER 9

# Pies

# Basic Pie Crust

*This versatile crust is flaky and satisfying—perfect for all of your pie recipes!*

**INGREDIENTS | MAKES 2 (9") CRUSTS OR 1 DOUBLE CRUST (8–16 SERVINGS)**

2 cups unbleached all-purpose flour

¼ teaspoon salt

½ cup vegetable shortening, cold

6 tablespoons vegan margarine, cold and cut into pieces

½ cup ice water

1. In a large bowl, whisk the flour and salt together. Cut the shortening and margarine into the flour with a pastry cutter or large fork until it resembles coarse crumbs. Sprinkle with 6–7 tablespoons of ice water and gently mix until just moistened, adding additional ice water if needed. Mixture should still be crumbly and somewhat dry.

2. Divide dough in half and roll into two balls. Wrap each ball in plastic wrap and press into a disk shape with your hands. Chill for at least 30–60 minutes, or until ready to use. On a lightly floured surface, roll out one disk at a time to fit a 9" or 10" pie pan, dusting with additional flour as needed to prevent sticking. Or roll dough out according to specific recipe directions. Place in a pie pan and trim edges. Dock the crust with the tines of a fork. Chill for 30–60 minutes.

3. For recipes calling for a prebaked crust, place a piece of parchment on top of the dough. Fill the crust with dried beans and place in a preheated 350°F oven for 20 minutes. Remove beans and parchment paper. Bake for another 10 minutes until golden brown. Cool before adding filling.

**PER ⅛ SERVING OF A SINGLE CRUST** Calories: 98 | Fat: 5 | Protein: 2 g | Sugar: 0 g | Fiber: 0 g | Carbohydrates: 12 g

# Graham Cracker Pie Crust

*Use a food processor to make graham cracker crumbs quickly,
or place crackers in a zip-top freezer bag and crush with a rolling pin.*

**INGREDIENTS | MAKES 1 PIE CRUST
(8 SERVINGS)**

1½ cups vegan graham cracker crumbs,
finely ground

¼ cup sugar

2 tablespoons brown sugar

6 tablespoons vegan margarine, melted

½ teaspoon cinnamon, optional

## Why Aren't Marshmallows Vegan?

They aren't even technically vegetarian!
Marshmallows contain gelatin, which is
extracted from boiled animal bones or
hides. Online specialty stores and some
natural foods stores may stock vegan
marshmallows, but check all labels
carefully.

1. Place graham cracker crumbs, sugar, and brown sugar in a food processor fitted with the "S" blade. Pulse a few times to combine.
2. Add melted margarine and optional cinnamon. Process until mixture resembles coarse crumbs. Press into a 9" or 10" pie pan.
3. Crust is ready to use according to pie recipe instructions. To prebake, place in a preheated 375°F oven for 8–10 minutes. Cool crust before adding filling.

**PER SERVING** Calories: 179 | Fat: 10 g | Protein: 1 g | Sugar: 14 g | Fiber: 0 g | Carbohydrates: 22 g

# Cookie Pie Crust

*Vanilla wafer-style cookies, chocolate cookies, gingersnaps,
and pecan sandies all make excellent pie crusts. Experiment with your favorites!*

**INGREDIENTS | MAKES 1 PIE CRUST
(8 SERVINGS)**

1½ cups cookie crumbs, finely ground

¼ cup sugar

8 tablespoons vegan margarine, melted

1. Place cookie crumbs and sugar in a food processor fitted with the "S" blade. Pulse a few times to combine.
2. Add melted margarine. Process until mixture resembles coarse crumbs. Press into a 9" or 10" pie pan.
3. Crust is ready to use according to pie recipe instructions. To prebake, place in a preheated 375°F oven for 8–10 minutes. Cool crust before adding filling.

**PER SERVING** Calories: 199 | Fat: 14 g | Protein: 1 g | Sugar: 6 g | Fiber: 0 g | Carbohydrates: 17 g

# Cereal Pie Crust

*This is a great way to use up extra cereal! When using a sweetened cereal,
reduce the amount of sugar added to the crust or skip the sugar altogether.*

**INGREDIENTS | MAKES 1 PIE CRUST
(8 SERVINGS)**

1½ cups finely ground cereal (about 5–6
cups, preground)

½ cup vegan margarine, melted

¼ cup sugar

1. Place cereal crumbs and sugar in a food processor fitted with the "S" blade. Pulse a few times to combine.
2. Add melted margarine. Process until mixture resembles coarse crumbs. Press into a 9" or 10" pie pan.
3. Crust is ready to use according to pie recipe instructions. To prebake, place in a preheated 375°F oven for 8–10 minutes. Cool crust before adding filling.

**PER SERVING** Calories: 265 | Fat: 12 g | Protein: 4 g | Sugar: 10 g | Fiber: 4 g | Carbohydrates: 38 g

# Empanada Dough

*Empanadas are convenient "hand pies" that can be stuffed with sweet
or savory fillings. They're perfect for lunchboxes and picnics.*

**INGREDIENTS | MAKES 4 LARGE OR 8
SMALL EMPANADAS**

2¼ cups unbleached all-purpose flour

½ teaspoon sea salt

8 tablespoons vegan margarine, cold
and cut into small pieces

Egg replacement equal to 1 egg

⅓ cup ice water

1 tablespoon apple cider vinegar

## Empanadas

From the Spanish and Portuguese word *empanar*, which means roughly "to wrap," these tasty fried turnovers can be found wherever the Spanish and Portuguese languages have taken hold. The pastries often are savory, filled with local meat and produce, but they also can be filled with your favorite vegan meat substitutes or sweets and enjoyed for breakfast or dessert.

1. In a large bowl, whisk together the flour and salt. Cut the cold margarine into the flour with a pastry cutter or large fork, until mixture has the consistency of coarse crumbs.
2. In a separate bowl, mix the egg replacement with the ice water and apple cider vinegar. Add wet ingredients to the flour mixture and stir until just moistened.
3. Turn dough out onto a lightly floured surface and gently knead only a couple of times to form a ball. Wrap in plastic wrap and gently press into a disk shape with the palm of your hand.
4. Chill dough for 1 hour before filling. For use on another day, place in a freezer bag and freeze.

**PER 1 SMALL SERVING OF EMPANADA DOUGH**
Calories: 230 | Fat: 11 g | Protein: 4 g | Sugar: 0 g | Fiber: 1 g | Carbohydrates: 27 g

# Apple Pie

*This recipe features cinnamon-spiced apples, tender and sweet,*
*in a flaky pie crust. It's an all-American favorite!*

**INGREDIENTS | SERVES 8**

8 cups Granny Smith apples, peeled and sliced

1 tablespoon lemon juice

½ cup brown sugar, packed

¾ cup sugar

1 teaspoon cinnamon

⅛ teaspoon nutmeg

1 Basic Pie Crust (9" double crust) (see recipe in this chapter)

2 tablespoons vegan margarine, cold and cut into pieces

1 tablespoon soymilk

1 tablespoon raw sugar, for dusting

## Cinnamon

This dried bark of the laurel tree, once used by the Egyptians in the embalming process of mummification, also has multiple health benefits for the living! Cinnamon may lower blood sugar, reduce blood clotting and inflammation, and is antimicrobial. Boost your intake of cinnamon by sprinkling it generously onto cereal, stirring into tea or coffee, or try adding a little bit to your next veggie stir-fry.

1. Preheat oven to 425°F.
2. Toss the apples with the lemon juice in a large bowl. Add the brown sugar, sugar, cinnamon, and nutmeg, stirring to combine. Set aside. On a lightly floured surface, roll out each piece of dough into a 13" circle, about ⅛" thick. Lay one piece in a 9" pie pan, allowing the extra dough to drape over the edge. Fill pie dough with the apple mixture. Dot the apple filling with the cold pieces of margarine.
3. Cover with the second piece of dough, allowing the extra dough to drape over the edge. Trim the extra dough away with a knife so that there is a ¾" edge all the way around the pie pan. Press the top and bottom edges together and fold the dough up so that it sits on top of the rim of the pie pan. Press with fingers to form a fluted pattern all the way around. Cut 4–5 slashes, about 2" long, in the top crust, in a wheel-spoke pattern. Brush crust with soymilk and dust with raw sugar.
4. Bake for 15 minutes. Turn heat down to 350°F and continue to bake for 40–45 minutes more until the juices are bubbling and the crust is golden brown. Cover the edge with a strip of aluminum foil if the crust begins to brown too quickly. Cool for 25–30 minutes.

**PER SERVING** Calories: 511 | Fat: 24 g | Protein: 4 g | Sugar: 45 g | Fiber: 2 g | Carbohydrates: 72 g

# Chocolate Cream Pie

*Delight your kids with this cool and creamy pie! Non-vegans won't miss the dairy at all.*

**INGREDIENTS | SERVES 8**

⅓ cup cornstarch

⅓ cup unsweetened cocoa powder

1½ cups sugar

¼ teaspoon sea salt

3 cups soymilk

2 teaspoons vanilla extract

3 tablespoons vegan margarine

1 prebaked Cookie Pie Crust made with vanilla wafer-style cookies (see recipe in this chapter)

Vegan whipped topping, optional

1. Whisk together cornstarch, cocoa powder, sugar, and salt in a medium saucepan. Mix in soymilk until blended.
2. Bring to a boil over medium heat, stirring constantly. Remove from heat and stir in vanilla extract and margarine. Pour into pie crust and spread in an even layer.
3. Refrigerate for 4–6 hours or overnight. Garnish with vegan whipped topping, if desired.

**PER SERVING** Calories: 443 | Fat: 20 g | Protein: 4 g | Sugar: 46 g | Fiber: 2 g | Carbohydrates: 64 g

# Coconut-Custard Pie

*This pie is loaded with coconut flavor. The toasted coconut takes it to another level!*

**INGREDIENTS | SERVES 8**

½ recipe Basic Pie Crust (single crust) dough, chilled (see recipe in this chapter)

6 ounces extra-firm silken tofu

1 cup canned coconut milk

1 cup sugar

1 tablespoon cornstarch

4 tablespoons vegan margarine, melted

2 teaspoons vanilla extract

1½ cups sweetened shredded coconut

⅓ cup sweetened shredded coconut, toasted

## Decorating with Stencils

You may have seen desserts where the tops are decorated with patterns of powdered sugar, cocoa, espresso powder, or colorful sugars. This type of decoration is often accomplished with the use of a stencil. Stencils are an elegant method of decorating cakes and cupcakes, and you will find many patterns available through cake decorating suppliers. Simply place over the top of the cake, and dust your ingredient over the stencil. Carefully remove the stencil, revealing the pattern of the decoration on the cake! If you've ever made paper snowflakes, you can use the same technique to make your own decorating stencils.

1. Preheat oven to 375°F.
2. On a lightly floured surface, roll dough out to a 10"–11" circle, about ⅛" thick. Place in a 9" pie pan. Fold edges up so the dough is resting on the rim of the pie pan. Press edge with fingers into a fluted shape. Cover with plastic wrap and refrigerate until ready to fill.
3. Place tofu in a food processor fitted with the "S" blade and process until smooth. Add the coconut milk, sugar, cornstarch, margarine, and vanilla extract. Process until well mixed. Stir in 1½ cups shredded coconut.
4. Pour filling into chilled pie crust. Bake for 45–50 minutes until the crust is golden brown. Pie will not appear to be completely set. Allow to cool for an hour, then sprinkle with ⅓ cup toasted coconut. Cool completely. Refrigerate leftovers.

**PER SERVING** Calories: 481 | Fat: 30 g | Protein: 4 g | Sugar: 35 g | Fiber: 1 g | Carbohydrates: 50 g

# Mixed Berry Pie

*Frozen berries will work in a pinch when fresh berries are not available!*
*Simply thaw and drain the berries, then proceed with the recipe instructions.*

**INGREDIENTS | SERVES 8**

2 cups blackberries

2 cups raspberries

2 cups blueberries

⅔ cup sugar

1 teaspoon lemon juice

½ teaspoon cinnamon

1½ tablespoons cornstarch

1 Basic Pie Crust dough (double crust)
(see recipe in this chapter)

2 tablespoons soymilk

2 tablespoons turbinado raw sugar

1. In a large bowl, combine blackberries, raspberries, blueberries, sugar, lemon juice, cinnamon, and cornstarch. Gently toss to coat. Allow to sit for 30 minutes.
2. Preheat oven to 400°F. Roll the bottom crust out to a 12" circle on a lightly floured surface and place in a 9" pie pan. Cover with plastic wrap and place in the refrigerator. Roll the top crust out to a 12" circle.
3. Fill the bottom crust with the berry mixture and cover with the top crust. Fold the overhanging edges up together, resting on the rim of the pie pan. Press with fingers to form a fluted shape all the way around the pie. Cut 4–5 slashes from the center of the pie out toward the edge, about 2" long, in a wheel-spoke pattern. Brush top with soymilk and sprinkle with raw sugar.
4. Place pie on a baking sheet to catch any overflow of juices. Bake for 30 minutes. Reduce heat to 350°F, lay a sheet of aluminum foil over the top and edges to protect the crust from burning, and bake for another 30 minutes, until the juices are bubbling and the crust is golden brown.

**PER SERVING** Calories: 438 | Fat: 22 g | Protein: 4 g | Sugar: 27 g | Fiber: 6 g | Carbohydrates: 58 g

# Empanadas de Papas y Rajas con Crema

*This is a creamy, spicy potato pie! The fire-roasted chile gives this dish the rich, wonderful flavor of outdoor cooking.*

**INGREDIENTS | SERVES 6**

1 large poblano chile
1½ tablespoons olive oil
½ small onion, thinly sliced
¼ teaspoon salt
1 clove garlic, crushed
2 cups red potatoes, boiled and peeled
¼ cup frozen corn kernels, thawed
⅓ cup vegan sour cream
1 recipe Empanada Dough (see recipe in this chapter)
2 tablespoons soymilk, for brushing

## Working with Chiles

The white membrane inside a chile contains the capsicum, which is the compound that creates the sensation of heat on the tongue. This stuff can create some discomfort, especially on tender, sensitive skin. To be safe, wear gloves when chopping chiles, and keep your hands away from your eyes. If you'd like less heat, remove the membrane and the seeds that attach to it.

1. Roast the chile on an outdoor grill or over an open flame on a stovetop burner, turning with tongs until the skin on all sides is charred and blistered. Immediately place in a plastic bag and seal. The steam from the chile will loosen the skin. After 15 minutes, remove the skin, stem, and seeds. Cut into strips about ¼" wide and 1" long.

2. Heat oil in a large skillet over medium heat. Add onion and salt. Cook until tender, stirring occasionally, about 7–10 minutes. Add garlic and chile strips and cook for another 4–5 minutes. Add potatoes and corn and continue to cook, stirring occasionally for 4–5 minutes, until potatoes are heated. Add sour cream, stirring to combine, and heat to just bubbling. Remove from heat and allow to cool.

3. Heat oven to 350°F. Roll dough out to about ⅛" thick on a lightly floured surface. Cut out 6 (6") circles, rerolling scraps as needed. Fill the center of each circle with ¼–⅓ cup filling, leaving a ½" border. Fold one side of dough over the filling in a half-moon shape and seal by crimping the border edges with the tines of a fork. Place on a baking sheet and brush tops with soymilk.

4. Bake for 15–20 minutes until golden brown. Allow to cool several minutes before serving.

**PER SERVING** Calories: 429 | Fat: 21 g | Protein: 7 g | Sugar: 2 g | Fiber: 3 g | Carbohydrates: 53 g

Fresh Fruit Tart
(Chapter 8)

Olive Oil Crackers
(Chapter 13)

Potato Bread
(Chapter 5)

Chinese Scallion Pancakes
(Chapter 6)

Sour Cream Coffee Cake
(Chapter 2)

Spinach and Mushroom Quiche
(Chapter 9)

Chocolate-Peanut Butter Cupcakes
(Chapter 12)

Vegan Cheeze Biscuits
(Chapter 3)

Red Velvet Cake with White Frosting
(Chapter 11)

Ratatouille Tarte Tatin
(Chapter 8)

Snowy Lemon Cookies
(Chapter 10)

Classic White Bread
(Chapter 15)

Currant-Cream Scones
(Chapter 3)

Old-Fashioned Peanut Butter Cookies
(Chapter 10)

Navajo Fry Bread
(Chapter 6)

Strawberry Crumble Bars
(Chapter 10)

Whole-Wheat Sandwich Loaf
(Chapter 15)

**Sun-Dried Tomato Pesto Focaccia**
(Chapter 5)

**Sweet Potato Braid**
(Chapter 5)

# Fruit Pie in the Raw

*This "pie" isn't actually cooked or baked at all, making it a fantastic, fruity, summertime dessert.*

**INGREDIENTS | SERVES 8**

1 cup raw almonds

¼ teaspoon sea salt

½ teaspoon cinnamon

1¼ cups pitted dates

2 bananas, sliced

1 cup fruit, such as peaches, thinly sliced

2 cups strawberries

½ cup raisins

½ cup blackberries

½ cup blueberries

1. Process almonds, salt, and cinnamon in a food processor until finely ground. Add dates and process until a small amount of the mixture holds together when pressed in your hand. Press mixture evenly into a 9" pie pan.
2. Layer banana slices over the crust. Layer sliced fruits over the bananas. In a blender or food processor, make a sauce by combining strawberries with the raisins. Blend until smooth. Pour over the pie. Smooth with the back of a spoon to get the sauce into all the gaps. Decorate pie with blackberries and blueberries.
3. Chill pie in the refrigerator for 2–3 hours.

**PER SERVING** Calories: 265 | Fat: 9 g | Protein: 6 g | Sugar: 15 g | Fiber: 7 g | Carbohydrates: 46 g

# Fresh Strawberry Pie

*Sweet strawberries, picked at the peak of the season, take center stage in this glistening, ruby-red pie!*

**INGREDIENTS | SERVES 8**

6 cups ripe strawberries, hulled, divided use

1 cup sugar

½ cup water

1 tablespoon lemon juice

3 tablespoons cornstarch

1 (9") Basic Pie Crust (½ recipe), baked (see recipe in this chapter)

1. In a large saucepan, mash 2 cups strawberries. Add sugar, water, lemon juice, and cornstarch. Bring to boil over medium heat, stirring constantly until thick and clear. Remove from heat. Allow to cool for 5–10 minutes.
2. Fill pie crust with remaining 4 cups strawberries. Pour sauce over strawberries.
3. Refrigerate pie for 1–2 hours before serving.

**PER SERVING** Calories: 294 | Fat: 11 g | Protein: 2 g | Sugar: 30 g | Fiber: 3 g | Carbohydrates: 48 g

# Roasted Butternut Squash Empanadas

*Serve yourself a warm, toasty handful of roasted squash goodness!*

INGREDIENTS | SERVES 6

3 cups butternut squash, peeled, seeded, and cubed

1 medium onion, quartered

1 clove garlic, unpeeled

2 tablespoons olive oil

½ teaspoon sea salt

¼ teaspoon cracked black pepper

1 tablespoon lemon juice

½ teaspoon dried thyme

¼ teaspoon cinnamon

1 recipe Empanada Dough (see recipe in this chapter)

6 ounces vegan cream cheese

2 tablespoons soymilk, for brushing

1. Preheat oven to 400°F. Place squash, onion, and garlic on a rimmed baking sheet. Toss with olive oil, salt, and pepper. Bake for 50–60 minutes, stirring every 15 minutes, until squash is soft and beginning to caramelize around the edges. Allow to cool.
2. Reduce oven temperature to 350°F. Peel the garlic clove. In a medium bowl, mash cooled squash with garlic, lemon juice, thyme, and cinnamon. Stir in more salt and pepper, if desired. Set aside. Roll empanada dough out to about ⅛" thick on a lightly floured surface. Cut out 6 (6") circles, rerolling scraps as needed.
3. Spread 2 tablespoons vegan cream cheese in a strip down the center of each circle, leaving a ½" border. Add ¼–⅓ cup squash filling. Fold one side of dough over the filling in a half-moon shape and seal by crimping the border edges with the tines of a fork. Place empanadas on a baking sheet and brush tops with soymilk.
4. Bake for 15–20 minutes until golden brown. Allow to cool several minutes before serving.

**PER SERVING** Calories: 473 | Fat: 25 g | Protein: 7 g | Sugar: 5 g | Fiber: 3 g | Carbohydrates: 56 g

# Spinach and Mushroom Quiche

*This quiche tastes great with other vegetables!*
*Try asparagus or zucchini with a bit of vegan cheese thrown in.*

**INGREDIENTS | SERVES 8–10**

2 tablespoons olive oil

1 small onion, diced

1 small clove garlic, minced

½ cup red bell pepper, diced

1 cup mushrooms, sliced

1 pound fresh spinach leaves, washed and chopped

1 pound firm tofu, drained and patted dry

½ teaspoon turmeric

¼ cup soymilk

1½ teaspoons sea salt

¼ teaspoon cracked black pepper

1 tablespoon fresh dill weed, chopped

1 prebaked 9" Basic Pie Crust (½ recipe) (see recipe in this chapter)

1. Preheat oven to 425°F.
2. Heat the oil in a medium saucepan over medium heat. Add onion, garlic, red bell pepper, and mushrooms. Cook until tender, stirring occasionally, for 8–10 minutes. Add the spinach and cook for 1–2 minutes, until spinach has wilted. Pour into a large bowl and set aside.
3. Blend tofu with turmeric, soymilk, salt, and pepper in a blender or food processor until smooth. Add dill weed and tofu mixture to the spinach and stir until combined. Pour into prebaked pie crust. Smooth the top with a spatula.
4. Bake for 30–35 minutes, until the crust is browned and the filling is set.

**PER SERVING** Calories: 237 | Fat: 15 g | Protein: 8 g | Sugar: 2 g | Fiber: 2 g | Carbohydrates: 17 g

# Pumpkin Pie

*For fresh pumpkin purée: Halve and remove the seeds of sugar pumpkins,*
*place cut-side down in a baking dish, cover with foil, and bake at 375°F for 90 minutes.*
*Scoop out the flesh and purée until smooth.*

**INGREDIENTS | SERVES 8**

2 cups canned or fresh pumpkin purée

½ cup brown sugar

¼ cup sugar

½ teaspoon salt

2 teaspoons ground cinnamon

½ teaspoon ground ginger

¼ teaspoon ground cloves

¼ teaspoon nutmeg

¼ teaspoon allspice

10 ounces firm tofu, drained and patted dry

1 unbaked 9" Basic Pie Crust (½ recipe) (see recipe in this chapter)

1. Preheat oven to 425°F.
2. In a food processor, blend pumpkin, brown sugar, sugar, salt, cinnamon, ginger, cloves, nutmeg, allspice, and tofu until smooth. Pour into pie crust and smooth with a spatula.
3. Bake for 15 minutes. Reduce oven temperature to 350°F and bake for an additional 40 minutes, until crust is golden brown. Filling may still be somewhat wobbly. Chill for several hours before serving.

**PER SERVING** Calories: 203 | Fat: 5 g | Protein: 3 g | Sugar: 22 g | Fiber: 3 g | Carbohydrates: 38 g

## Homemade Pumpkin Pie Spice Mix

Craving pumpkin pie but find that you are out of pumpkin pie spice mix? No worries! Fresher-tasting, homemade pumpkin pie spice mix is easy to make. Simply combine 4 tablespoons ground cinnamon, 2 tablespoons ground ginger, 2 teaspoons cloves, 1 teaspoon nutmeg, and 1 teaspoon allspice. Mix well and store in an airtight container.

# Mango-Pineapple Empanadas

*This sweet, fruity hand pie has the flavors of a tropical paradise.*
*Add a teaspoon of rum extract to the filling for an extra kick!*

## INGREDIENTS | SERVES 6

1½ cups fresh pineapple, chopped into small pieces

1½ cups fresh mango, diced in ½" cubes

½ cup pineapple or apricot preserves

2 tablespoons lemon juice

⅛ teaspoon salt

1 tablespoon cornstarch

1 tablespoon water

1 recipe Empanada Dough (see recipe in this chapter)

2 tablespoons soymilk

Raw turbinado sugar, for dusting (optional)

1. Preheat oven to 350°F.
2. Combine the pineapple, mango, preserves, lemon juice, and salt in a medium saucepan. Cook over medium heat, stirring constantly for about 10 minutes, until fruit is soft. In a small bowl, mix the cornstarch with the water until blended, then stir into the fruit mixture. Remove from heat and allow to cool.
3. Roll dough out to about ⅛" thick on a lightly floured surface. Cut out 6 (6") circles, rerolling scraps as needed. Fill the center of each circle with ¼–⅓ cup filling, leaving a ½" border. Fold one side of dough over the filling in a half-moon shape and seal by crimping the border edges with the tines of a fork. Place on an ungreased baking sheet and brush tops with soymilk. Sprinkle with raw sugar, if desired.
4. Bake for 15–20 minutes until golden brown. Allow to cool several minutes before serving.

**PER SERVING** Calories: 425 | Fat: 15 g | Protein: 6 g | Sugar: 21 g | Fiber: 2 g | Carbohydrates: 67 g

# Blueberry Pie

*Tempt your family and friends with antioxidant-rich blueberry filling surrounded by a decadent, flaky pie crust!*

INGREDIENTS | SERVES 8

1 full recipe 9" Basic Pie Crust dough, chilled (see recipe in this chapter)

8 cups blueberries

2 tablespoons lemon juice

4 tablespoons cornstarch

½ cup sugar

2 tablespoons vegan margarine, cut into small pieces

2 tablespoons soy creamer

2 tablespoons raw turbinado sugar

## Is Your Soy Cheese Vegan?

Many nondairy products do actually contain dairy, even if it says "nondairy" right there on the package! Nondairy creamer and soy cheeses are notorious for this. Look for casein or whey on the ingredients list, particularly if you suffer from dairy allergies, and, if you're allergic to soy, look for nut- or rice-based vegan cheeses.

1. Preheat oven to 350°F.
2. Remove dough for bottom crust from the refrigerator. Roll dough out to a 12" circle on a lightly floured surface. Press dough into 9" pie pan. Cover with plastic and return to refrigerator. Remove top piece of dough and roll out to a 12" circle. Fold in half, and in half again. Wrap in plastic wrap and refrigerate.
3. In a large bowl, mash 1 cup of the blueberries. Add the remaining blueberries, lemon juice, cornstarch, and sugar. Stir gently to combine. Remove bottom crust from the refrigerator and fill with berry mixture so the berries are slightly higher in the center. Dot blueberries with margarine pieces.
4. Remove top crust from refrigerator, and unfold over pie. Press overhanging edges together with fingers, and fold up and pinch to form a fluted pattern resting on top of the rim of the pie. Brush top crust and edges with soy creamer. Sprinkle top with raw sugar, if desired. Bake for 40–50 minutes until crust is golden brown and filling is bubbling. If edges begin to brown too quickly, place a strip of aluminum foil around the rim of the pie. Allow to cool 30 minutes before serving.

**PER SERVING** Calories: 386 | Fat: 13 g | Protein: 4 g | Sugar: 31 g | Fiber: 4 g | Carbohydrates: 65 g

# Vegetable Potpie

*Potpies, with their buttery crust, tender vegetables,
and creamy sauces, are a stick-to-the-ribs comfort food!*

## INGREDIENTS | SERVES 6

3 tablespoons vegan margarine

1 cup onion, diced

1 clove garlic, minced

2 medium celery stalks, thinly sliced

¼ cup all-purpose flour

3 cups vegetable broth

2 medium carrots, ¼" dice

1 large russet potato, ½" diced

½ cup green beans, cut into 1" pieces

1 cup mushrooms, sliced

1½ teaspoons dried thyme

1½ teaspoons salt

1 teaspoon cracked black pepper

½ cup frozen peas, thawed

½ cup vegan sour cream

¾ batch Basic Pie Crust (see recipe in this chapter)

2 tablespoons soy creamer

1. Melt margarine over medium heat in a large skillet. Add onion, garlic, and celery; cook for 3–4 minutes. Stir in flour, vegetable broth, carrots, potato, green beans, mushrooms, thyme, salt, and pepper. Bring to a boil and simmer, stirring occasionally until sauce has thickened and vegetables are nearly tender, about 15–20 minutes. Stir in peas and sour cream. Pour into a lightly greased 9" × 13" baking dish.

2. Preheat oven to 400°F. Roll the Basic Pie Crust dough to about ⅛" thick and to fit the baking dish without any dough hanging over the edges. Drape dough over the filling and tuck the edges between the filling and the sides of the dish. Cut a few slits in the dough to vent. Brush top with soy creamer. Place the baking dish on a foil-lined, rimmed baking sheet to catch any overflow.

3. Bake 45–50 minutes, or until sauce is bubbly and crust is golden brown.

**PER SERVING** Calories: 413 | Fat: 19 g | Protein: 7 g | Sugar: 6 g | Fiber: 5 g | Carbohydrates: 54 g

# Chocolate-Banana Pie

*Surprise your guests with a sweet layer of bananas in the middle of this pie. It's great served with vegan whipped topping or a drizzle of chilled Strawberry Glaze (see Chapter 14).*

**INGREDIENTS | SERVES 10**

1 (12.3-ounce) package firm silken tofu

10 ounces vegan chocolate chips, melted

1 teaspoon vanilla extract

Splenda or powdered stevia, to taste

1–4 tablespoons soy creamer

1 (9") prepared chocolate Cookie Pie Crust (see recipe this chapter)

2–3 medium bananas

1. In a blender, process tofu until smooth. Add melted chocolate chips and vanilla extract. Blend until smooth. Blend in soymilk until desired consistency is achieved. Sweeten with Splenda, to taste.
2. Pour half the chocolate mixture into the pie crust and smooth with a rubber spatula. Thinly slice bananas and layer over the filling. Pour the rest of the filling over the bananas and smooth the top.
3. Refrigerate pie for 2–4 hours before serving.

**PER SERVING** Calories: 349 | Fat: 20 g | Protein: 5 g | Sugar: 23 g | Fiber: 3 g | Carbohydrates: 39 g

# Cheezecake

*This is a nice, plain cheesecake that can be topped any number of ways— try using fresh fruit, fruit sauce, or even chocolate sauce. Let your imagination fly!*

**INGREDIENTS | SERVES 10**

2 (8-ounce) containers vegan cream cheese, softened

1 cup sugar

1 tablespoon lemon juice

1 teaspoon vanilla powder

2 tablespoons cornstarch

1 prebaked Graham Cracker Pie Crust (see recipe in this chapter)

1. Preheat oven to 350°F.
2. In a blender, combine cream cheese, sugar, lemon juice, and vanilla powder. Add cornstarch and blend until smooth. Pour into crust.
3. Bake cheesecake for 45 minutes. Cheesecake should be puffed up and lightly browned. Cool completely and refrigerate. Decorate or serve with toppings as desired.

**PER SERVING** Calories: 294 | Fat: 12 g | Protein: 2 g | Sugar: 33 g | Fiber: 0 g | Carbohydrates: 46 g

# CHAPTER 10

# Cookies and Bars

# Cherry-Applesauce Cookies

*Applesauce gives these cookies a tender, cake-like texture,
cherries provide a sweet-tart zing, and walnuts chime in with a satisfying crunch!*

**INGREDIENTS | YIELDS: APPROXIMATELY
4 DOZEN COOKIES**

½ cup vegan margarine, softened

¾ cup sugar

¼ cup brown sugar, lightly packed

Egg replacement equal to 1 egg

1¼ cups applesauce

2⅔ cups flour

¼ teaspoon salt

1 teaspoon baking soda

1½ teaspoons cinnamon

1 cup dried, sweetened cherries,
coarsely chopped

½ cup walnuts, chopped

1. Preheat oven to 400°F.
2. Cream margarine, sugar, and brown sugar together in a large bowl. Stir in egg replacement and applesauce.
3. In a separate bowl, mix flour, salt, baking soda, and cinnamon. Add a third of the flour mixture to the wet ingredients and mix well. Repeat until wet and dry mixtures are combined. Stir in cherries and walnuts.
4. Drop by tablespoon onto ungreased cookie sheet. Bake for 11–13 minutes.
5. Remove from baking sheet to cool.

**PER 1 COOKIE** Calories: 80 | Fat: 3 g | Protein: 1 g | Sugar: 6 g | Fiber: 1 g | Carbohydrates: 13 g

# Snowy Lemon Cookies

*Longing for that box of powdered sugar–covered lemon cookies
from your childhood? Well, here they are!*

**INGREDIENTS | YIELDS: APPROXIMATELY
3 DOZEN COOKIES**

½ cup powdered sugar

⅓ cup sugar

3 tablespoons vegan margarine

2 tablespoons vegetable shortening

Egg replacement equal to 1 egg

1 teaspoon vanilla extract

¼ teaspoon salt

1 tablespoon fresh lemon juice

1 tablespoon lemon zest

1½ cups flour

1½ teaspoons baking powder

1 cup powdered sugar mixed with 1
teaspoon unsweetened lemonade drink
mix

1. Preheat oven to 325°F.
2. Cream together the powdered sugar, sugar, margarine, shortening, egg replacement, vanilla extract, salt, lemon juice, and lemon zest.
3. In a separate bowl, combine the flour and baking powder. Add the dry mixture to the wet mixture and combine until the dough is crumbly. Form into 1" balls and place about 1" apart on an ungreased baking sheet. Bake for 13–15 minutes.
4. Once cookies are baked, but still hot, place 5 or 6 at a time into a gallon-size sealable plastic bag filled with the powdered sugar–lemonade mixture and shake gently to coat.
5. Cool completely.

**PER 1 COOKIE** Calories: 51 | Fat: 2 g | Protein: 1 g | Sugar: 4 g | Fiber: 0 g | Carbohydrates: 9 g

# Scottish Shortbread

*This delightfully crumbly, buttery-tasting cookie is even more delicious with a bit of fresh lemon curd and a hot cup of tea.*

### INGREDIENTS | YIELDS 32 COOKIES

½ cup sugar

1 cup vegan margarine, cold

1¾ cups flour

### That's a Beautiful Cookie!

Shortbread can easily become an ornate work of art when prepared with artistically designed pans, stamps, molds, and tiles. Check your favorite baking or kitchen supply store or online resources. There are gorgeous patterns to suit almost any occasion, including Victorian, floral, holiday, snowflakes, scenery, and Celtic knotwork.

1. Preheat oven to 350°F.
2. Combine sugar, cold margarine, and flour with a large fork or pastry cutter. Dough will have a crumbly texture like sand. Refrigerate for 10 minutes.
3. Press chilled dough evenly into an ungreased 8" × 8" baking pan. Dock with a fork. Bake for 40–45 minutes until the edges are lightly browned. Cool in the pan.
4. When cookies are cooled, cut to make 32 rectangular pieces by slicing one side of the pan into 4 rows, then turning the pan a quarter turn and slicing into 8 rows.

**PER 1 COOKIE** Calories: 87 | Fat: 6 g | Protein: 1 g | Sugar: 3 g | Fiber: 0 g | Carbohydrates: 8 g

# Chocolate–Peanut Butter No-Bake Cookies

*You could argue that this flourless, eggless, favorite childhood delectable is really more candy than cookie . . . in fact, they're not even baked! They're just too yummy to leave out. Be careful to use quick-cooking oats, not instant oats, for this recipe.*

### INGREDIENTS | YIELDS APPROXIMATELY 40 COOKIES

2 cups quick-cooking oats

1 cup shredded coconut

2 cups sugar

½ cup soymilk

½ cup unsweetened cocoa powder

Pinch salt

½ cup vegan margarine

1 cup natural peanut butter, chunky-style

1 teaspoon vanilla extract

1. Combine oats and coconut in a large bowl and set aside.
2. Combine sugar, soymilk, cocoa, salt, and margarine in a heavy saucepan. Stirring constantly with a wooden spoon, bring to boil over medium heat and boil for exactly 1 minute.
3. Remove from heat and stir in peanut butter and vanilla extract. Pour peanut butter mixture over oat mixture and stir until combined.
4. Drop by tablespoon onto baking sheets lined with wax paper. Cool completely.

**PER 1 COOKIE** Calories: 128 | Fat: 7 g | Protein: 2 g | Sugar: 12 g | Fiber: 1 g | Carbohydrates: 16 g

# Whole-Wheat Persimmon Cookies

*Sweet and spicy persimmon cookies are a delicious way to celebrate the holiday season!*

**INGREDIENTS | YIELDS APPROXIMATELY 32 COOKIES**

1½ cups brown sugar

½ cup vegan margarine

1 teaspoon vanilla extract

Egg replacement equal to 2 eggs

¾ cup ripe persimmon pulp, mashed

1¾ cups flour

1 cup whole-wheat flour

¼ teaspoon salt

½ teaspoon baking soda

1½ teaspoons cinnamon

¼ teaspoon cloves

⅔ cup raisins

1 cup walnuts

1. Preheat oven to 375°F.
2. In a large bowl, cream brown sugar, vegan margarine, vanilla extract, and egg replacement. Stir in persimmon pulp.
3. In a separate bowl, combine the flours, salt, baking soda, and spices. Add the dry mixture one third at a time to the wet mixture until just mixed. Stir in raisins and nuts, being careful to not overmix.
4. Drop by tablespoon at least 1" apart onto an ungreased cookie sheet and bake for 10–12 minutes until cookies spring back when lightly touched.
5. Remove cookies to a cooling rack to cool.

**PER 1 COOKIE** Calories: 138 | Fat: 5 g | Protein: 2 g | Sugar: 12 g | Fiber: 1 | Carbohydrates: 22 g

## Is It Ripe Yet?

Persimmons are ripe when very soft. They ripen at room temperature, but placing them in a paper bag will speed up the process. Adding an apple to the bag will ripen them even more quickly! Apples emit ethylene gas, which hastens the ripening of persimmons, as well as other fruits such as avocados, peaches, nectarines, and some melons.

# Cocoa Pecan Drops

*Pecan cookies with a little something extra . . . chocolate! Try adding a half-teaspoon of ground cinnamon to the cocoa–powdered sugar coating mixture for a traditional Mexican flavor combination.*

**INGREDIENTS | YIELDS APPROXIMATELY 3 DOZEN COOKIES**

1 cup vegan margarine, softened
½ cup sugar
¼ cup brown sugar, packed
2 teaspoons vanilla extract
1 tablespoon soymilk
2 cups sifted flour
½ teaspoon salt
¼ cup plus 2 tablespoons unsweetened cocoa powder
¾ cup pecans, ground
¼ cup pecans, chopped
½ cup powdered sugar

1. Preheat oven to 350°F.
2. In a large bowl, cream margarine, sugar, and brown sugar. Stir in vanilla extract and soymilk. In a separate bowl, combine flour, salt, and ¼ cup cocoa powder. Gradually add the flour mixture to the wet ingredients. Stir in ground and chopped pecans. Chill dough for 30 minutes.
3. Form dough into 1" balls and place on an ungreased cookie sheet 1" apart. Bake for 18–22 minutes. While cookies are baking, mix remaining 2 tablespoons cocoa powder with powdered sugar.
4. Remove cookies from the oven and allow to cool for 2 minutes on the cookie sheet. Then, while cookies are still hot, toss them in the cocoa-sugar mixture to coat.
5. Allow to cool completely, then coat with the cocoa-sugar mixture a second time.

**PER 1 COOKIE** Calories: 113 | Fat: 7 g | Protein: 1 g | Sugar: 5 g | Fiber: 1 g | Carbohydrates: 11 g

# Almond Cookies

*Sweet and bursting with the flavor of almonds, these cookies*
*are a classic complement to your favorite Chinese meal, or any meal!*

**INGREDIENTS | YIELDS APPROXIMATELY 42 COOKIES**

3 or 4 tablespoons slivered almonds

¼ cup vegan margarine, softened

¼ cup vegetable shortening, softened

¾ cup sugar

Egg replacement equal to 1 egg

½ teaspoon almond extract

1 cup flour

1 cup almond meal

¼ teaspoon baking powder

## The Scoop on Shortening

Shortening is a popular ingredient in baked goods because it gives products made with wheat flour a crumbly texture. Wheat flour contains a protein called gluten. Gluten, when allowed to develop in long protein strands, is responsible for the chewy texture in foods like breads and pizza crusts. When a more tender product is desired, shortening "shortens" dough by interfering with gluten formation, resulting in shorter protein strands.

1. Preheat oven to 350°F.
2. Toast slivered almonds in a dry pan over low heat until lightly browned. Transfer to a small bowl and set aside. In a large bowl, combine margarine, shortening, and sugar at medium speed with an electric mixer. Stir in egg replacement and almond extract.
3. In a separate bowl, combine flour, almond meal, and baking powder. Stir the dry ingredients into the wet ingredients. Cover the bowl and refrigerate for 2–3 hours.
4. Form the chilled dough into ¾" balls and place on a lightly greased cookie sheet about 2" apart. Flatten slightly with the bottom of a glass. Press 2 or 3 toasted almond slivers into the top of each cookie. Bake at 350°F for 11–13 minutes.
5. Allow to cool for 3 minutes on cookie sheet before placing on wire rack. Cool completely.

**PER 1 COOKIE** Calories: 63 | Fat: 4 g | Protein: 1 g | Sugar: 4 g | Fiber: 1 g | Carbohydrates: 7 g

# Everything Cookies

*Crispy, crunchy, gooey, and chewy . . . the only thing missing is the kitchen sink!*
*The corn flake cereal in this recipe can be substituted with other cereals.*
*Try crispy rice, crushed bran flakes, or Chex-type cereals.*

**INGREDIENTS** | YIELDS APPROXIMATELY
4 DOZEN COOKIES

1 cup vegan margarine

1 cup sugar

½ cup brown sugar, packed

Egg replacement equal to 2 eggs

1 teaspoon vanilla extract

1¼ cups sifted flour

1 cup sifted whole-wheat flour

1 teaspoon baking soda

½ teaspoon baking powder

½ teaspoon salt

1 cup quick-cooking oats

1 cup corn flakes cereal, crushed

½ cup shredded coconut

½ cup currants or raisins

½ cup walnuts, chopped

1 cup vegan chocolate chips

1. Preheat oven to 375°F.
2. In a large bowl, cream margarine, sugar, and brown sugar. Stir in egg replacement and vanilla extract. In a separate bowl, combine flour, whole-wheat flour, baking soda, baking powder, and salt.
3. Gradually combine the flour mixture with the wet ingredients.
4. Stir in the oats, corn flakes, coconut, currants, walnuts, and chocolate chips. Drop by tablespoon onto an ungreased cookie sheet. Bake 9–11 minutes until the edges are golden brown.
5. Remove from the oven and allow to cool on the cookie sheet for 2 minutes. Transfer to wire racks and cool completely.

**PER 1 COOKIE** Calories: 132 | Fat: 6 g | Protein: 2 g | Sugar: 11 g | Fiber: 1 g | Carbohydrates: 18 g

# Autumn Applesauce Cookies

*The aromatic spices in this cookie will have you reminiscing about fall colors and the feel of the crisp, cool air . . . a welcome sign that summer is waning and autumn is about to begin.*

**INGREDIENTS | YIELDS: APPROXIMATELY 4 DOZEN COOKIES**

½ cup vegan margarine, softened

¾ cup sugar

¼ cup brown sugar, lightly packed

Egg replacement equal to 1 egg

1¼ cups applesauce

2⅔ cups flour

¼ teaspoon salt

1 teaspoon baking soda

2 teaspoons cinnamon

1 teaspoon cloves

¼ teaspoon ground ginger

¼ teaspoon cardamom

¼ teaspoon allspice

¾ cup raisins

¾ cup walnuts, chopped

1. Preheat oven to 400°F.
2. Cream margarine, sugar, and brown sugar together in a large bowl. Stir in egg replacement and applesauce.
3. In a separate bowl, mix flour, salt, baking soda, and all spices. Gradually combine the flour mixture with the wet ingredients. Stir in raisins and walnuts.
4. Drop by tablespoon onto ungreased cookie sheet. Bake for 11–13 minutes.
5. Remove from baking sheet to cool.

**PER 1 COOKIE** Calories: 81 | Fat: 3 g | Protein: 1 g | Sugar: 6 g | Fiber: 1 g | Carbohydrates: 13 g

## Chai Tea

Infuse water with chai spice flavor by simmering 4 cups water with 2 cinnamon sticks, 8 cloves, 8 cardamom pods, and a 1" chunk of fresh ginger for 10 minutes. Strain. Discard spices. Bring spiced water to a boil and remove from heat. Add 2 or 3 black teabags according to desired strength and allow to steep 3–5 minutes. Add soymilk and sweetener to taste.

# Chocolate Chip Cookies

*Inspired by a well-known recipe, this version is a bit healthier
with all vegan ingredients and the goodness of whole-wheat flour.*

**INGREDIENTS | YIELDS APPROXIMATELY
5 DOZEN COOKIES**

¾ cup vegan margarine, softened

¼ cup vegetable shortening

¾ cup sugar

¾ cup brown sugar, packed

1 teaspoon vanilla extract

Egg replacement equal to 2 eggs

1½ cups flour

1 cup whole-wheat flour

½ teaspoon salt

1 teaspoon baking soda

2 cups vegan chocolate chips or carob chips

1 cup walnuts, coarsely chopped (optional)

1. Preheat oven to 375°F.
2. In a large bowl, cream margarine, shortening, sugar, brown sugar, and vanilla extract until smooth. Stir in egg replacement.
3. In a separate bowl, combine flour, whole-wheat flour, salt, and baking soda. Gradually combine flour mixture with wet ingredients. Stir in vegan chocolate chips and walnuts.
4. Drop by tablespoon onto an ungreased baking sheet and bake 9–11 minutes. Cool on baking sheet for 1 minute; transfer to wire racks to cool completely.

**PER 1 COOKIE** Calories: 99 | Fat: 5 g | Protein: 1 g | Sugar: 8 g | Fiber: 1 g | Carbohydrates: 13 g

## Carob, the Chocolate Impostor

Often used as a "healthy chocolate," carob is lower in fat than cocoa powder and does not contain addictive stimulants, such as theobromine and caffeine, which are present in chocolate. It is the pod of the carob tree—not the seed—that is ground to make carob powder. Carob seeds are used to make carob bean gum, also known as locust bean gum, a thickening agent found in processed foods like salad dressings and ice cream.

# Old-Fashioned Peanut Butter Cookies

*The original purpose of the hatch-mark pattern remains a mystery. The simplest explanation is that this classic pattern makes it easy to distinguish between peanut butter cookies and other cookies. Whatever the purpose, these cookies taste peanut-buttery and delicious!*

**INGREDIENTS | YIELDS APPROXIMATELY 52 COOKIES**

½ cup vegan margarine

½ cup vegetable shortening

1 cup sugar

1 cup brown sugar, packed

Egg replacement equal to 2 eggs

2 teaspoons vanilla extract

1 cup natural peanut butter, chunky-style

2½ cups flour

½ teaspoon baking soda

1 teaspoon baking powder

¼ teaspoon salt

1. Preheat oven to 375°F.
2. Cream margarine, shortening, sugar, and brown sugar in a large bowl. Stir in egg replacement, vanilla extract, and peanut butter. In a separate bowl, sift flour, baking soda, baking powder, and salt together. Gradually combine flour mixture with wet ingredients.
3. Roll pieces of dough by hand into 1" balls and place on ungreased cookie sheet about 1" apart. Refrigerate the dough for a few minutes if it seems too soft to roll easily. Use a fork to flatten each cookie with a crisscross pattern.
4. Bake for 10–12 minutes until golden brown around the edges. Cool completely on a wire rack.

**PER 1 COOKIE** Calories: 116 | Fat: 6 g | Protein: 2 g | Sugar: 8 g | Fiber: 1 g | Carbohydrates: 14 g

# Oatmeal Raisin Cookies

*Chewy, hearty, and satisfying! Did you know that oatmeal cookies have their own national holiday? There is confusion about whether the actual date for this holiday is March 18 or April 30, so celebrate by having oatmeal cookies on both days!*

**INGREDIENTS | YIELDS APPROXIMATELY 3 DOZEN COOKIES**

½ cup vegan margarine

⅓ cup sugar

½ cup brown sugar, packed

Egg replacement equal to 1 egg

1 teaspoon vanilla extract

1 cup flour

½ teaspoon baking soda

1½ teaspoons ground cinnamon

1¼ cups rolled or quick oats

1 cup raisins

½ cup walnuts, chopped (optional)

1. Preheat oven to 350°F.
2. Cream margarine, sugar, and brown sugar together in a large bowl. Stir in egg replacement and vanilla extract until blended. In a separate bowl, combine flour, baking soda, and cinnamon. Gradually combine flour mixture with wet ingredients, then stir in oats, raisins, and walnuts, if desired.
3. Chill the dough for about an hour. Drop by tablespoon onto a lightly greased cookie sheet and bake for 10–12 minutes until the edges are golden brown.
4. Allow to cool on cookie sheet for 3 minutes before transferring to wire racks. Cool completely.

**PER 1 COOKIE** Calories: 79 | Fat: 3 g | Protein: 1 g | Sugar: 8 g | Fiber: 1 g | Carbohydrates: 13 g

## Raisin Revival

Bring those hard, dried-up raisins back to life by soaking 1 cup of raisins in 1 cup of hot water. Within a few minutes or up to 1 hour they'll plump right up. For a surprising flavor boost, try soaking raisins in rum or brandy before adding them to your recipes! Remember to drain soaked raisins before you use them. This works well with other dried fruits too.

# Sugar Cookies

*Crispy with just the right amount of sweetness, these cookies are sure to delight!*
*Decorating these cookies is a snap. Lightly press decorating or sanding sugar onto the top*
*of the cookie dough before it is baked; or after they're baked and cooled, paint with cookie icing.*

**INGREDIENTS | YIELDS APPROXIMATELY 3 DOZEN COOKIES**

¾ cup vegan margarine, softened

1¼ cups sugar

Egg replacement equal to 1 egg

1 teaspoon vanilla extract

2 tablespoons soymilk

2½ cups flour

½ teaspoon baking powder

¼ teaspoon baking soda

¼ teaspoon salt

## Uneven Baking?

Are you frustrated that the results of your baking efforts are often inconsistent even when you know you've followed the recipe correctly? If foods are always under- or overbaked, the oven may not be calibrated correctly. Get the oven fixed and buy yourself an oven thermometer. If foods are overly browned on just one side of the pan, while other areas appear fine or underdone, it could be that your oven has a hot spot. Try rotating the pan at the halfway point of the baking process to even out the baking.

1. Preheat oven to 375°F.
2. In a large bowl, cream the margarine and sugar. Beat in the egg replacement, vanilla extract, and soymilk. In a separate bowl, sift together flour, baking powder, baking soda, and salt. Gradually add the flour mixture to the wet ingredients. Divide dough in half, wrap each half in plastic wrap, and flatten into a 6" disk with the palm of your hand.
3. Chill dough 2–3 hours. Roll each dough ball to a thickness of ¼" on a floured surface and cut out with your favorite cookie cutters. Keep each ball of dough refrigerated until you are ready to use it.
4. Place at least 1" apart on a lightly greased cookie sheet and bake for 10–11 minutes until the edges are lightly browned. Leave cookies on baking sheet for 1 minute and then transfer to wire racks.

**PER 1 COOKIE** Calories: 90 | Fat: 4 g | Protein: 1 g | Sugar: 7 g | Fiber: 0 g | Carbohydrates: 13 g

# Orange-Spice-Molasses Cookies

*Warm and spicy, these cookies are perfect for cookie sliders!*
*Soften vegan vanilla "ice cream" for a few minutes and sandwich a few tablespoons*
*between 2 cookies. Freeze for 20–30 minutes before serving.*

**INGREDIENTS | YIELDS APPROXIMATELY 24 COOKIES**

¾ cup vegan margarine, softened

¼ cup sugar

¾ cup brown sugar, packed

Egg replacement equal to 1 egg

¼ cup molasses

1 teaspoon vanilla extract

1 tablespoon orange zest, finely minced or grated

2¼ cups flour

1 teaspoon baking soda

¼ teaspoon salt

1½ teaspoons ground cinnamon

1 teaspoon ground cloves

1 teaspoon ground ginger

⅛ teaspoon ground nutmeg

Granulated sugar for rolling (optional)

1. Preheat oven to 375°F.
2. In a large bowl, cream margarine and sugars until smooth. Mix in egg replacement, molasses, and vanilla extract. Stir in the orange zest. In a separate bowl sift together flour, baking soda, salt, and spices.
3. Gradually add flour mixture to wet ingredients. Shape dough into walnut-sized balls. Place 2" apart on a lightly greased cookie sheet. If desired, roll balls in granulated sugar before placing on the cookie sheet. Bake for 10–12 minutes.
4. Allow to cool on cookie sheet for 5 minutes, then transfer to wire rack.

**PER 1 COOKIE** Calories: 139 | Fat: 6 g | Protein: 1 g | Sugar: 11 g | Fiber: 0 g | Carbohydrates: 21 g

## What Is Molasses, Anyway?

Molasses is a byproduct of the process of refining sugar from sugar cane and sugar beets. Like olive oil and maple syrup, molasses is available in several grades, primarily determined by the quality of the sugar source (cane or beet) and the degree of processing. Nutritionally, blackstrap molasses is a grade of molasses that is a great source of iron and calcium. This natural sweetener gives a caramel-like flavor to cookies and gingerbread.

# Snickerdoodles

*These are similar to a sugar cookie but add a delicious cinnamon kick.*

**INGREDIENTS | YIELDS APPROXIMATELY 4 DOZEN COOKIES**

½ cup vegan margarine, softened

½ cup vegetable shortening

1½ cups sugar

Egg replacement equal to 2 eggs

1 teaspoon vanilla extract

2 teaspoons cream of tartar

1 teaspoon baking soda

¼ teaspoon salt

2¾ cups flour

1 tablespoon ground cinnamon, for coating

3 tablespoons sugar, for coating

1. Preheat oven to 375°F.
2. In a large bowl, cream margarine, shortening, and sugar. Beat in egg replacement, vanilla extract, cream of tartar, baking soda, and salt until fluffy. Gradually combine flour with wet ingredients. Chill dough for 2–3 hours.
3. Combine cinnamon and sugar for coating together in a small bowl. Remove chilled dough from the refrigerator.
4. Form dough into 1" balls and roll in cinnamon-sugar to coat. Place on ungreased cookie sheet about 2" apart.
5. Bake for 10–11 minutes until lightly browned. Allow to cool for 1 minute on cookie sheet, then transfer to wire rack. Cool completely.

**PER 1 COOKIE** Calories: 90 | Fat: 4 g | Protein: 1 g | Sugar: 7 g | Fiber: 0 g | Carbohydrates: 13 g

## Cream of Tartar

You may have heard of the type of tartar that accumulates on teeth, but *cream of tartar* is not the concern of a dentist! Cream of tartar is an acidic byproduct of winemaking. In baking, cream of tartar reacts with baking soda as a leavening agent to create air bubbles of carbon dioxide. This helps make baked goods lighter and less dense. Cream of tartar is also used as a stabilizer to give volume to beaten egg whites for meringues. It also prevents crystallization of sugar-containing foods, like frosting, and when made into a paste with lemon juice, it can be an effective, natural cleaner for brass and copper cookware!

# Chocolate Cheesecake Bars

*Packaged cake mixes are often dairy-free and make a great shortcut to a delicious dessert!*
*Make sure to select a cake mix without pudding in the mix.*

**INGREDIENTS | YIELDS 24 BARS**

1 package chocolate cake mix

4 ounces vegan cream cheese, cold

6 tablespoons vegan margarine, cold

20 ounces vegan cream cheese, softened

⅔ cup sugar

1 teaspoon vanilla extract

Egg replacement equal to 2 eggs

1 cup vegan chocolate chips (optional)

1. Preheat oven to 350°F.
2. In a large bowl, combine cake mix, cream cheese, and margarine with a pastry cutter or large fork until crumbly. Remove 1½ cups of cake mixture; stir in optional chocolate chips and set aside for topping. Press remaining cake mixture into a lightly greased 9" × 13" baking dish and bake 12 minutes. Cool.
3. Beat softened cream cheese, sugar, vanilla extract, and egg replacement on low speed with an electric mixer until smooth. Spread evenly over baked cake layer.
4. Lightly press reserved chocolate chip–cake mixture over cream cheese layer. Bake 40–45 minutes.
5. Cool completely, then cover with plastic wrap and refrigerate 4–6 hours. Cut into squares.

**PER 1 BAR** Calories: 262 | Fat: 13 g | Protein: 3 g | Sugar: 21 g | Fiber: 1 g | Carbohydrates: 36 g

# Strawberry Crumble Bars

*This is a rich, decadent bar, combining ripe, sweet strawberries with a buttery cookie crust and a brown sugar–oatmeal crumble topping. You may want to keep these all for yourself!*

### INGREDIENTS | YIELDS 16 BARS

½ cup vegan margarine, cold

¼ plus ⅓ cup sugar, divided use

1¾ cups flour, divided use

2 cups strawberries, hulled and halved

⅓ cup orange juice

2 tablespoons cornstarch

1 tablespoon lemon juice

¾ cup oats

½ cup brown sugar, packed

¼ teaspoon baking soda

Dash salt

¼ cup vegan margarine, melted

## Cookies on Demand!

It's easy to have fresh, hot-from-the-oven cookies within minutes, any time you want them! Simply place cookie dough on baking sheets, as though you're about to bake them, but freeze them instead. Once frozen, you can transfer them from the cookie sheet to freezer bags. When you're ready for some fresh, hot cookies, place them on a cookie sheet and bake, adding a few minutes to the baking time.

1. Preheat oven to 350°F.
2. Cream cold margarine and ¼ cup sugar. Add 1 cup flour and combine. Press into a greased 8" × 8" pan and bake at 350°F for 20 minutes. Remove from oven. Cool.
3. While crust cools, combine strawberries, ⅓ cup sugar, orange juice, cornstarch, and lemon juice in a heavy saucepan. Simmer over low heat about 4–5 minutes until thickened, stirring frequently. Spread mixture over cooled crust.
4. In a large bowl, combine remaining ¾ cup flour, oats, brown sugar, baking soda, and salt. Add melted margarine and combine. Spread evenly over strawberry filling. Bake 30–35 minutes at 350°F. Cool completely then cut into squares.

**PER 1 BAR** Calories: 206 | Fat: 9 g | Protein: 2 g | Sugar: 15 g | Fiber: 1 g | Carbohydrates: 30 g

# Lemon Bars

*A lemon bar with no eggs and no dairy? Absolutely! How is that possible, you ask? The magic ingredient giving the lemon filling the creamy texture of a good lemon curd is . . . silken soft tofu!*

**INGREDIENTS | YIELDS 16 BARS**

½ cup vegan margarine, cold

1½ cups sugar, divided

½ teaspoon salt

1 cup plus 2 tablespoons flour, divided

¾ cup silken soft tofu, drained and patted dry

½ cup fresh lemon juice

3 tablespoons cornstarch

Zest from 2 lemons

Powdered sugar for sifting over the top (optional)

1. Preheat oven to 350°F. Lightly grease and flour an 8" × 8" pan.
2. Cream margarine, ¼ cup sugar, and salt with a pastry cutter or large fork. Cut in 1 cup flour until the dough is in small pieces. Chill dough for 10–15 minutes, then press into the bottom of the prepared baking dish. Bake for 20 minutes until lightly browned. Cool.
3. While crust cools, blend tofu in food processor until smooth. Add remaining 1¼ cups sugar, lemon juice, cornstarch, and remaining 2 tablespoons flour. Process until blended, then stir in the lemon zest. Pour mixture over the prebaked crust.
4. Bake at 350°F for 35–40 minutes, until filling is set and lightly browned. Cool completely and sift powdered sugar over the top, if desired.

**PER 1 BAR** Calories: 167 | Fat: 6 g | Protein: 1 g | Sugar: 19 g | Fiber: 0 g | Carbohydrates: 28 g

# Apricot-Almond Oatmeal Bars

*Sticky, apricot-ty, and almond-y oatmeal goodness!*
*These bars are rich and dense with dried apricots, nuts, and oats.*

**INGREDIENTS | YIELDS 16 BARS**

½ cup vegan margarine, softened

½ cup brown sugar, packed

3 cups oats, divided use

1 cup dried apricots, diced

⅓ cup apricot preserves

1 tablespoon lemon juice

Egg replacement equal to 2 eggs

1 cup brown sugar, lightly packed

1 teaspoon vanilla extract

¼ teaspoon baking powder

½ cup sliced almonds

1. Preheat oven to 350°F.
2. Cream margarine and packed brown sugar. Stir in 2 cups oats. Press into a lightly greased 8" × 8" pan and bake for 15 minutes. Cool. While crust cools, combine apricots, apricot preserves, and lemon juice in a heavy saucepan over low heat for about 5–6 minutes until apricots are softened. Set aside.
3. In a large bowl, combine egg replacement, lightly packed brown sugar, vanilla extract, and baking powder. Stir in apricot mixture, almonds, and remaining oats. Spread evenly over cooled crust.
4. Bake 30–35 minutes. Cool completely.

**PER 1 BAR** Calories: 188 | Fat: 8 g | Protein: 3 g | Sugar: 14 g | Fiber: 3 g | Carbohydrates: 28 g

# Walnut-Date Squares

*These treats are moist, gooey, and delicious. For a special occasion, serve these warm with a dollop of your favorite vegan whipped topping, or a scoop of vegan vanilla ice cream.*

**INGREDIENTS | YIELDS 16 SQUARES**

1 cup chopped dates, packed
1 cup packed brown sugar, divided use
½ cup orange juice
1 teaspoon vanilla extract
¾ cup flour
¾ cup oats
1 teaspoon cinnamon
⅛ teaspoon ground cloves
¼ teaspoon baking soda
Pinch salt
½ cup vegan margarine, cold
¾ cup walnuts, coarsely chopped

## A Date for Your Health!

Commonly used dates include Medjool and Deglet Noor, but did you know that there are more than twenty different varieties of dates? Other varieties include Amir Hajj, Zahidi, Barnhi, and honey dates. Historically, dates have been a staple food for the desert cultures of North Africa and the Middle East. Nutritionally, dates are a great source of carbohydrates, fiber, calcium, iron, and potassium. Store dates in the refrigerator in an airtight container for up to 6 months.

1. Preheat oven to 350°F. Lightly grease and flour an 8" × 8" baking pan.
2. Combine dates, ½ cup brown sugar, and orange juice in a saucepan. Heat to boiling over medium-low heat. Reduce heat and simmer for 4 minutes to thicken, stirring frequently. Remove from heat, then stir in vanilla extract.
3. In a separate bowl, combine flour, oats, remaining ½ cup brown sugar, cinnamon, cloves, baking soda, and salt. Cut margarine into pieces and combine with flour mixture until crumbly. Press ½ of the flour mixture into the bottom of the baking pan to form the crust.
4. Sprinkle walnuts in an even layer and lightly press into the crust. Spread the date mixture over the crust and then top with the remaining flour mixture.
5. Bake at 350°F for 30 minutes, until lightly browned. Place pan on wire rack to cool. Cut into squares to serve.

**PER 1 BAR** Calories: 212 | Fat: 9 g | Protein: 2 g | Sugar: 14 g | Fiber: 2 g | Carbohydrates: 31 g

# Chocolate-Walnut Brownies

*Make these for the times when only a dense, chewy, and chocolaty brownie will do! These brownies are great with vegan ice cream, hot fudge, and vegan whipped topping for a decadent brownie sundae.*

**INGREDIENTS | SERVES 16**

1¼ cups all-purpose flour, divided use

½ cup water

1½ teaspoons baking powder

6 tablespoons vegan margarine

⅓ cup cocoa powder

1 cup sugar

¼ teaspoon salt

½ teaspoon vanilla extract

⅓ cup vegan chocolate chips

½ cup walnuts, chopped

## Do You Know Your Cocoa from Your Cacao?

While the words "cocoa" and "cacao" (pronounced *ka-kow*) are often used interchangeably, the tree that chocolate grows on, its pods, and the beans inside the pods are referred to as cacao. Cacao beans are fermented, dried, roasted, and then ground into a paste called chocolate liquor. The natural fat pressed from this chocolate liquor is cocoa butter. Once the cocoa butter is pressed out, the remaining solid product, cocoa presscake, is milled into cocoa powder. Some cocoa powder is treated with an alkali—this is known as Dutch-process cocoa powder. You can use either type of cocoa powder for baking; however, since Dutch-process cocoa powder is less acidic and will not react with baking soda, it is best used in recipes that contain baking powder.

1. Preheat oven to 350°F.
2. Mix ¼ cup flour with water in a small saucepan. Stirring constantly, cook over medium heat until it has a thick, paste-like consistency. Remove from heat and cool completely.
3. Whisk the remaining flour and baking powder together and set aside. In a large saucepan, melt margarine over low heat and stir in cocoa powder.
4. With a wooden spoon, beat sugar, salt, and vanilla extract into the cooked flour mixture. Add this to the melted margarine and cocoa, and mix well. Then stir in the dry flour mixture. Fold in chocolate chips and walnuts.
5. Spread batter evenly in a lightly greased 8" × 8" pan and bake for 20–25 minutes. Cool and cut into squares.

**PER SERVING** Calories: 176 | Fat: 8 g | Protein: 2 g | Sugar: 15 g | Fiber: 1 g | Carbohydrates: 25 g

# Pecan Blondies

*Many blondie recipes call for vanilla extract, but the almond extract in this recipe gives this sweet treat a wonderful warm, rich flavor you're going to love.*

**INGREDIENTS | SERVES 16**

1¼ cups all-purpose flour, divided use

½ cup water

1½ teaspoons baking powder

½ cup sugar

½ cup brown sugar, packed

¼ teaspoon salt

½ teaspoon almond extract

4 tablespoons vegan margarine, melted

¾ cup pecans, chopped

## Flavor Conundrum?

Confused about extracts, flavorings, and flavored oils? Commonly used for home cooking and baking, extracts are made by soaking a flavor source, such as vanilla beans, almonds, or lemon peel, in ethyl alcohol and water. Less potent than extracts, flavorings are usually extracts that are diluted with imitation flavors. The most concentrated flavor of all comes from flavored oils, which are derived by pressing the natural oils from the flavor source.

1. Preheat oven to 350°F.
2. Mix ¼ cup flour with water in a medium saucepan. Stirring constantly, cook over medium heat until mixture has a thick, paste-like consistency. Remove from heat and cool completely.
3. Whisk together remaining flour and baking powder and set aside.
4. With a wooden spoon, beat sugars, salt, and almond extract into the cooked flour mixture. Add the melted margarine and mix well. Then stir in the dry flour mixture. Fold in pecans.
5. Spread batter evenly in a lightly greased 8" × 8" pan and bake for 20–25 minutes. Cool and cut into squares.

**PER SERVING** Calories: 147 | Fat: 7 g | Protein: 1 g | Sugar: 13 g | Fiber: 1 g | Carbohydrates: 21 g

# CHAPTER 11

# Cakes

# Fresh Apple Cake

*This cake is spicy, super moist, and bursting with apples.*
*Try adding walnuts and rum-soaked raisins for your next special occasion!*

## INGREDIENTS | SERVES 18

2 cups rapadura or Sucanat sugar

Egg replacement equal to 2 eggs

½ cup canola oil

2 teaspoons vanilla extract

2 tablespoons soymilk

2 cups all-purpose flour

1½ teaspoons baking soda

2 teaspoons cinnamon

¼ teaspoon nutmeg

¼ teaspoon ground cloves

4 cups unpeeled apples, diced

1. Preheat oven to 325°F.
2. On medium-low speed, beat sugar and egg replacement with an electric mixer. Add oil, vanilla extract, and soymilk; continue to mix until well blended.
3. Sift flour, baking soda, and spices together in a separate bowl. Gradually blend into wet ingredients. Fold in apples.
4. Spread batter into a lightly greased and floured 9" × 13" pan. Bake for 1 hour.

**PER SERVING** Calories: 208 | Fat: 6 g | Protein: 2 g | Sugar: 25 g | Fiber: 1 g | Carbohydrates: 37 g

## That's a Lotta Apples!

With more than 7,500 varieties of apples grown worldwide, you could enjoy a different type of apple every day for over twenty years and still not try them all! Apples like cool temperatures, so store them in the refrigerator or in a cool basement or cellar to keep them fresh. To prevent browning of apples for salads or for eating as-is, dip cut apples in acidulated water. To make acidulated water, mix 1 part lemon juice with 3 parts water.

# Pineapple Upside-Down Cake

*Caramelized sugar adds a rich depth of flavor to this moist cake.*
*To create a pineapple upside-down cake with visual pizzazz, lay pecan halves and maraschino cherries*
*in the melted sugar in a decorative pattern before you add the pineapple layer.*

**INGREDIENTS | SERVES 8**

1 cup vegan margarine, softened, divided use

½ cup light brown sugar, packed

2 (20-ounce) cans crushed pineapple, drained

3 tablespoons silken soft tofu

½ cup vegan sour cream, divided use

1 teaspoon vanilla extract

1½ cups all-purpose flour

¾ cup sugar

1 teaspoon baking soda

¼ teaspoon salt

1 tablespoon apple cider vinegar

1. Preheat oven to 350°F. Place rack in lower third of oven.
2. Melt 6 tablespoons of the margarine in a 9" or 10" cast-iron skillet. Add brown sugar and stir until melted. Remove from heat. Press extra juice out of pineapple in a colander and then spread pineapple over melted brown-sugar mixture in skillet.
3. In a medium bowl, mix tofu, 2 tablespoons of the sour cream, and vanilla extract on medium speed until smooth. Set aside.
4. In a large bowl, whisk flour, sugar, baking soda, and salt together until well blended. Add remaining sour cream and margarine, and mix on low speed to moisten the dry ingredients. Mixture will be quite lumpy.
5. Gradually add the tofu mixture to the flour mixture and beat on medium speed for 1 minute, scraping down the sides of the bowl as needed. Quickly mix in the vinegar.
6. Spread batter evenly over pineapple with a spatula. Bake for 40–50 minutes, or until a toothpick inserted in the center of the cake comes out clean.
7. Remove from the oven and immediately run a knife around the edge of the skillet to loosen the cake. Carefully invert onto a serving plate. Serve warm or at room temperature.

**PER SERVING** Calories: 519 | Fat: 50 g | Protein: 4 g | Sugar: 48 g | Fiber: 2 g | Carbohydrates: 71 g

# Chocolate-Peppermint Bundt Cake

*This chocolate-mint deliciousness isn't reserved for only the holiday season! Enjoy this cake all year long.*

**INGREDIENTS | SERVES 16**

2 cups soymilk

2 teaspoons vinegar

2¼ cups unbleached all-purpose flour

2 cups sugar

¾ cup unsweetened cocoa

1 teaspoon baking powder

1 teaspoon baking soda

1 teaspoon salt

⅔ cup canola oil

1½ teaspoons peppermint extract

1 teaspoon vanilla extract

½ batch Chocolate Ganache (see Chapter 14)

⅓ cup crushed peppermint candies

1. Preheat oven to 350°F.
2. Combine soymilk and vinegar in a medium bowl. Allow to sit for 10 minutes to thicken. In a large bowl, whisk together the flour, sugar, cocoa, baking powder, baking soda, and salt. Set aside. Add oil, peppermint extract, and vanilla extract to the soymilk mixture, whisking to combine. Add wet ingredients to the flour mixture, stirring gently until there are no large lumps.
3. Pour batter into a greased and floured bundt cake pan. Bake 45–50 minutes, or until a toothpick comes out clean when inserted into the center of the cake. Cool cake for 10 minutes, then invert onto a serving platter. Cool completely.
4. Prepare vegan Chocolate Ganache and cool for 10 minutes. Pour over cake. Sprinkle top of cake with crushed peppermint candies.

**PER SERVING** Calories: 348 | Fat: 16 g | Protein: 3 g | Sugar: 29 g | Fiber: 2 g | Carbohydrates: 50 g

# Cinnamon Coffee Cake

*Here's a moist, tender cake with an inner swirl of cinnamon and nuts!*

**INGREDIENTS | SERVES 12**

1¼ cups sugar, divided use

1 tablespoon cinnamon

½ cup walnuts, chopped

½ cup vegan margarine, softened

Egg replacement equal to 2 eggs

1 teaspoon vanilla extract

1 cup vegan sour cream

2 cups all-purpose flour

1 teaspoon baking powder

1 teaspoon baking soda

½ teaspoon salt

1. Preheat oven to 350°F.
2. Combine ¼ cup sugar, cinnamon, and walnuts in a small bowl. Set aside.
3. In a large bowl, cream margarine and the remaining 1 cup sugar on low speed. Beat in egg replacement, vanilla extract, and sour cream until smooth. Sift the flour, baking powder, baking soda, and salt together. Increase mixer speed to medium and gradually add the dry ingredients to margarine mixture.
4. Sprinkle half of the cinnamon-nut mixture in the bottom of a lightly greased bundt pan. Spread half of the batter over the cinnamon-nut mixture. Sprinkle the rest of the cinnamon-nut mixture over the batter layer. Spread the remaining batter over the top. Bake for 45 minutes.
5. Cool cake for 10 minutes, then invert onto a serving platter. Serve warm or at room temperature.

**PER SERVING** Calories: 317 | Fat: 48 g | Protein: 4 g | Sugar: 22 g | Fiber: 1 | Carbohydrates: 45 g

# Spice Cake

*An old-fashioned favorite, this Spice Cake will conjure warm, comfy feelings and memories of Grandma's kitchen.*

**INGREDIENTS | SERVES 12**

½ cup soymilk

2 teaspoons vinegar

¾ cup vegan margarine, softened

¾ cup sugar

¾ cup brown sugar, lightly packed

Egg replacement equal to 4 eggs

½ cup vegan sour cream

1 teaspoon vanilla extract

2¼ cups all-purpose flour

1 teaspoon baking powder

1 teaspoon baking soda

½ teaspoon salt

1½ teaspoons cinnamon

½ teaspoon nutmeg

2 teaspoons ground ginger

½ teaspoon ground cloves

1 batch Cream Cheeze Frosting (see Chapter 14)

1. Preheat oven to 325°F.
2. Combine soymilk and vinegar in a small bowl, whisking to blend. Set aside for 10 minutes to thicken. In a large bowl, cream margarine, sugar, brown sugar, egg replacement, sour cream, and vanilla extract on low speed until blended.
3. In a separate bowl, sift flour, baking powder, baking soda, salt, cinnamon, nutmeg, ginger, and cloves together. Gradually add to wet ingredients, one third at a time, beating on low speed for 30 seconds each time, or until well incorporated. Increase speed to medium and beat for 1½ minutes.
4. Divide batter between 2 greased and floured 9" round cake pans. Bake for 30–35 minutes or until a toothpick comes out clean when inserted into the center of the cakes.
5. Cool cake 10–15 minutes in the pans. Run a knife around the edges to loosen and remove from pans. Cool completely. Place one cake on the serving platter and spread 1 cup of Cream Cheeze Frosting over the top. Place the second cake on top and frost with the remaining frosting.

**PER SERVING** Calories: 373 | Fat: 16 g | Protein: 3 g | Sugar: 33 g | Fiber: 1 g | Carbohydrates: 55 g

# Whoopie Pies

*While some folks can't agree whether to call
these cakes or cookies, everyone agrees to call them delicious!*

**INGREDIENTS | SERVES 10**

1 cup soymilk

1 tablespoon apple cider vinegar

2 cups all-purpose flour

½ cup unsweetened cocoa powder

¼ teaspoon cinnamon

1 teaspoon baking powder

1¼ teaspoons baking soda

½ teaspoon salt

½ cup vegan margarine, softened

1 cup brown sugar, packed

Egg replacement to equal 1 egg

1 teaspoon vanilla extract

½ batch Cream Cheeze Filling or White Frosting (see Chapter 14)

1. Preheat oven to 400°F.
2. Stir together soymilk and vinegar in a small bowl and allow to sit for 10 minutes. Whisk together flour, cocoa, cinnamon, baking soda, baking powder, and salt in a separate bowl until combined.
3. Beat together margarine and brown sugar in a large bowl with an electric mixer at medium-high speed for about 3 minutes, or until pale and fluffy. Then add egg replacement and vanilla extract, beating until combined.
4. Reduce speed to low and add flour mixture and soymilk mixture alternately, in batches, until smooth. Scrape down the sides of the bowl, as needed. Scoop ¼-cup mounds of batter onto a greased baking sheet about 2" apart.
5. Bake 10–12 minutes, or until top springs back when lightly touched. Transfer to wire racks and cool completely.
6. Once cakes are cool, turn 5 cakes with the flat sides up and spread with Cream Cheeze Filling. Top with plain cakes. Wrap each Whoopie Pie in plastic wrap and refrigerate for 1 hour.

**PER ½ PIE** Calories: 377 | Fat: 14 g | Protein: 5 g | Sugar: 35 g | Fiber: 2 g | Carbohydrates: 60 g

# Key Lime Cake

*This is a tangy, refreshing dessert for a warm summer evening!*

## INGREDIENTS | SERVES 12

2 cups soymilk

3 tablespoons Key lime juice

2½ cups unbleached all-purpose flour

2 cups sugar

1 teaspoon baking powder

1 teaspoon baking soda

1 teaspoon salt

⅔ cup canola oil

1 teaspoon vanilla extract

2 tablespoons Key lime zest, chopped

1 batch Key Lime Cream Cheeze Frosting (see Chapter 14)

1. Preheat oven to 350°F.
2. Combine soymilk and Key lime juice in a medium bowl. Allow to sit for 10 minutes to thicken. In a large bowl, whisk together the flour, sugar, baking powder, baking soda, and salt. Set aside. Add oil, vanilla extract, and Key lime zest to the soymilk mixture, whisking to combine.
3. Add wet ingredients to the flour mixture, stirring gently until there are no large lumps. Divide batter evenly between 2 greased and floured 8" round cake pans.
4. Bake for 35–40 minutes or until a toothpick comes out clean when inserted into the center of the cakes.
5. Cool 10–15 minutes in the pans. Run a knife around the edges of the cakes and remove from the pans. Cool completely. Place one cake on a serving platter and frost with one cup of Key Lime Cream Cheeze Frosting. Place the second cake on top and frost with the remaining frosting.

**PER SERVING** Calories: 364 | Fat: 17 g | Protein: 2 g | Sugar: 35 g | Fiber: 0.g | Carbohydrates: 52 g

## Stop and *Taste* the Flowers!

Available in many markets today, fresh, edible flowers are a beautiful and tasty way to decorate and add flavor to salads and desserts. Take care to select flowers whose flavor profile will complement your dish. Rose, violet, and lavender petals have a sweet flavor, while flowers such as nasturtiums taste peppery. But beware! Flowers from nurseries and florist shops are not safe to eat as they may have been treated with pesticides or other chemicals. Only flowers that are pesticide-free and truly edible should be consumed. So do your research—either grow your own edible flowers or purchase packages that are clearly marked for consumption.

# Yellow Layer Cake

*A wonderful, homey, basic cake! The turmeric adds a beautiful yellow hue without adding flavor.*

**INGREDIENTS | SERVES 16**

2 cups soymilk

2 teaspoons apple cider vinegar

2½ cups unbleached all-purpose flour

1¾ cups sugar

1 teaspoon baking powder

1 teaspoon baking soda

½ teaspoon salt

⅔ cup canola oil

2 teaspoons vanilla extract

⅛–¼ teaspoon turmeric

1 batch Dark Chocolate Frosting (see Chapter 14)

1. Preheat oven to 350°F.
2. Combine soymilk and vinegar in a medium bowl. Allow to sit for 10 minutes to thicken. In a large bowl, whisk together the flour, sugar, baking powder, baking soda, and salt. Set aside. Add oil, vanilla extract, and turmeric to the soymilk mixture, whisking to combine.
3. Add wet ingredients to the flour mixture, stirring gently until there are no large lumps. Divide batter evenly between 2 greased and floured 8" round cake pans.
4. Bake for 35–40 minutes or until a toothpick comes out clean when inserted into the center of the cakes.
5. Cool cakes 10–15 minutes in the pans. Run a knife around the edges to loosen and remove from pans. Cool completely. Place 1 cake on a serving platter and spread a layer of Dark Chocolate Frosting over the top. Place the second cake on top and frost the entire cake as desired.

**PER SERVING** Calories: 410 | Fat: 16 g | Protein: 3 g | Sugar: 47 g | Fiber: 1 g | Carbohydrates: 64 g

# Red Velvet Cake with White Frosting

*This shockingly red cake is also delicious with a cream cheese frosting.*

**INGREDIENTS | SERVES 16**

2 cups soymilk

2 teaspoons apple cider vinegar

2½ cups unbleached all-purpose flour

2 cups sugar

¼ cup unsweetened cocoa powder

1 teaspoon baking powder

1 teaspoon baking soda

1 teaspoon salt

⅔ cup canola oil

1–2 tablespoons red food coloring

4 teaspoons vanilla extract

1 teaspoon almond extract

½ batch White Frosting (see Chapter 14)

## The Red in Red Velvet Cake

Food writers have surmised that the red color of early red velvet cakes was a result of the chemical reaction between the anthocyanin pigments in cocoa and the acids in buttermilk, which will give a red color. However, food science does not support this conclusion. Therefore, red food coloring is used to achieve the desired bright red color. Home cooks, wanting to avoid using red food coloring, have experimented with puréed beets, beet juice, and beet powder with unsatisfactory results. When beets are used in sufficient amounts to significantly color the cake, the cake may taste like beets! If you don't mind a red velvet cake that isn't red, you could omit the red food coloring. The cake will still taste great!

1. Preheat oven to 350°F.
2. Combine soymilk and vinegar in a medium bowl. Allow to sit for 10 minutes to thicken. In a large bowl, whisk together the flour, sugar, cocoa, baking powder, baking soda, and salt. Set aside. Add oil, food coloring, vanilla extract, and almond extract to the soymilk mixture, whisking to combine.
3. Add wet ingredients to the flour mixture, stirring gently until there are no large lumps. Divide batter evenly between 2 greased and floured 8" round cake pans.
4. Bake for 25–30 minutes or until a toothpick comes out clean when inserted into the center of the cakes.
5. Cool cakes 10–15 minutes in the pans. Run a knife around the edges to loosen and carefully remove from pans. Cool completely. Place one cake on a serving platter and spread a layer of White Frosting over the top. Place the second cake on top and frost with the remaining frosting.

**PER SERVING** Calories: 337 | Fat: 13 g | Protein: 3 g | Sugar: 37 g | Fiber: 1 g | Carbohydrates: 53 g

# Peach Kuchen

*Bursting with fruit, this rustic cake can also be made with apricots, nectarines, or Italian plums. Don't worry about peeling the fruit.*

**INGREDIENTS | SERVES 12**

½ cup vegan margarine

⅓ cup sugar plus ¼ cup sugar, divided use

1 teaspoon vanilla extract

Egg replacement equal to 1 egg

1 tablespoon vegan sour cream

1½ cups all-purpose flour

1 teaspoon baking powder

2 cups fresh or canned peaches, sliced

½ teaspoon cinnamon

½ batch Tofu Custard Filling, uncooked (Chapter 14)

1. Preheat oven to 375°F.
2. Cream the margarine, sugar, and vanilla extract with an electric mixer on low speed in a large bowl until creamy. Whisk in the egg replacement and sour cream. Sift flour and baking powder together in a small bowl. Gradually add this to the wet mixture and beat for 1 minute on medium-low speed. Spread dough in the bottom and slightly up the sides of a greased springform pan.
3. Place the sliced peaches in a decorative pattern over the dough. Combine remaining ¼ cup sugar with cinnamon and sprinkle over peaches. Bake for 30 minutes. Pour prepared Tofu Custard over the top and bake for another 15 minutes, or until custard is set. Cool 15–20 minutes before removing from the springform pan. Serve warm or at room temperature.

**PER SERVING** Calories: 182 | Fat: 8 g | Protein: 3 g | Sugar: 10 g | Fiber: 1 g | Carbohydrates: 24 g

# Strawberry Cake

*Pretty in pink and tasting of strawberries! This is a wonderful cake for a birthday celebration.*

**INGREDIENTS | SERVES 16**

1 cup soymilk

2 teaspoons apple cider vinegar

2½ cups all-purpose flour

2 cups sugar

1 teaspoon baking powder

1 teaspoon baking soda

½ teaspoon salt

⅔ cup canola oil

2–3 teaspoons red food coloring

1 teaspoon vanilla extract

1¼ cups puréed strawberries

½ batch Strawberry Frosting (see Chapter 14)

## Kids in the Kitchen

Kids love helping in the kitchen, and this kid-friendly recipe is truly cake in a hurry! To make Chocolate Hurry Cake: In a large coffee mug, mix 3½ tablespoons flour, ¼ teaspoon baking powder, 2 tablespoons unsweetened cocoa powder, and 2 tablespoons sugar. Stir in egg replacement equal to 1 egg, 3 tablespoons soymilk, 1 tablespoon oil, and 1 tablespoon water. Microwave for 3 minutes until cake is set. Dump cake out onto a plate and enjoy while it's warm!

1. Preheat oven to 350°F.
2. Combine soymilk and vinegar in a medium bowl. Allow to sit for 10 minutes to thicken. In a large bowl, whisk together the flour, sugar, baking powder, baking soda, and salt. Set aside. Add oil, food coloring, vanilla extract, and strawberries to the soymilk mixture, whisking to combine.
3. Add wet ingredients to the flour mixture, stirring gently until there are no large lumps. Divide batter evenly between 2 greased and floured 8" round cake pans.
4. Bake for 25–35 minutes or until a toothpick comes out clean when inserted into the center of the cakes.
5. Cool cakes 10–15 minutes in the pans. Run knife around the edge of the cakes to loosen and carefully remove from pans. Place one cake on a serving platter and spread a layer of Strawberry Frosting over the top. Place the second cake on top and frost the top layer.

**PER SERVING** Calories: 373 | Fat: 16 g | Protein: 3 g | Sugar: 41 g | Fiber: 1 g | Carbohydrates: 57 g

# Gingerbread Cake

*A dollop of nondairy whipped topping is the perfect complement to this moist, dark, and spicy cake.*

**INGREDIENTS | SERVES 8**

½ cup vegetable shortening

¼ cup brown sugar, packed

Egg replacement equal to 1 egg

1 cup molasses

2⅓ cups all-purpose flour

1½ teaspoons baking soda

½ teaspoon salt

2 teaspoons ground ginger

1½ teaspoons ground cinnamon

¼ teaspoon nutmeg

¼ teaspoon allspice

⅛ teaspoon ground cloves

1 cup boiling water

1. Preheat oven to 350°F.
2. With an electric mixer, cream shortening and brown sugar together in a large bowl on low speed until fluffy. Beat in egg replacement and then molasses.
3. In a separate bowl, sift together flour, baking soda, salt, ginger, cinnamon, nutmeg, allspice, and cloves. Gradually add flour mixture, alternating with water, to wet ingredients, beating after each addition. Mix until smooth. Pour batter into a greased and floured 8" × 8" pan.
4. Bake 35–40 minutes or until a toothpick comes out clean when inserted into the center of the cake. Serve warm or cold.

**PER SERVING** Calories: 400 | Fat: 13 g | Protein: 4 g | Sugar: 30 g | Fiber: 1 g | Carbohydrates: 67 g

## A Veggie Sneak Attack!

When it comes to getting your picky child or spouse to eat nutritious veggies, nothing is more devious than concealing them in sweet treats! Carrot cake and zucchini bread are well-known and loved, but what about adding puréed spinach to chocolate cake? Or adding mashed sweet potatoes to brownies? Chocolate is a strong flavor that will mask the flavor of many incognito veggies. Look for recipes online or use your own creativity to see what you can get away with!

# Chocolate Layer Cake

*This dark, rich cake also tastes great with White Frosting (see Chapter 14).*

**INGREDIENTS | SERVES 18**

3 cups unbleached all-purpose flour

2 cup sugar

½ cup cocoa powder

2 teaspoons baking soda

1 teaspoon salt

⅔ cup canola oil

2 teaspoons vanilla extract

2 teaspoons vinegar

2 cups water

1 batch Milk Chocolate Frosting (see Chapter 14)

## How to Toast Coconut

Toasting coconut is a simple way to enhance the nuttiness and coconut flavor, while adding color and crispiness. To toast coconut in the oven, spread a thin layer of coconut on a baking sheet and bake at 350°F for approximately 10–15 minutes or until golden brown, stirring every few minutes. On the stovetop, place a thin layer in a skillet over medium heat, stirring frequently. For the microwave, spread 1 cup coconut on a microwave-safe plate and heat for approximately 3 minutes, stirring every 30 seconds. Store toasted coconut in an airtight container in the refrigerator for up to 1 month.

1. Preheat oven to 350°F.
2. In a large bowl, whisk together flour, sugar, cocoa powder, baking soda, and salt. Set aside.
3. In a separate bowl, whisk together oil, vanilla extract, vinegar, and water until smooth. Gently stir wet ingredients into flour mixture, stirring until there are no large lumps. Divide batter evenly between 2 greased and floured 8" round cake pans. Bake for 25–30 minutes or until a toothpick comes out clean when inserted into the center of the cakes.
4. Cool cakes 10–15 minutes in the pans. Run a knife around the edges to loosen the cakes and carefully remove from pans. Place one cake on a serving platter and spread with a layer of Milk Chocolate Frosting. Place the second cake on top and frost the entire cake, as desired.

**PER SERVING** Calories: 395 | Fat: 14 g | Protein: 3 g | Sugar: 48 g | Fiber: 2 g | Carbohydrates: 67 g

# Cherry-Pineapple Dump Cake

*Using a packaged cake mix and cherry pie filling makes this delicious recipe quick and easy!*

**INGREDIENTS | SERVES 12**

1 (20-ounce) can crushed pineapple with juice

1 (20-ounce) can cherry pie filling

1 box vegan yellow cake mix

½ cup vegan margarine, melted

1 cup walnuts, chopped

## Cheating the Vegan Way

Baking cakes has never been easier for vegans! Today, health food stores and markets carry specialty vegan cake mixes; you can even order them online. But did you know that many regular, commercially packaged cake mixes do not contain eggs or dairy products in the ingredients? Read the ingredient list carefully and avoid packages with pudding in the mix. Simply replace the eggs called for in the directions with an equal amount of applesauce or other egg replacement of your choice, and prepare the cake according to the package directions. Sometimes, cheating is a good thing!

1. Preheat oven to 350°F.
2. Spread pineapple and juice in a greased 9" × 13" baking pan. Spread cherry pie filling evenly over pineapple. Sprinkle cake mix evenly over cherry layer. Sprinkle walnuts evenly over the top and drizzle with melted margarine.
3. Bake 45–50 minutes or until top is golden brown. Filling will be very hot. Allow to cool 10–15 minutes before serving.

**PER SERVING** Calories: 396 | Fat: 19 g | Protein: 4 g | Sugar: 24 g | Fiber: 2 g | Carbohydrates: 54 g

# CHAPTER 12

# Cupcakes

# Red Velvet Cupcakes

*Luscious red velvet cake smothered with Cream Cheeze Frosting is totally irresistible!*

**INGREDIENTS | SERVES 14**

1 cup soymilk

1 teaspoon apple cider vinegar

1½ cups unbleached all-purpose flour

1 cups sugar

2 tablespoons unsweetened cocoa powder

½ teaspoon baking powder

1 teaspoon baking soda

½ teaspoon salt

⅓ cup canola oil

1 tablespoon red food coloring

2 teaspoons vanilla extract

½ teaspoon almond extract

½ batch Cream Cheeze Frosting (see Chapter 14)

1. Preheat oven to 350°F.
2. Combine soymilk and vinegar in a medium bowl. Allow to sit for 10 minutes to thicken. In a large bowl, whisk together the flour, sugar, cocoa, baking powder, baking soda, and salt. Set aside. Add oil, food coloring, vanilla extract, and almond extract to the soymilk mixture, whisking to combine.
3. Bake 18–22 minutes or until a toothpick comes out clean when inserted into the center of the cupcakes. Allow to cool in the pans for 10 minutes, then remove from pans and place on wire racks to cool completely.
4. Frost cupcakes with Cream Cheeze Frosting. Store in the refrigerator in an airtight container.

**PER SERVING** Calories: 232 | Fat: 9 g | Protein: 2 g | Sugar: 24 g | Fiber: 1 g | Carbohydrates: 37 g

# Peanut Butter and Jelly Cupcakes

*This is a perennial kids' favorite, transformed into a fun cupcake!*

**INGREDIENTS | MAKES 14 CUPCAKES**

1⅓ cups unbleached all-purpose flour

1 cup sugar

1 teaspoon baking soda

½ teaspoon salt

¼ cup canola oil

3 tablespoons peanut butter

1 teaspoon vanilla extract

1 teaspoon apple cider vinegar

1 cup water

½ cup grape jelly ·

½ batch Peanut Butter Frosting (see Chapter 14)

## Make Your Own Jams and Jellies

Making jams and jellies is a great way to take advantage of sale prices on fruit or to use up an excess of ripe homegrown fruit! Homemade jams and jellies don't have to be complicated to make and they are wonderful and impressive gifts. Contact your local cooperative extension office for information or search for information online. Makers of canning products are a great place to start.

1. Preheat oven to 350°F.
2. In a large bowl, whisk together flour, sugar, baking soda, and salt. Set aside.
3. In a separate bowl, whisk together oil, peanut butter, vanilla extract, vinegar, and water until smooth. Gently stir wet ingredients into flour mixture, stirring until there are no large lumps. Pour batter into paper-lined cupcake pans until ¾ full.
4. Bake 20–22 minutes or until a toothpick comes out clean when inserted into the center of the cupcakes. Allow to cool in the pans for 10 minutes, then remove from pans and place on wire racks to cool completely.
5. To fill, cut a small core from the top center of each cupcake. Place 1–2 teaspoons of grape jelly in each cupcake. Trim the core pieces to fit and use them to cover the hole in each cupcake. Frost with Peanut Butter Frosting.
6. Store in the refrigerator in an airtight container.

**PER SERVING** Calories: 297 | Fat: 14 g | Protein: 4 g | Sugar: 28 g | Fiber: 1 g | Carbohydrates: 41 g

# Caramel Apple Cupcakes

*This tasty apple cake with caramel filling will have you feeling like a kid again.*

**INGREDIENTS | MAKES 20 CUPCAKES**

½ cup soymilk

1 teaspoon apple cider vinegar

Egg replacement equal to 2 eggs

½ cup canola oil

2 teaspoons vanilla extract

2 cups unbleached all-purpose flour

1 cup rapadura or Sucanat sugar

1 teaspoon baking powder

2 teaspoons baking soda

1 teaspoon salt

2 teaspoons cinnamon

¼ teaspoon nutmeg

¼ teaspoon ground cloves

4 cups unpeeled apples, diced

1 cup Caramel Topping (see Chapter 14)

1–2 cups White Frosting (see Chapter 14)

1. Preheat oven to 350°F.
2. Combine soymilk with vinegar in a large bowl. Allow to sit for 10 minutes to thicken. Add egg replacement, oil, and vanilla extract to the soymilk mixture, whisking until blended. Set aside. In a separate bowl, whisk together the flour, sugar, baking powder, baking soda, salt, cinnamon, nutmeg, and cloves. Add flour mixture to the wet ingredients. Mix gently until there are no large lumps. Gently stir in apples.
3. Fill paper-lined cupcake tins ¾ full. Bake 20–25 minutes or until a toothpick comes out clean when inserted into the center of the cupcakes. Allow to cool in the pans for 10 minutes, then remove from pans and place on wire racks to cool completely.
4. To fill, cut a small core from the top center of each cupcake. Place 1–2 tablespoons of the caramel topping in each cupcake. Trim the core pieces to fit and use them to cover the hole in each cupcake. Frost with White Frosting.
5. Store in the refrigerator in an airtight container.

**PER SERVING** Calories: 282 | Fat: 12 g | Protein: 2 g | Sugar: 32 g | Fiber: 1 g | Carbohydrates: 43 g

# Strawberry Cupcakes

*These cupcakes are a triple strawberry hit with Strawberry Cake, Strawberry Glaze, and Strawberry Frosting. You won't be able to resist them!*

**INGREDIENTS | SERVES 14**

½ cup soymilk

1 teaspoon apple cider vinegar

1¼ cups all-purpose flour

1 cups sugar

1 teaspoon baking powder

1 teaspoon baking soda

¼ teaspoon salt

⅓ cup canola oil

1–2 teaspoons red food coloring

1 teaspoon vanilla extract

¾ cups puréed strawberries

½ batch Strawberry Glaze (see Chapter 14)

½ batch Strawberry Frosting (see Chapter 14)

## Butterfly Cupcakes

Make these creative cupcakes with your favorite cake and fillings. Using a sharp knife, cut a cone-shaped piece, ¾" deep by 1¼" wide, from the top of each cupcake. Cut tops in half. Spoon 1–2 tablespoons filling into each hole. Position the cake top halves on top of the filling to resemble wings. Dust with powdered sugar or decorate using your imagination!

1. Preheat oven to 350°F.
2. Combine soymilk and vinegar in a medium bowl. Allow to sit for 10 minutes to thicken. In a large bowl, whisk together the flour, sugar, baking powder, baking soda, and salt. Set aside. Add oil, food coloring, vanilla extract, and strawberries to the soymilk mixture, whisking to combine.
3. Add wet ingredients to the flour mixture, stirring gently until there are no large lumps. Pour batter into paper-lined cupcake pans until ¾ full.
4. Bake 20–25 minutes or until a toothpick comes out clean when inserted into the center of the cupcakes. Allow to cool in the pans for 10 minutes, then remove from pans and place on wire racks to cool completely.
5. To fill, cut a small core from the top center of each cupcake. Place 1–2 tablespoons of Strawberry Glaze in each cupcake. Trim the core pieces to fit and use them to cover the hole in each cupcake. Frost with Strawberry Frosting.
6. Store in the refrigerator in an airtight container.

**PER SERVING** Calories: 299 | Fat: 12 g | Protein: 2 g | Sugar: 33 g | Fiber: 1 g | Carbohydrates: 46 g

# Double Chocolate Cupcakes

*Chocolate lovers will adore these cupcakes—there's chocolate on chocolate goodness!*

**INGREDIENTS | MAKES 14 CUPCAKES**

1½ cups unbleached all-purpose flour

1 cup sugar

¼ cup cocoa powder

1 teaspoon baking soda

½ teaspoon salt

⅓ cup canola oil

1 teaspoon vanilla extract

1 teaspoon apple cider vinegar

1 cup water

½ batch Dark Chocolate Frosting (see Chapter 14)

1. Preheat oven to 350°F.
2. In a large bowl, whisk together flour, sugar, cocoa powder, baking soda, and salt. Set aside.
3. In a separate bowl, whisk together oil, vanilla extract, vinegar, and water until smooth. Gently stir wet ingredients into flour mixture, stirring until there are no large lumps. Pour batter into paper-lined cupcake pans until ¾ full.
4. Bake 20–25 minutes or until a toothpick comes out clean when inserted into the center of the cupcakes. Allow to cool in the pans for 10 minutes, then remove from pans and place on wire racks to cool completely.
5. Frost cupcakes with Dark Chocolate Frosting.
6. Store in the refrigerator in an airtight container.

**PER SERVING** Calories: 247 | Fat: 9 g | Protein: 2 g | Sugar: 28 g | Fiber: 1 g | Carbohydrates: 40 g

# Classic Vanilla Cupcakes

*This traditional flavor, yummy in its own right, is easily paired with other flavorings!*

**INGREDIENTS | MAKES 14 CUPCAKES**

1 cup soymilk

1 teaspoon apple cider vinegar

1¼ cups unbleached all-purpose flour

¾ cup sugar

½ teaspoon baking powder

1 teaspoon baking soda

¼ teaspoon salt

⅓ cup canola oil

2 teaspoons vanilla extract

½ batch White Frosting (see Chapter 14)

1. Preheat oven to 350°F.
2. Combine soymilk and vinegar in a medium bowl. Allow to sit for 10 minutes to thicken. In a large bowl, whisk together the flour, sugar, baking powder, baking soda, and salt. Set aside. Add oil and vanilla extract to the soymilk mixture, whisking to combine.
3. Add wet ingredients to the flour mixture, stirring gently until there are no large lumps. Pour batter into paper-lined cupcake pans until ¾ full.
4. Bake 20–25 minutes or until a toothpick comes out clean when inserted into the center of the cupcakes. Allow to cool in the pans for 10 minutes, then remove from pans and place on wire racks to cool completely. Frost cupcakes with White Frosting.
5. Store in the refrigerator in an airtight container.

**PER SERVING** Calories: 216 | Fat: 9 g | Protein: 2 g | Sugar: 24 g | Fiber: 0 g | Carbohydrates: 33 g

# Orange Creamsicle Cupcakes

*Enjoy these orange-flavored cupcakes with a cloud of creamy white frosting!*

**INGREDIENTS | MAKES 14 CUPCAKES**

½ cup soymilk

1 teaspoon apple cider vinegar

1¼ cups unbleached all-purpose flour

¾ cup sugar

½ teaspoon baking powder

1 teaspoon baking soda

¼ teaspoon salt

½ cup soy creamer

⅓ cup canola oil

1 tablespoon orange extract

½ teaspoon vanilla extract

½ batch White Frosting (see Chapter 14)

1. Preheat oven to 350°F.
2. Combine soymilk and vinegar in a medium bowl. Allow to sit for 10 minutes to thicken. In a large bowl, whisk together the flour, sugar, baking powder, baking soda, and salt. Set aside. Add soy creamer, oil, orange extract, and vanilla extract to the soymilk mixture, whisking to combine.
3. Add wet ingredients to the flour mixture, stirring gently until there are no large lumps. Pour batter into paper-lined cupcake pans until ¾ full.
4. Bake 20–25 minutes or until a toothpick comes out clean when inserted into the center of the cupcakes. Allow to cool in the pans for 10 minutes, then remove from pans and place on wire racks to cool completely. Frost cupcakes with White Frosting.
5. Store in the refrigerator in an airtight container.

**PER SERVING** Calories: 221 | Fat: 9 g | Protein: 1 g | Sugar: 24 g | Fiber: 0 g | Carbohydrates: 33 g

# Chocolate-Chile Cupcakes

*Cinnamon and chile pepper give this chocolate cupcake an ancient Aztec kick.*

**INGREDIENTS | MAKES 14 CUPCAKES**

1½ cups unbleached all-purpose flour

1 cup sugar

¼ cup cocoa powder

1 teaspoon baking soda

½ teaspoon salt

¾ teaspoon ground cinnamon, divided use

¾ teaspoon ground cayenne pepper, divided use

⅓ cup canola oil

1 teaspoon vanilla extract

1 teaspoon apple cider vinegar

1 cup water

½ batch Dark Chocolate Frosting (see Chapter 14)

1. Preheat oven to 350°F.
2. In a large bowl, whisk together flour, sugar, cocoa powder, baking soda, salt, ½ teaspoon cinnamon, and ½ teaspoon ground cayenne pepper. Set aside.
3. In a separate bowl, whisk together oil, vanilla extract, vinegar, and water until smooth. Gently stir wet ingredients into flour mixture, stirring until there are no large lumps. Pour batter into paper-lined cupcake pans until ¾ full.
4. Bake 20–22 minutes or until a toothpick comes out clean when inserted into the center of the cupcakes. Allow to cool in the pans for 10 minutes, then remove from pans and place on wire racks to cool completely.
5. Combine remaining ¼ teaspoon cinnamon and ¼ teaspoon cayenne with Dark Chocolate Frosting and spread on cupcakes.
6. Store in the refrigerator in an airtight container.

**PER SERVING** Calories: 246 | Fat: 9 g | Protein: 2 g | Sugar: 28 g | Fiber: 1 g | Carbohydrates: 40 g

## Aztec Hot Chocolate

The ancient Aztecs are credited with creating the first hot chocolate; however, unlike the sweet chocolaty beverage you may be used to, the chocolate of the Aztecs was a bitter, unsweetened beverage which was often flavored with cinnamon and ground chile pepper. Sound enticing? Bring to boil over medium heat 2 cups soymilk, 3 tablespoons sugar, ¼ teaspoon cinnamon, and a pinch of ground red pepper in a small saucepan. Reduce heat and simmer for 3 minutes. Whisk in ¼ cup unsweetened cocoa powder and a dash of vanilla extract. Pour into cups and serve with vegan whipped topping, if desired.

# Banana Pudding Cupcakes

*These cupcakes are miniature versions of your favorite banana pudding trifle. They're a sweet combination of banana cake, vanilla pudding, fresh bananas, vanilla frosting, and vanilla cookie crumbles!*

**INGREDIENTS | MAKES 14 CUPCAKES**

⅓ cup soymilk

1 teaspoon apple cider vinegar

1¼ cups all-purpose flour

1 cup sugar

½ teaspoon baking powder

1 teaspoon baking soda

¼ teaspoon salt

⅓ cup canola oil

1 teaspoon vanilla extract

¼ cup bananas, mashed

½ cup bananas, diced

1 cup Vanilla Pudding Filling (see Chapter 14)

½ batch White Frosting (see Chapter 14)

½ cup vegan vanilla wafer–style cookies, crumbled

## Ripen Fruit in a Hurry

Many fruits, such as peaches and nectarines, ripen in the presence of ethylene gas. Placing unripe fruit in a paper bag will speed up the ripening process, as the bag will hold the fruit in contact with the small amounts of ethylene gas emitted by the fruit. To ripen fruit even more quickly, you can increase the amount of ethylene gas in the bag by placing a ripe banana or apple in the bag along with the unripe fruit.

1. Preheat oven to 350°F.
2. Combine soymilk and vinegar in a medium bowl. Allow to sit for 10 minutes to thicken. In a large bowl, whisk together the flour, sugar, baking powder, baking soda, and salt. Set aside. Add oil, vanilla extract, and mashed bananas to the soymilk mixture, whisking to combine.
3. Add wet ingredients to the flour mixture, stirring gently until there are no large lumps. Pour batter into paper-lined cupcake pans until ¾ full.
4. Bake 20–25 minutes or until a toothpick comes out clean when inserted into the center of the cupcakes. Allow to cool in the pans for 10 minutes, then remove from pans and place on wire racks to cool completely.
5. To fill, cut a small core from the top center of each cupcake. Combine diced bananas with Vanilla Pudding Filling and spoon 1–1½ tablespoons into each cupcake. Trim the core pieces to fit and use them to cover the hole in each cupcake. Frost with White Frosting and sprinkle with crumbled cookies.
6. Store in the refrigerator in an airtight container.

**PER SERVING** Calories: 276 | Fat: 10 g | Protein: 2 g | Sugar: 31 g | Fiber: 1 g | Carbohydrates: 45 g

# Chocolate-Covered Cherry Cupcakes

*Chocolate and cherries are in perfect harmony for this sweet treat!*

**INGREDIENTS | MAKES 14 CUPCAKES**

1 cup soymilk

1 teaspoon apple cider vinegar

1½ cups unbleached all-purpose flour

¾ cup sugar

½ teaspoon baking powder

1 teaspoon baking soda

½ teaspoon salt

⅓ cup canola oil

1 tablespoon red food coloring

1 teaspoon vanilla extract

1 tablespoon cherry liqueur

1½ cups maraschino cherries, drained and finely chopped, divided use

½ batch Chocolate Ganache (see Chapter 14)

1. Preheat oven to 350°F.
2. Combine soymilk and vinegar in a medium bowl. Allow to sit for 10 minutes to thicken. In a large bowl, whisk together the flour, sugar, baking powder, baking soda, and salt. Set aside. Add oil, food coloring, vanilla extract, and cherry liqueur to the soymilk mixture, whisking to combine.
3. Add wet ingredients to the flour mixture, stirring gently until there are no large lumps. Fold in 1 cup maraschino cherry bits. Pour batter into paper-lined cupcake pans until ¾ full.
4. Bake 20–25 minutes or until a toothpick comes out clean when inserted into the center of the cupcakes. Allow to cool in the pans for 10 minutes, then remove from pans and place on wire racks to cool completely.
5. Drizzle cooled cupcakes with Chocolate Ganache. Sprinkle remaining ½ cup maraschino cherry bits on top.
6. Store in the refrigerator in an airtight container.

**PER SERVING** Calories: 249 | Fat: 10 g | Protein: 3 g | Sugar: 26 g | Fiber: 2 g | Carbohydrates: 38 g

# Raspberry–Lemon Curd Cupcakes

*These cupcakes are a perfect summer treat. Serve them at your next soiree or with afternoon tea.*

**INGREDIENTS | MAKES 14 CUPCAKES**

1 cup soymilk

1 teaspoon apple cider vinegar

1½ cups unbleached all-purpose flour

¾ cup sugar

½ teaspoon baking powder

1 teaspoon baking soda

½ teaspoon salt

⅓ cup canola oil

2 teaspoons red food coloring

½ teaspoon vanilla extract

2 tablespoons raspberry liqueur

1 batch Lemon Curd Filling (see Chapter 14)

1 batch Raspberry Glaze (see Chapter 14)

1. Preheat oven to 350°F.
2. Combine soymilk and vinegar in a medium bowl. Allow to sit for 10 minutes to thicken. In a large bowl, whisk together the flour, sugar, baking powder, baking soda, and salt. Set aside. Add oil, food coloring, vanilla extract, and raspberry liqueur to the soymilk mixture, whisking to combine.
3. Add wet ingredients to the flour mixture, stirring gently until there are no large lumps. Pour batter into paper-lined cupcake pans until ¾ full.
4. Bake 20–25 minutes or until a toothpick comes out clean when inserted into the center of the cupcakes. Allow to cool in the pans for 10 minutes, then remove from pans and place on wire racks to cool completely.
5. To fill, cut a small core from the top center of each cupcake. Place 1–2 tablespoons of Lemon Curd Filling in each cupcake. Trim the core pieces to fit and use them to cover the hole in each cupcake. Drizzle with Raspberry Glaze.
6. Store in the refrigerator in an airtight container.

**PER SERVING** Calories: 236 | Fat: 10 g | Protein: 2 g | Sugar: 22 g | Fiber: 0 g | Carbohydrates: 34 g

# Coconut Cupcakes

*These cupcakes pack a coconut-flavored punch—they combine coconut cake with rich Coconut Cream Cheeze Frosting and toasted coconut.*

**INGREDIENTS | MAKES 14 CUPCAKES**

½ cup soymilk

1 teaspoon apple cider vinegar

1¼ cups unbleached all-purpose flour

¾ cup sugar

½ teaspoon baking powder

1 teaspoon baking soda

¼ teaspoon salt

⅓ cup canola oil

½ cup coconut milk

1 teaspoon vanilla extract

1 teaspoon almond extract

1¼ cups sweetened shredded coconut

½ batch Coconut Cream Cheeze Frosting (see Chapter 14)

½ cup toasted coconut, optional

1. Preheat oven to 350°F.
2. Combine soymilk and vinegar in a medium bowl. Allow to sit for 10 minutes to thicken. In a large bowl, whisk together the flour, sugar, baking powder, baking soda, and salt. Set aside. Add oil, coconut milk, vanilla extract, and almond extract to the soymilk mixture, whisking to combine.
3. Add wet ingredients to the flour mixture, stirring gently until there are no large lumps. Gently fold in the shredded coconut. Pour batter into paper-lined cupcake pans until ¾ full.
4. Bake 20–25 minutes or until a toothpick comes out clean when inserted into the center of the cupcakes. Allow to cool in the pans for 10 minutes, then remove from pans and place on wire racks to cool completely.
5. Spread Coconut Cream Cheeze Frosting over cooled cupcakes; top with toasted coconut, if desired.
6. Store in the refrigerator in an airtight container.

**PER SERVING** Calories: 286 | Fat: 14 g | Protein: 2 g | Sugar: 28 g | Fiber: 1 g | Carbohydrates: 40 g

# Mocha Cupcakes

*Coffee and chocolate are meant for each other. You'll agree as soon as you try these cupcakes.*

**INGREDIENTS | MAKES 14 CUPCAKES**

1½ cups unbleached all-purpose flour

1 cup sugar

3 tablespoons cocoa powder

1 tablespoon instant espresso powder

1 teaspoon baking soda

½ teaspoon salt

⅓ cup canola oil

1 teaspoon vanilla extract

1 teaspoon apple cider vinegar

1 cup water

½ batch Coffee Frosting (see Chapter 14)

Cocoa powder for dusting, optional

## Make Friends with Marzipan

Marzipan is a paste made from finely ground almonds and sugar. It has many uses, including candymaking, baking, and cake decorating. Very sweet and tasting strongly of almonds, marzipan can take a little getting used to for some. Not sure if you've tasted marzipan? Marzipan, or almond paste (which is nearly identical), is the primary flavoring ingredient in Bear Claw pastries!

1. Preheat oven to 350°F.
2. In a large bowl, whisk together flour, sugar, cocoa powder, espresso powder, baking soda, and salt. Set aside.
3. In a separate bowl, whisk together oil, vanilla extract, vinegar, and water until smooth. Gently stir wet ingredients into flour mixture, stirring until there are no large lumps. Pour batter into paper-lined cupcake pans until ¾ full.
4. Bake 20–22 minutes or until a toothpick comes out clean when inserted into the center of the cupcakes. Allow to cool in the pans for 10 minutes, then remove from pans and place on wire racks to cool completely.
5. Spread Coffee Frosting on cooled cupcakes; dust with cocoa powder, if desired.
6. Store in the refrigerator in an airtight container.

**PER SERVING** Calories: 251 | Fat: 9 g | Protein: 2 g | Sugar: 31 g | Fiber: 1 g | Carbohydrates: 42 g

# Chocolate Mint-Chip Cupcakes

*Rich chocolate cupcakes with refreshing mint–chocolate chip frosting are always a hit!*

## INGREDIENTS | MAKES 14 CUPCAKES

1½ cups unbleached all-purpose flour

1 cup sugar

¼ cup cocoa powder

1 teaspoon baking soda

½ teaspoon salt

⅓ cup canola oil

1 teaspoon peppermint extract

1 teaspoon apple cider vinegar

1 cup water

½ cup vegan chocolate chips, chopped

½ batch Peppermint Frosting (see Chapter 14), without crushed candies

3–4 drops green food coloring

1. Preheat oven to 350°F.
2. In a large bowl, whisk together flour, sugar, cocoa powder, baking soda, and salt. Set aside.
3. In a separate bowl, whisk together oil, peppermint extract, vinegar, and water until smooth. Gently stir wet ingredients into flour mixture, stirring until there are no large lumps. Pour batter into paper-lined cupcake pans until ¾ full.
4. Bake 20–22 minutes or until a toothpick comes out clean when inserted into the center of the cupcakes. Allow to cool in the pans for 10 minutes, then remove from pans and place on wire racks to cool completely.
5. Combine chocolate chips with Peppermint Frosting and add food coloring as desired. Spread frosting on the cooled cupcakes.
6. Store in the refrigerator in an airtight container.

**PER SERVING** Calories: 281 | Fat: 11 g | Protein: 2 g | Sugar: 32 g | Fiber: 1 g | Carbohydrates: 44 g

## Easy Crushed Nuts

When a recipe calls for crushed nuts, it can be challenging to crush them without sending bits of nuts flying all over your kitchen. Try this simple trick. Pour nuts in a zip-top plastic bag up to ⅓ full and close the seal, pressing out as much air from the bag as you can. Lay the bag on a counter or cutting board and crush the nuts by rolling a rolling pin across the bag until all nuts are broken into the desired size. Pour the crushed nuts from the bag into your recipe. Throw away the bag and cleanup is complete!

# Root Beer Float Cupcakes

*These cupcakes embody the fun and flavor of the summery treat.*
*The secret ingredient is a childhood favorite: root beer barrel candies!*

**INGREDIENTS | MAKES 14 CUPCAKES**

½ cup soymilk

1 teaspoon apple cider vinegar

1½ cups unbleached all-purpose flour

⅔ cup sugar

½ teaspoon baking powder

1 teaspoon baking soda

¼ teaspoon salt

⅓ cup canola oil

½ teaspoon vanilla extract

½ teaspoon root beer extract

½ cup root beer soda

½ batch White Frosting (see Chapter 14)

½ cup root beer barrel candies, crushed

1. Preheat oven to 350°F.
2. Combine soymilk and vinegar in a medium bowl. Allow to sit for 10 minutes to thicken. In a large bowl, whisk together the flour, sugar, baking powder, baking soda, and salt. Set aside. Add oil, vanilla extract, root beer extract, and root beer soda to the soymilk mixture, whisking to combine.
3. Add wet ingredients to the flour mixture, stirring gently until there are no large lumps. Pour batter into paper-lined cupcake pans until ¾ full.
4. Bake 20–25 minutes or until a toothpick comes out clean when inserted into the center of the cupcakes. Allow to cool in the pans for 10 minutes, then remove from pans and place on wire racks to cool completely.
5. Spread White Frosting over cupcakes and sprinkle the crushed root beer candies over the top.
6. Store in the refrigerator in an airtight container.

**PER SERVING** Calories: 248 | Fat: 9 g | Protein: 2 g | Sugar: 28 g | Fiber: 0 g | Carbohydrates: 40 g

## Evoke Childhood Memories with Nostalgic Candies

People love the long-lost candies from their childhood! Fortunately, some of these vintage candies are available at specialty shops or online. Try decorating cakes and cupcakes with childhood favorites like Pez, Necco Wafers, Boston Baked Beans, Lemonheads, and chopped up Bit-O-Honey candies. Smiles are guaranteed!

# Chocolate-Coconut Cupcakes

*Try adding toasted almonds to the cake for a popular candy-bar taste!*

## INGREDIENTS | MAKES 14 CUPCAKES

1½ cups unbleached all-purpose flour

1 cup sugar

¼ cup cocoa powder

1 teaspoon baking soda

½ teaspoon salt

⅓ cup canola oil

½ teaspoon coconut extract

½ teaspoon apple cider vinegar

1 cup water

¾ cup sweetened shredded coconut, toasted

½ batch Coconut Cream Cheeze Frosting (see Chapter 14)

Additional toasted coconut for garnish, optional

1. Preheat oven to 350°F.
2. In a large bowl, whisk together flour, sugar, cocoa powder, baking soda, and salt. Set aside.
3. In a separate bowl, whisk together oil, coconut extract, vinegar, and water until smooth. Gently stir wet ingredients into flour mixture, stirring until there are no large lumps. Fold in ¾ cup toasted coconut. Pour batter into paper-lined cupcake pans until ¾ full.
4. Bake 20–22 minutes or until a toothpick comes out clean when inserted into the center of the cupcakes. Allow to cool in the pans for 10 minutes, then remove from pans and place on wire racks to cool completely.
5. Spread Coconut Cream Cheeze Frosting over cooled cupcakes; sprinkle with toasted coconut, if desired.
6. Store in the refrigerator in an airtight container.

**PER SERVING** Calories: 304 | Fat: 12 g | Protein: 2 g | Sugar: 34 g | Fiber: 1 g | Carbohydrates: 48 g

## Great News about Coconut

You may have been taught that coconut meat and coconut oil, which are high in saturated fats, are a dietary no-no because excess saturated fats can lead to high cholesterol levels and heart disease. In the case of many saturated fats, such as fat from animal products, they're composed of long-chain fatty acids. However, the saturated fats in coconut are primarily composed of medium-chain triglycerides, which are digested and metabolized by the body in a way that doesn't cause heart disease! Try cooking with virgin coconut oil, which contains neither the smell nor taste of coconut.

# Chocolate–Peanut Butter Cupcakes

*You'll love the classic combination of chocolate cake and peanut butter frosting.*
*These cupcakes are tender, moist, and decadent!*

**INGREDIENTS | MAKES 14 CUPCAKES**

1½ cups unbleached all-purpose flour

1 cup sugar

¼ cup cocoa powder

1 teaspoon baking soda

½ teaspoon salt

¼ cup canola oil

3 tablespoons peanut butter

1 teaspoon vanilla extract

1 teaspoon vinegar

1 cup water

½ batch Peanut Butter Frosting (see Chapter 14)

1 cup Chocolate Ganache (see Chapter 14)

1. Preheat oven to 350°F.
2. In a large bowl, whisk together flour, sugar, cocoa powder, baking soda, and salt. Set aside.
3. In a separate bowl, whisk together oil, peanut butter, vanilla extract, vinegar, and water until smooth. Gently stir wet ingredients into flour mixture, stirring until there are no large lumps. Pour batter into paper-lined cupcake pans until ¾ full.
4. Bake 20–22 minutes or until a toothpick comes out clean when inserted into the center of the cupcakes. Allow to cool in the pans for 10 minutes, then remove from pans and place on wire racks to cool completely.
5. Frost cupcakes with Peanut Butter Frosting and drizzle with Chocolate Ganache.
6. Store in the refrigerator in an airtight container.

**PER SERVING** Calories: 342 | Fat: 18 g | Protein: 5 g | Sugar: 27 g | Fiber: 2 g | Carbohydrates: 42 g

## Never Feed Chocolate to Dogs

First of all, it's a waste of good chocolate. Secondly, chocolate is toxic to dogs! Chocolate contains the stimulant theobromine, which in sufficient quantities can cause dogs to experience symptoms of poisoning, up to and including death. So, no matter how persistently Fido begs or how cute he acts, take care to keep chocolate and goodies made with chocolate out of his reach.

# Piña Colada Cupcakes

*Pineapple, coconut, and cake are combined here . . . are you smiling yet?*

**INGREDIENTS | MAKES 14 CUPCAKES**

1 cup soymilk

1 teaspoon apple cider vinegar

1¼ cups unbleached all-purpose flour

¾ cup sugar

½ teaspoon baking powder

1 teaspoon baking soda

¼ teaspoon salt

⅓ cup canola oil

¼ teaspoon lemon extract

½ teaspoon vanilla extract

½ teaspoon coconut extract

¾ cup crushed pineapple, drained

½ batch Coconut Cream Cheeze Frosting (see Chapter 14)

1. Preheat oven to 350°F.
2. Combine soymilk and vinegar in a medium bowl. Allow to sit for 10 minutes to thicken. In a large bowl, whisk together the flour, sugar, baking powder, baking soda, and salt. Set aside. Add oil, lemon extract, vanilla extract, and coconut extract to the soymilk mixture, whisking to combine.
3. Add wet ingredients to the flour mixture, stirring gently until there are no large lumps. Fold in the crushed pineapple. Pour batter into paper-lined cupcake pans until ¾ full.
4. Bake 20–25 minutes or until a toothpick comes out clean when inserted into the center of the cupcakes. Allow to cool in the pans for 10 minutes, then remove from pans and place on wire racks to cool completely. Frost cooled cupcakes with Coconut Cream Cheeze Frosting.
5. Store in the refrigerator in an airtight container.

**PER SERVING** Calories: 272 | Fat: 11 g | Protein: 2 g | Sugar: 31 g | Fiber: 1 g | Carbohydrates: 42 g

# CHAPTER 13

# Crackers, Crumbles, Crisps, and Cobblers

# Basic Crackers

*These crackers are crispy and great with any topping!*
*Serve them at your next party, or enjoy them yourself with hummus.*

**INGREDIENTS | YIELDS 48 CRACKERS**

3 cups all-purpose flour

1½ tablespoons sugar

1½ teaspoons salt

⅓ cup vegetable shortening, cold

⅓ cup vegan margarine, cold

¾ cup ice water

1½ teaspoons coarse sea salt

1. In a large bowl, sift together flour, sugar, and salt. Cut in shortening and margarine with a large fork or pastry cutter until mixture is crumbly. Add ice water and mix with a fork until incorporated. Dust hands with flour and shape dough into 4 equal-sized balls. Wrap in plastic wrap and refrigerate at least 30 minutes.

2. Preheat oven to 375°F. Place oven rack in the lower third of oven.

3. Divide each dough ball into 12 same-sized pieces. Roll each piece on a lightly floured surface to ⅛" thickness. Place on lightly floured baking sheets and sprinkle with sea salt. Press sea salt lightly into crackers. Bake for 10 minutes or until golden brown.

4. Cool on wire racks. Store in an airtight container.

**PER 1 CRACKER** Calories: 54 | Fat: 3 g | Protein: 1 g | Sugar: 0 g | Fiber: 0 g | Carbohydrates: 6 g

# Sweet Potato Crackers

*These delicious crackers are great with soups!*
*Try them with your favorite bean chili or classic tomato soup.*

**INGREDIENTS | YIELDS APPROXIMATELY 4 DOZEN CRACKERS**

2 cups sweet potato, peeled and cubed
½ cup soymilk
3 cups all-purpose flour
5 tablespoons baking powder
1 teaspoon salt
6 tablespoons vegan margarine
Coarsely ground sea salt, optional

1. Preheat oven to 350°F.
2. Boil sweet potato until tender; drain. Blend with soymilk until smooth.
3. In a large bowl, whisk flour, baking powder, and salt together. Cut margarine into the flour mixture with a large fork or pastry cutter until texture is crumbly. Add sweet potato mixture and mix well until all ingredients are incorporated. Knead by hand on a floured surface or in a stand mixer with a dough-hook attachment for 3–5 minutes.
4. Divide dough into 4 equal balls. Roll each ball to ⅛" thickness, cut into 12 same-sized pieces, and place on an ungreased baking sheet. Prick with a fork and sprinkle with coarse sea salt, if desired. Bake 10 minutes, flip crackers over, and bake 3 more minutes, until lightly browned.
5. Cool completely on a wire rack. Store in an airtight container.

**PER 1 CRACKER** Calories: 53 | Fat: 2 g | Protein: 1 g | Sugar: 1 g | Fiber: 1 g | Carbohydrates: 9 g

# Peach-Berry Cobbler

*You'll love this beautiful presentation of peaches and blackberries.*

**INGREDIENTS | SERVES 6**

3 cups peaches, peeled, if desired, and sliced

2 cups blackberries

¾ cup sugar, divided use

2 tablespoons cornstarch

⅔ cup soymilk

1 tablespoon canola oil

1 teaspoon vanilla extract

1½ cups all-purpose flour

2 teaspoons baking powder

¼ teaspoon salt

## My Fruit Cobbler Is Better than Yours!

How do you prefer your cobbler? Biscuit-topped? Topped with cake, or pie crust? How about cake-bottomed with the fruit on top? People have strong personal opinions about what constitutes a proper cobbler, often based upon memories from their childhood and regional influences. However, while there may not be agreement about whose cobbler is made the right way, everyone agrees that no matter how it's made, cobbler is good!

1. Preheat oven to 375°F.
2. Combine peaches, blackberries, ¼ cup sugar, and cornstarch in a large bowl. Let stand for 30 minutes, stirring occasionally.
3. Mix soymilk, oil, and vanilla extract in a large bowl. In a separate bowl, combine flour, remaining ½ cup sugar, salt, and baking powder. Stir flour mixture into wet ingredients.
4. Pour the fruit mixture into a greased 8" × 8" pan. Drop the batter by spoonfuls over the fruit. Spread batter to cover, but don't try to make it perfect. Bake for 30–40 minutes until golden brown and bubbly.

**PER SERVING** Calories: 304 | Fat: 3 g | Protein: 5 g | Sugar: 35 g | Fiber: 5 g | Carbohydrates: 65 g

# Apple Crisp

*Try using a combination of different apples, such as Granny Smith and Golden Delicious.*

**INGREDIENTS | SERVES 6**

5 cups Granny Smith apples, cored and peeled

3 tablespoons lemon juice

¼ cup sugar

1 teaspoon lemon zest

½ cup raisins, optional

½ cup all-purpose flour

½ cup brown sugar, packed

1 teaspoon cinnamon

Pinch salt

⅓ cup chopped nuts, optional

6 tablespoons vegan margarine, cold

1. Preheat oven to 375°F.
2. Slice apples into a large bowl and toss with lemon juice. Mix in sugar, lemon zest, and raisins, if desired. Pour into a greased 8" × 8" baking dish. Set aside.
3. In a food processor, combine flour, brown sugar, cinnamon, salt, and nuts, if desired. Cut margarine into pieces and add to processor. Pulse until mixture becomes small crumbles, then pour in an even layer to cover the apples.
4. Bake for 35–40 minutes until the top is golden brown and apple are tender.

**PER SERVING** Calories: 287 | Fat: 11 g | Protein: 1 g | Sugar: 36 g | Fiber: 2 g | Carbohydrates: 47 g

# Olive Oil Crackers

*Enjoy these crackers with Garlicky Hummus, fresh fruit, and a glass of wine for a light meal!*

**INGREDIENTS | MAKES 30 CRACKERS**

3 cups all-purpose flour

1 teaspoon salt

⅓ cup extra-virgin olive oil

1 cup warm water

Olive oil, as needed

## Garlicky Hummus

In a food processor, blend 3 cloves mashed garlic, 1½ teaspoons sea salt, 2 tablespoons tahini, 3 tablespoons lemon juice, and 1 (15-ounce) can garbanzo beans, drained. Start processing, gradually adding ¼ cup olive oil. Blend until smooth and creamy, adding additional oil as needed for consistency. Adjust flavor with additional lemon juice and salt. Pour in serving dish. Garnish with cracked black pepper, paprika, and drizzle with more olive oil. Serve with crackers, raw veggies, or pita bread.

1. Sift flour and salt together in a large bowl. Mix in the extra-virgin olive oil and water. Either by hand on a floured surface, or in a stand mixer with a dough-hook attachment, knead dough for 5–7 minutes.

2. Shape dough into a ball, adding more flour as necessary, so dough is not too sticky. Cut into 20 same-sized pieces then form each piece into a ball. Rub a few drops of olive oil on each ball, cover with a dish towel, and allow to rest at room temperature for 1 hour.

3. Preheat oven to 450°F. Roll each dough ball to approximately ⅛" thick and place on a floured baking sheet. Prick each cracker with fork. Bake 10–12 minutes, or until golden brown. Cool completely. Store in an airtight container

**PER 1 CRACKER** Calories: 67 | Fat: 2 g | Protein: 1 g | Sugar: 0 g | Fiber: 0 g | Carbohydrate: 10 g

# Cheezy Crackers

*You may have given up cheese, but you don't have to give up cheesy flavor!*

**INGREDIENTS | YIELDS APPROXIMATELY 30 CRACKERS**

3 cups all-purpose flour

½ cup nutritional yeast

1½ tablespoons sugar

1½ teaspoons salt

1½ teaspoons baking soda

1½ teaspoons garlic powder

1½ teaspoons onion powder

1½ teaspoons paprika

½ teaspoon turmeric

¼ teaspoon white pepper

⅛ teaspoon ground cayenne

⅓ cup vegan margarine, cold

1½ teaspoons white vinegar

¾ cup ice water

1½ teaspoons coarse sea salt

1. Preheat oven to 375°F.
2. In a large bowl, whisk together flour, nutritional yeast, sugar, salt, baking soda, garlic powder, onion powder, paprika, turmeric, white pepper, and cayenne. Cut in cold margarine with a large fork or pastry cutter until crumbly.
3. Combine vinegar with water and gradually stir into the dry mixture to form a dough. Add a bit more flour or water as needed if dough is either too sticky or too dry. Cover dough with plastic wrap and chill for 15–30 minutes.
4. Roll dough to ⅛" thickness on a floured surface and cut out small cracker shapes by hand or with a small cookie cutter. Place on an ungreased baking sheet, and sprinkle lightly with sea salt. Bake for 10–12 minutes. Cool completely and store in an airtight container.

**PER 1 CRACKER** Calories: 75 | Fat: 2 g | Protein: 2 g | Sugar: 1 g | Fiber: 1 g | Carbohydrates: 12 g

# Mixed Berry Cobbler

*It's a triple-berry threat! Feel free to experiment with other berry combinations.*

**INGREDIENTS | SERVES 6**

1 cup flour
1 teaspoon baking powder
1¼ cups sugar, divided use
1 cup soymilk
¼ teaspoon vanilla extract
½ cup vegan margarine, melted
2 tablespoons cornstarch
1 cup blueberries
1 cup blackberries
1 cup raspberries
2 tablespoons raw turbinado sugar

1. Preheat oven to 350°F.
2. Combine flour, baking powder, and 1 cup sugar in a medium bowl. Whisk in soymilk, vanilla extract, and margarine. Pour batter in a greased 8" × 8" pan. Combine remaining ¼ cup sugar and cornstarch with berries and spread over the batter.
3. Bake for 1 hour. Sprinkle raw turbinado sugar over the top when cobbler has baked for 50 minutes.

**PER SERVING** Calories: 326 | Fat: 3 g | Protein: 4 g | Sugar: 50 g | Fiber: 4 g | Carbohydrates: 73 g

# Nectarine-Plum Crumble

*The blush tones from the combination of gold nectarines and purple plums make this a visually appealing dessert!*

**INGREDIENTS | SERVES 6**

2 cups nectarines
2 cups plums
¼ cup sugar
2 tablespoons cornstarch
3 tablespoons orange juice
1 cup quick-cooking oats
½ cup all-purpose flour
¾ cup brown sugar, packed
½ teaspoon cinnamon
Pinch salt
½ cup vegan margarine, melted

1. Preheat oven to 350°F.
   Chop nectarines and plums into 1" pieces and combine with sugar, cornstarch, and orange juice in a large bowl. Pour into the bottom of a greased 8" × 8" baking pan. In a separate bowl combine oats, flour, brown sugar, cinnamon, salt, and melted margarine. Spread the oat mixture in an even layer over the fruit.
2. Bake for 55–60 minutes until golden brown and bubbly.

**PER SERVING** Calories: 384 | Fat: 16 g | Protein: 4 g | Sugar: 35 g | Fiber: 3 g | Carbohydrates: 58 g

# Oat Crackers

*This is a rustic snack cracker with the goodness of oats. Serve it with hot dips or your favorite stews.*

**INGREDIENTS | YIELDS APPROXIMATELY 20 CRACKERS**

1½ cups rolled oats, coarsely ground
1 cup whole-wheat flour
1 teaspoon salt
2 teaspoons sugar
3 tablespoons vegan margarine
½ cup water
2 tablespoons olive oil

1. Combine oats, flour, salt, and sugar in a large bowl. Cut in margarine with a large fork or pastry cutter until crumbly. Mix in water and olive oil. Shape into a ball, cover, and refrigerate for 1 hour.
2. Preheat oven to 350°F. Place dough onto a lightly greased, rimless baking sheet. Roll dough to ⅛" thick. Score dough with a knife in desired cracker shapes. Bake 10–15 minutes, or until lightly browned.
3. Cool completely in the pan. Break along score lines. Store in an airtight container.

**PER 1 CRACKER** Calories: 72 | Fat: 4 g | Protein: 2 g | Sugar: 0 g | Fiber: 1 g | Carbohydrate: 9 g

# Whole-Grain Cherry Crumble

*This recipe tastes like cherry pie, but without all the fuss!*

**INGREDIENTS | SERVES 12**

5 cups sour cherries, pitted
¼ cup cornstarch
1 cup sugar
1 cup white whole-wheat flour
1 cup quick-cooking oats
1 cup brown sugar, packed
1 teaspoon cinnamon
¼ teaspoon baking powder
¼ teaspoon baking soda
½ cup vegan margarine, melted

1. Preheat oven to 350°F.
2. Combine cherries, cornstarch, and sugar, and spread into the bottom of a greased 9" × 13" baking pan.
3. Combine the flour, oats, brown sugar, cinnamon, baking powder, and baking soda in a medium bowl. Stir in melted margarine. Spread oat mixture in an even layer over cherries. Bake for 40–50 minutes until browned and bubbly.

**PER SERVING** Calories: 303 | Fat: 8 g | Protein: 3 g | Sugar: 40 g | Fiber: 3 g | Carbohydrates: 57 g

# Mango-Blueberry Crisp

*Be sure to select mangoes that are firm but ripe, and not mushy!*

## INGREDIENTS | SERVES 6

4 cups mango, ripe but firm

1½ cups blueberries

2 teaspoons lemon juice

½ cup sugar

½ cup all-purpose flour

½ cup brown sugar, packed

Pinch of salt

6 tablespoons vegan margarine, cold

## How to Cut a Mango

Cutting a beautiful, luscious mango is easy once you locate the pit! The mango pit is long and flat. Stand the mango up on one of the skinnier edges, holding the palm of your hand against the side. Place the knife blade lengthwise across the top edge of the fruit and slice down, exposing the flat pit on one side. Turn the fruit around so your hand is against the exposed pit side and slice the fruit from the other side of the pit. Now you can either peel the two halves and slice or cube as desired, or you can score the fruit inside the skin, turn inside out, and cut the resulting mango cubes from the skin.

1. Preheat oven to 375°F.
2. Cut mango into cubes. Combine cubed mango and blueberries in a large bowl and toss with lemon juice and sugar. Pour into a greased 8" × 8" baking dish. Set aside.
3. In a food processor, combine flour, brown sugar, and salt. Cut margarine into pieces and add to processor. Pulse until mixture becomes small crumbles, then pour in an even layer to cover the fruit.
4. Bake for 35–40 minutes until golden brown and bubbly.

**PER SERVING** Calories: 366 | Fat: 12 g | Protein: 2 g | Sugar: 55 g | Fiber: 3 g | Carbohydrates: 67 g

# Cracked Pepper Crackers

*Try using a blend of several different types of peppercorns.*
*Black, green, or white peppercorns would all be great in this recipe.*

**INGREDIENTS** | YIELDS APPROXIMATELY
30 CRACKERS

3 cups flour
1½ tablespoons sugar
1½ tablespoons salt
1 teaspoon freshly ground black pepper
3 tablespoons vegan margarine, cold
1 cup soymilk
1 teaspoon coarsely ground sea salt
2 teaspoons freshly cracked pepper, any type

1. Sift together flour, sugar, salt, and ground black pepper. Cut in margarine with a large fork or pastry cutter until crumbly. Stir in soymilk.
2. Transfer dough to a floured surface and knead 5 minutes. Form into a ball. Divide dough into 4 same-sized pieces and form into balls. Cover dough with plastic wrap and refrigerate for 1 hour.
3. Preheat oven to 375°F. Place each dough ball on a rimless, ungreased baking sheet and roll out to ⅛" thick. Score with a knife into 2" squares. Lightly press coarse salt and cracked pepper onto tops of crackers. Bake for 10–15 minutes or until golden brown.
4. Allow to cool completely on the pans. Break along score lines. Store in an airtight container.

**PER 1 CRACKER** Calories: 61 | Fat: 1 g | Protein: 2 g | Sugar: 1 g | Fiber: 0 g | Carbohydrates: 11 g

# Whole-Grain Apple-Cranberry Crumble

*Save yourself some time and work at your next holiday celebration—*
*this recipe is an easy alternative to making apple pie!*

**INGREDIENTS | SERVES 6**

3½ cups Granny Smith Apples, cored and peeled

2 tablespoons lemon juice

1½ cups cranberries, fresh or frozen

¾ cup sugar

1 cup quick-cooking oats

½ cup whole-wheat flour

¾ cup brown sugar, packed

1 teaspoon cinnamon

Pinch salt

½ cup vegan margarine, melted

¾ cup walnuts, chopped

1. Preheat oven to 350°F.
2. Chop apples and combine with lemon juice, cranberries, and sugar in a large bowl. Pour into bottom of a greased 8" × 8" baking pan. In a separate bowl combine oats, flour, brown sugar, cinnamon, salt, and melted margarine. Stir in walnuts. Spread oat mixture evenly over fruit.
3. Bake for 55–60 minutes until golden brown and bubbly.

**PER SERVING** Calories: 560 | Fat: 25 g | Protein: 6 g | Sugar: 60 g | Fiber: 6 g | Carbohydrates: 83 g

## The Right Apple for the Job!

Some apples are better for eating whole while others are better for cooking! Good cooking apples—such as Granny Smith, Pippin, Cortland, Winesap, and Rome Beauty—hold their shape well and are flavorful when cooked.

# Cinnamon Grahams

*These Cinnamon Grahams are healthier than their non-vegan alternatives—they're sweetened with agave syrup and lightly sprinkled with cinnamon sugar!*

**INGREDIENTS | MAKES 20 CRACKERS**

½ cup brown sugar, packed

½ cup vegan margarine, softened

⅓ cup agave syrup

1½ teaspoons vanilla extract

2¼ cups whole-wheat flour

¾ cup all-purpose flour

1 teaspoon baking powder

½ teaspoon baking soda

¼ teaspoon salt

½ cup soymilk

1 teaspoon cinnamon

3 tablespoons sugar

1. Cream brown sugar, margarine, agave syrup, and vanilla extract in a large bowl until fluffy. Sift together flours, baking powder, baking soda, and salt in a separate large bowl. Gradually add flour mixture to wet ingredients, alternating with soymilk. Cover dough with plastic wrap and refrigerate for at least 2 hours.

2. Preheat oven to 350°F. Cut chilled dough into 4 equal-sized pieces. Working with one piece at a time, roll out each piece on a floured surface into a 5" × 15" rectangle. Place on ungreased baking sheets. Cut each rectangle on the long side into 5 smaller 5" × 3" rectangles. Score each smaller rectangle down the center without cutting through completely.

3. Dock each cracker with the tines of a fork for an authentic graham cracker appearance. Combine cinnamon and sugar in a small bowl and sprinkle on crackers.

4. Bake for 13–15 minutes. Cool completely on wire racks. Store in an airtight container.

**PER ½ CRACKER** Calories: 75 | Fat: 2 g | Protein: 1 g | Sugar: 4 g | Fiber: 1 g | Carbohydrates: 10 g

# Chocolate-Pear Crisp

*This is a perfect dessert after a romantic meal.*

**INGREDIENTS | SERVES 6**

4 cups ripe Bartlett pears, peeled and cored

1 tablespoon lemon juice

1 tablespoon cornstarch

½ cup sugar

¼ teaspoon cinnamon

1 cup all-purpose flour

½ cup brown sugar, packed

Pinch salt

½ cup vegan margarine, cold

1 cup vegan chocolate chips, coarsely chopped

## A Pear Pick-Me-Up

Pears are juicy, have a high amount of natural sugars, and they're a good source of potassium, making them a great snack choice for physically active people! And with 4.5 grams of fiber per unpeeled fruit, pears are a great choice to help you meet your fiber goals.

1. Preheat oven to 375°F. Place rack in lower third of oven.
2. Cut pears into ⅛" slices and combine with lemon juice, cornstarch, sugar, and cinnamon in a large bowl. Pour into a greased 8" × 8" pan.
3. In a food processor, combine flour, brown sugar, and salt. Cut margarine into pieces and add to processor. Pulse until mixture becomes small crumbles. Stir in chocolate chips then pour in an even layer to cover the fruit.
4. Bake for 35–40 minutes until golden brown and bubbly.

**PER SERVING** Calories: 617 | Fat: 26 g | Protein: 5 g | Sugar: 65 g | Fiber: 6 g | Carbohydrates: 93 g

# Rosemary Whole-Wheat Crackers

*These are a much healthier—and more elegant—version of the rosemary crackers you can buy at the grocery store. Enjoy them with your favorite vegan dips, or sprinkled into soups.*

**INGREDIENTS | YIELDS APPROXIMATELY 30 CRACKERS**

2 cups whole-wheat flour

1 cup all-purpose flour

1½ teaspoons baking powder

¾ teaspoon salt

1 cup warm water

½ cup extra-virgin olive oil

⅛ cup fresh rosemary, chopped

Coarse sea salt, optional

1. Preheat oven to 400°F.
2. In a large bowl, sift together whole-wheat flour, all-purpose flour, baking powder, and salt. Mix in water, oil, and rosemary until dough is formed. Shape dough into a ball. Cover with a towel or plastic wrap and refrigerate for 1 hour.
3. Divide dough into 3 equal pieces. Lightly grease 3 rimless baking sheets. Place one dough ball on each baking sheet and roll out dough to ⅛" thick. Score dough with a knife into 2" squares. Lightly press coarse sea salt into crackers, if desired.
4. Bake for 10–15 minutes, or until crackers are golden brown. Allow to cool completely on the pans. Store in an airtight container.

**PER 1 CRACKER** Calories: 74 | Fat: 4 g | Protein: 2 g | Sugar: 0 g | Fiber: 1 g | Carbohydrates: 9 g

# Blueberry–Sour Cream Cobbler

*This dessert tastes rich from the sour cream, but is bursting with the goodness of blueberries!*

**INGREDIENTS | SERVES 12**

6 cups blueberries

2 tablespoons cornstarch

¾ cup sugar, divided use

1½ cups all-purpose flour

1 teaspoon baking powder

¼ teaspoon salt

¾ cup vegan margarine, cold

1 cup vegan sour cream

1 tablespoon raw turbinado sugar

1. Preheat oven to 350°F.
2. Combine blueberries, cornstarch, and ½ cup sugar in a large bowl. Pour into greased 9" × 13" baking pan. Sift flour, remaining ¼ cup sugar, baking powder, and salt in a large bowl. Cut cold margarine into pieces and cut into flour mixture with a large fork or pastry cutter into a coarse meal texture. Add vegan sour cream and mix well.
3. Divide dough into 8 spoonfuls and drop over berry mixture to make 8 biscuits. Press a large pinch of raw turbinado sugar onto the top of each biscuit.
4. Bake 45–50 minutes until browned and bubbly.

**PER SERVING** Calories: 313 | Fat: 15 g | Protein: 3 g | Sugar: 22 g | Fiber: 2 g | Carbohydrates: 44 g

# Rhubarb Crisp

*Try replacing half the rhubarb with strawberries for a classic combination.*

**INGREDIENTS | SERVES 6**

4 cups rhubarb, cut into 1" pieces

¾ cup sugar

2 tablespoons cornstarch

½ cup all-purpose flour

½ cup brown sugar, packed

½ teaspoon cinnamon

Pinch salt

6 tablespoons vegan margarine, cold

1. Preheat oven to 375°F.
2. In a large bowl, combine rhubarb, sugar, and cornstarch. Pour into a greased 8" × 8" baking dish. Set aside.
3. In a food processor, combine flour, brown sugar, cinnamon, and salt. Cut margarine into pieces and add to processor. Pulse until mixture becomes small crumbles, then pour in an even layer to cover the rhubarb.
4. Bake for 35–40 minutes until the top is golden brown and rhubarb is tender.

**PER SERVING** Calories: 332 | Fat: 11 g | Protein: 2 g | Sugar: 44 g | Fiber: 2 g | Carbohydrates: 57 g

# Apricot-Pineapple Cobbler

*Here's a new twist on the traditional cobbler.*
*Pineapple adds a bit of island flair to this comforting classic!*

**INGREDIENTS | SERVES 6**

3 cups apricots, sliced

1 cup pineapple, diced

¾ cup sugar, divided use

2 tablespoons cornstarch

⅔ cup soymilk

1 tablespoon canola oil

1 teaspoon vanilla extract

1½ cups all-purpose flour

¼ teaspoon salt

2 teaspoons baking powder

## Leftover Pineapple Juice?

Marinated and grilled tofu is a great way to use leftover pineapple juice from canned pineapple! Simply marinate slices of extra-firm tofu that have been pressed (to remove excess moisture) with ¼ pineapple juice, 1 teaspoon soy sauce, 1 tablespoon olive oil, 1 clove mashed garlic, 2 teaspoons brown sugar, and 1 teaspoon minced fresh ginger. Marinate overnight, then cook tofu slices on an oiled grill to desired doneness.

1. Combine apricots, pineapple, ¼ cup sugar, and cornstarch in a large bowl. Let stand for 30 minutes, stirring occasionally.
2. Mix soymilk, oil, and vanilla extract in a large bowl. In a separate bowl, combine flour, the remaining ½ cup sugar, salt, and baking powder. Stir flour mixture into wet ingredients.
3. Preheat oven to 375°F. Pour the fruit mixture into a greased 8" × 8" pan. Drop the batter by spoonfuls over the fruit. Spread batter to cover, but don't try to make it perfect. Bake for 30–40 minutes until golden brown and bubbly.

**PER SERVING** Calories: 305 | Fat: 3 g | Protein: 5 g | Sugar: 36 g | Fiber: 3 g | Carbohydrates: 65 g

# Strawberry-Walnut Crisp

*Crunchy and sweet, this dish is perfect with vegan vanilla ice cream or as a decadent weekend breakfast.*

## INGREDIENTS | SERVES 6

¾ cup walnut pieces

4 cups strawberries, hulled and halved

½ cup sugar

2 tablespoons cornstarch

¾ cup all-purpose flour

½ cup brown sugar, packed

¼ teaspoon nutmeg

Pinch salt

6 tablespoons vegan margarine, cold

## Fresh or Frozen Berries?

When fresh berries are not in season, frozen berries are a great alternative! It may be necessary to thaw and drain some berries, such as strawberries, because the high water content may otherwise make your recipe soggy during cooking. Sometimes additional cooking time or adding a little extra cornstarch or flour mixed with the berries will correct this problem. Frozen blueberries, however, may be thrown in as-is!

1. Preheat oven to 350°F. Toast walnuts in a dry pan over medium-low heat until aromatic and lightly browned, stirring often. Set aside.
2. In a large bowl, combine strawberries, sugar, and cornstarch. Pour into a greased 8" × 8" baking dish. Set aside.
3. In a food processor, combine flour, brown sugar, nutmeg, and salt. Cut margarine into pieces and add to processor. Pulse until mixture becomes small crumbles. Add walnuts and pulse for a few seconds more. Then spread in an even layer over the berries.
4. Bake for 35–40 minutes until the top is golden brown.

**PER SERVING** Calories: 429 | Fat: 21 g | Protein: 5 g | Sugar: 40 g | Fiber: 3 g | Carbohydrates: 59 g

# CHAPTER 14

# Toppings, Glazes, and Fillings

# Cream Cheeze Frosting

*This rich and creamy frosting has the classic cream cheese tang without the dairy!*

**INGREDIENTS | MAKES 2½–3 CUPS**

8 ounces vegan cream cheese

4 tablespoons vegan margarine, softened

1 teaspoon vanilla extract

2 cups powdered sugar

1. In a large bowl, beat together cream cheese and margarine on medium speed until blended.
2. Add vanilla extract and powdered sugar and continue to beat until smooth.
3. Store covered in the refrigerator for up to 1 week.

**PER 1-TABLESPOON SERVING** Calories: 51 | Fat: 2 g | Protein: 0 g | Sugar: 6 g | Fiber: 0 g | Carbohydrates: 8 g

# Chocolate Ganache

*This is a silky-smooth chocolate icing, perfect for cakes and pastries. Substitute plain or vanilla soymilk when soy creamer is not available.*

**INGREDIENTS | MAKES 2½ CUPS**

¾ cup soy creamer

4 tablespoons vegan margarine

12 ounces vegan chocolate chips

1. Place soy creamer and margarine in a bowl over a pan of gently simmering water and heat until the margarine melts.
2. Add the vegan chocolate chips and continue to heat, stirring constantly until the mixture is smooth.
3. Store in the refrigerator in an airtight container. Reheat in a bowl over warm water as needed.

**PER 1-TABLESPOON SERVING** Calories: 59 | Fat: 4 g | Protein: 1 g | Sugar: 4 g | Fiber: 1 g | Carbohydrates: 6 g

### Chocolate-Dipped Strawberries

For a beautiful and romantic treat, dip ripe, long-stemmed strawberries halfway into 2 cups vegan semisweet chocolate that has been melted with 1 tablespoon shortening in a bowl over gently simmering water. The chocolate should be just melted, but not hot. Place dipped strawberries 1" apart on a wax paper–lined baking sheet and cool until chocolate is set. Remember to share with your sweetie!

# Key Lime Cream Cheeze Frosting

*Indulge in this refreshing, sweet-tart frosting! If you want the frosting to have a lime-green color to match the lime flavor, just add a few drops of green food coloring.*

**INGREDIENTS | MAKES 2 CUPS**

8 ounces vegan cream cheese, softened

½ cup vegan margarine, softened

2 cups powdered sugar

1 tablespoon Key lime juice

1 teaspoon Key lime zest, chopped

¼ teaspoon vanilla extract

1 teaspoon soy creamer or soymilk, if needed

1. Beat cream cheese and margarine on medium speed until blended.
2. Beat in powdered sugar. Then add Key lime juice, zest, and vanilla extract. Beat 1–2 minutes until smooth and creamy, adding soy creamer if needed.
3. Store in the refrigerator in an airtight container.

**PER 1-TABLESPOON SERVING** Calories: 76 | Fat: 4 g | Protein: 0 g | Sugar: 8 g | Fiber: 0 g | Carbohydrates: 10 g

# Cranberry Glaze

*Cranberry Glaze is striking—it's beautifully ruby-red! Use it on sweet breads or chocolate cake at your next holiday celebration.*

**INGREDIENTS | MAKES APPROXIMATELY 1 CUP**

1½ cups cranberries, chopped

½ cup sugar

½ cup water

1 teaspoon orange zest, optional

1. Combine cranberries, sugar, water, and orange zest (if using) in a medium saucepan. Bring to a boil over medium heat, stirring occasionally. Reduce heat and simmer, stirring constantly, for approximately 10 minutes. Mixture will thicken.
2. Remove from heat and cool to room temperature.
3. Store in the refrigerator in an airtight container.

**PER 1-TABLESPOON SERVING** Calories: 14 | Fat: 0 g | Protein: 0 g | Sugar: 3 g | Fiber: 0 g | Carbohydrates: 4 g

## Cranberries at Sea

You've probably heard the history of English sailors who consumed limes as a source of vitamin C to prevent scurvy on long voyages, but did you know that early American sailors also used cranberries for this purpose? Cranberries are high in vitamin C and fiber and are protective against bladder infections. Buy extra bags of fresh cranberries when they're available and pop them in the freezer. Frozen cranberries last nearly a year!

# Cream Cheeze Filling

*This versatile filling is great in many sweets and pastries,
including layer cakes, shortbread, tarts, and Danish.*

**INGREDIENTS | MAKES 1¼ CUPS**

8 ounces vegan cream cheese, softened
½ cup powdered sugar
4 tablespoons vegan margarine, softened

1. Combine cream cheese, powdered sugar, and margarine in a large bowl.
2. Beat with an electric mixer on medium speed until smooth.
3. Store in the refrigerator in an airtight container until ready to use.

**PER 1-TABLESPOON SERVING** Calories: 66 | Fat: 4 g | Protein: 0 g | Sugar: 4 g | Fiber: 0 g | Carbohydrates: 7 g

# Raspberry Sauce

*Raspberry sauce is a perfect pairing for poached pears or apple dumplings.*

**INGREDIENTS | MAKES APPROXIMATELY 1 CUP**

½ cup water
1 tablespoon cornstarch
¼ raw sugar or more for desired sweetness
1 tablespoon orange or lemon juice
2 cups raspberries

1. Whisk water, cornstarch, sugar, and orange juice together in a medium saucepan until cornstarch is dissolved. Add raspberries and bring to a boil over medium heat. Reduce heat and simmer for about 2–3 minutes, stirring constantly, until mixture thickens.
2. Carefully purée the sauce and strain through a fine sieve to remove the seeds, if desired.
3. Store in the refrigerator in an airtight container.

**PER 1-TABLESPOON SERVING** Calories: 22 | Fat: 0 g | Protein: 0 g | Sugar: 4 g | Fiber: 1 g | Carbohydrates: 6 g

## Poached Pears

In a large saucepan, bring 1½ cups water, ⅓ cup sugar, 2 tablespoons lemon juice, and a cinnamon stick to a boil. While waiting for liquid to boil, peel, halve, and core 2 ripe, firm pears. Submerge pear halves in boiling syrup and simmer over medium-low heat 15 minutes or until pears are just tender. Cool, drain, and serve at room temperature drizzled with Raspberry Sauce or chocolate sauce.

# Chocolate Frosting

*Classic chocolate flavor! Try substituting another flavor extract,*
*like rum or raspberry, for 1 teaspoon of the vanilla extract.*

**INGREDIENTS | MAKES 2½–3 CUPS**

¾ cup vegan margarine, softened

3 cups powdered sugar, divided use

6 tablespoons unsweetened cocoa powder

4 tablespoons soy creamer

1½ teaspoons vanilla extract

1. In a large bowl, cream margarine and 1 cup powdered sugar together until blended.
2. In a separate bowl, sift remaining 2 cups powdered sugar with cocoa powder. Gradually beat cocoa mixture into margarine on medium speed, alternating with soy creamer, until fluffy. Beat in vanilla extract.
3. Store in the refrigerator in an airtight container.

**PER 1-TABLESPOON SERVING** Calories: 69 | Fat: 4 g | Protein: 0 g | Sugar: 9 g | Fiber: 0 g | Carbohydrates: 10 g

# Strawberry Frosting

*Pink and berrylicious! For frosting with no seeds, purée the berries*
*and strain through a fine mesh sieve, then proceed with the recipe.*

**INGREDIENTS | MAKES 4 CUPS**

½ cup frozen strawberries, thawed and drained

¾ cup vegetable shortening

¼ cup vegan margarine, softened

4–5 cups powdered sugar

Soymilk, as needed, to thin

1. Purée strawberries and pour into a large bowl. Add shortening, margarine, and 2 cups powdered sugar. Beat on medium speed until blended.
2. Beat in 2 more cups powdered sugar until smooth.
3. Thin with soymilk, or thicken with additional powdered sugar, as needed, to achieve desired consistency.
4. Store in the refrigerator in an airtight container.

**PER 1-TABLESPOON SERVING** Calories: 58 | Fat: 3 g | Protein: 0 g | Sugar: 8 g | Fiber: 0 g | Carbohydrates: 8 g

## Are You a Strawberry Fanatic?

There are many festivals held in celebration of strawberries where fans can enjoy strawberry offerings ranging from the traditional and classic strawberry shortcake to the heart-stopping fried strawberry butter! And while strawberries are available in certain regional markets nearly year round, the tastiest strawberries are seasonal and locally grown. Buy locally to support the farmers in your area and to get the best-tasting strawberries around!

# Tofu Custard Filling

*Although this custard is meant to be baked as a filling in tart or kuchen recipes,
it can be eaten as a stand-alone custard by pouring into ramekins
on a baking sheet and baking at 375°F for 15–20 minutes until set.*

**INGREDIENTS | MAKES 2 CUPS**

1 pound silken firm tofu, drained and pressed

2 teaspoons vanilla extract

¼ cup sugar

2 teaspoons cornstarch

1. Place pressed tofu, vanilla extract, and sugar in a blender and blend until smooth.
2. Add cornstarch and continue blending until creamy.
3. Custard is ready to use in your tart or kuchen recipe. Store in the refrigerator in an airtight container.

**PER 2-TABLESPOON SERVING** Calories: 32 | Fat: 1 g | Protein: 2 g | Sugar: 4 g | Fiber: 0 g | Carbohydrates: 4 g

# Coconut Cream Cheeze Frosting

*The coconut in this recipe gives the frosting texture as well as great flavor!*

**INGREDIENTS | MAKES 3–4 CUPS**

8 ounces vegan cream cheese, softened

½ cup vegan margarine, softened

2 tablespoons coconut cream

1 teaspoon vanilla extract

4 cups powdered sugar

½ cup sweetened shredded coconut

1. In a large bowl, cream the cream cheese and margarine on medium speed until smooth. Blend in coconut cream and vanilla extract.
2. Gradually add powdered sugar, continuing to beat at medium speed until smooth. Stir in shredded coconut.
3. Store in the refrigerator in an airtight container.

**PER 1-TABLESPOON SERVING** Calories: 76 | Fat: 3 g | Protein: 0 g | Sugar: 10 g | Fiber: 0 g | Carbohydrates: 12 g

# Dark Chocolate Frosting

*Semisweet dark chocolate has a hint of bitterness that beautifully complements the sweetness of cake!*

**INGREDIENTS | MAKES 2 CUPS**

½ cup vegan margarine, softened

⅓ cup unsweetened cocoa powder

1 teaspoon vanilla extract

¼ cup semisweet vegan chocolate chips, melted

3 cups powdered sugar

Soymilk, as needed

1. Cream together margarine and cocoa powder in a large bowl on medium speed.
2. Add vanilla extract and chocolate chips. Gradually add the powdered sugar, continuing to beat at medium speed until smooth.
3. If frosting is too thick, add a few drops of soymilk until desired consistency is achieved. Store in the refrigerator in an airtight container.

**PER 1-TABLESPOON SERVING** Calories: 81 | Fat: 3 g | Protein: 0 g | Sugar: 12 g | Fiber: 0 g | Carbohydrates: 13 g

# Vanilla Pudding Filling

*This filling is so yummy you'll be tempted to eat it with a spoon!*

**INGREDIENTS | MAKES 2 CUPS**

1 cup soy creamer

1 cup soymilk

5 tablespoons cornstarch

⅓ cup sugar

Pinch salt

2 teaspoons vanilla extract

1. Whisk soy creamer, soymilk, and cornstarch together in medium saucepan until cornstarch is dissolved. Add sugar and salt and heat over medium heat until mixture comes to a boil.
2. Reduce heat and continue to cook at a gentle simmer, whisking constantly for 3–4 minutes until thickened. Remove from heat and stir in the vanilla extract.
3. Transfer to a bowl, cover with plastic wrap and allow to cool completely at room temperature. Refrigerate for at least 2 hours. Pudding is ready to be enjoyed as is or used as a filling.

**PER 2-TABLESPOON SERVING** Calories: 48 | Fat: 1 g | Protein: 0 g | Sugar: 5 g | Fiber: 0 g | Carbohydrates: 8 g

## Custard Powder

Popular in the UK and Australia, custard powder is a combination of cornstarch, salt, vanilla, and annatto (for color). To make custard, this mix is traditionally cooked with sugar and dairy milk. For a vegan version, simply substitute soymilk, almond milk, or other non-dairy milk of your choice. Bird's Custard Powder is a readily available brand in U.S. markets.

# Chocolate Pudding Filling

*Creamy, cool, and comforting! This makes a great filling for layer cakes, pastries, and chocolate pie.*

**INGREDIENTS | MAKES 2 CUPS**

1 cup soy creamer

¾ cup soymilk

5 tablespoons cornstarch

½ cup sugar

Pinch salt

⅓ cup vegan semisweet chocolate chips, melted

½ teaspoon vanilla extract

1. Whisk soy creamer, soymilk, and cornstarch together in a medium saucepan until cornstarch is dissolved. Add sugar and salt, and cook over medium heat until mixture comes to a boil.
2. Reduce heat and continue to cook at a gentle simmer, whisking constantly for 3–4 minutes until thickened. Remove from heat and stir in the chocolate chips until mixture is smooth. Stir in vanilla extract.
3. Transfer to a bowl, cover with plastic wrap, and allow to cool completely at room temperature. Refrigerate for at least 2 hours. Pudding is ready to be enjoyed as is or used as a filling.

**PER 2-TABLESPOON SERVING** Calories: 40 | Fat: 1 g | Protein: 0 g | Sugar: 5 g | Fiber: 0 g | Carbohydrates: 7 g

# Coffee Frosting

*Simply add ⅔ cup of cocoa powder to transform this into a delicious mocha frosting.*

**INGREDIENTS | MAKES APPROXIMATELY 3 CUPS**

¼ cup vegetable shortening

¼ cup vegan margarine, softened

4 cups powdered sugar, divided use

¼ cup strong brewed coffee, cold

1 teaspoon vanilla extract

1. In a large bowl, beat shortening, margarine, and 2 cups powdered sugar at medium speed until smooth.
2. Beat in coffee and vanilla extract. Add remaining powdered sugar and continue to beat until fluffy.
3. Store in the refrigerator in an airtight container.

**PER 1-TABLESPOON SERVING** Calories: 57 | Fat: 2 g | Protein: 0 g | Sugar: 10 g | Fiber: 0 g | Carbohydrates: 10 g

# Raspberry Glaze

*Glazes and sauces with raspberries are so simple to make, and they always impress!*

**INGREDIENTS | MAKES APPROXIMATELY ¾ CUP**

½ cup raspberry jam, seedless
¼ cup apple juice

1. Combine raspberry jam and apple juice in a small saucepan.
2. Cook over low heat, stirring constantly, until mixture is smooth and beginning to thicken. Remove from heat.
3. Store in an airtight container in the refrigerator.

**PER 1-TABLESPOON SERVING** Calories: 39 | Fat: 0 g | Protein: 0 g | Sugar: 7 g | Fiber: 0 g | Carbohydrates: 10 g

# Milk Chocolate Frosting

*With frosting this rich and creamy, and this easy to make, who needs canned frosting?*

**INGREDIENTS | MAKES APPROXIMATELY 3 CUPS**

¼ cup vegetable shortening
¼ cup vegan margarine, softened
4 cups powdered sugar, divided use
¼ cup unsweetened cocoa powder
3 tablespoons soy creamer or soymilk

1. In a large bowl, beat shortening, margarine, and 2 cups powdered sugar on medium speed until smooth.
2. Add cocoa, soy creamer, and remaining powdered sugar and continue to beat until fluffy.
3. Store in the refrigerator in an airtight container.

**PER 1-TABLESPOON SERVING** Calories: 59 | Fat: 2 g | Protein: 0 g | Sugar: 10 g | Fiber: 0 g | Carbohydrates: 10 g

### Carob, the Counterfeit Chocolate

Carob, also known as St. John's Bread, is a powder made from the pods of the carob tree, which has been used in recipes for years as a substitute for chocolate. Although carob has a distinctive flavor, it works well in place of chocolate, providing a welcome alternative for individuals who are allergic to chocolate or who wish to avoid the stimulating effect of theobromine, a caffeine-like substance present in chocolate but not in carob. To use carob, simply substitute an equal amount of carob powder for cocoa powder.

# Lemon Glaze

*This Lemon Glaze has the perfect amount of sweet and tart.*
*Serve it with cakes or breads, or drizzled over fruit and vegan ice cream.*

**INGREDIENTS | MAKES APPROXIMATELY ¾ CUP**

1 tablespoon vegan margarine
2 cups powdered sugar
3 tablespoons lemon juice

1. Melt margarine over low heat in a small saucepan. Remove from heat and whisk in sugar and lemon juice until smooth.
2. Drizzle glaze over cookies or cakes. Allow to firm up for 10 minutes before serving.
3. Store unused glaze in the refrigerator in an airtight container.

**PER 1-TABLESPOON SERVING** Calories: 87 | Fat: 1 g | Protein: 0 g | Sugar: 20 g | Fiber: 0 g | Carbohydrates: 20 g

# Apricot Glaze

*The intense apricot flavor makes this glaze a wonderful topping for your favorite vegan vanilla ice cream.*

**INGREDIENTS | MAKES ½ CUP**

½ cup apricot preserves
1 tablespoon orange juice or pineapple juice

1. Place preserves in a small saucepan and stir in orange or pineapple juice.
2. Bring to a boil over medium heat, stirring constantly. Remove from heat and strain if desired.
3. Cool. Store in the refrigerator in an airtight container.

**PER 1-TABLESPOON SERVING** Calories: 49 | Fat: 0 g | Protein: 0 g | Sugar: 9 g | Fiber: 0 g | Carbohydrates: 13 g

## Using Liqueurs in Frostings and Glazes

Liqueurs can be used to give frostings and glazes a rich, complex flavor profile. Instead of the flavor extract or juice called for in a recipe, try substituting an equal amount of a similarly flavored liqueur. For example, use Grand Marnier in place of orange juice or Amaretto in place of almond extract. You will be delighted with the results!

# Caramel Topping

*This topping is warm, gooey, and perfect for dipping apples, filling cupcakes, or topping your favorite sundaes.*

**INGREDIENTS | MAKES APPROXIMATELY 1 CUP**

1 cup sugar
6 tablespoons vegan margarine
½ cup soy creamer

1. Melt sugar in a large, heavy saucepan over medium heat, stirring constantly, until the sugar begins to boil. Whisk in the margarine until blended. Remove from heat.
2. Slowly add the soy creamer, whisking until smooth. Be careful, as mixture may foam up and will be very hot.
3. Allow caramel to cool for 3–4 minutes, then pour into a glass jar or bowl. Cool completely. Cover and store in the refrigerator.

**PER 1-TABLESPOON SERVING** Calories: 93 | Fat: 5 g | Protein: 0 g | Sugar: 12 g | Fiber: 0 g | Carbohydrates: 13 g

# Vanilla Glaze

*You'll love this simple glaze with the wonderful flavor and aroma of vanilla!*

**INGREDIENTS | MAKES ¾ CUP**

1 teaspoon vegan margarine, softened
2 cups powdered sugar
3 tablespoons soymilk
Pinch salt
¼ teaspoon vanilla extract

1. Melt the margarine in a medium saucepan. Remove from heat.
2. Add powdered sugar, soymilk, salt, and vanilla extract. Whisk until creamy.
3. Drizzle over cookies or cakes. Store in the refrigerator in an airtight container.

**PER 1-TABLESPOON SERVING** Calories: 82 | Fat: 0 g | Protein: 0 g | Sugar: 20 g | Fiber: 0 g | Carbohydrates: 20 g

# Maple Glaze

*Maple has a complex bouquet of flavors that are rich, sweet, and aromatic!*

**INGREDIENTS | MAKES APPROXIMATELY ¾ CUP**

2 cups powdered sugar
½ teaspoon maple extract
3 tablespoons soy creamer or soymilk

1. Combine all ingredients in a medium bowl and mix well.
2. Add additional powdered sugar or soy creamer to achieve desired consistency.
3. Store in the refrigerator in an airtight container.

**PER 1-TABLESPOON SERVING** Calories: 82 | Fat: 0 g | Protein: 0 g | Sugar: 20 g | Fiber: 0 g | Carbohydrates: 20 g

# Peppermint Frosting

*Sweet, creamy, cool, and refreshing—this frosting adds great flavor to any special dessert.*

**INGREDIENTS | MAKES APPROXIMATELY 3 CUPS**

4 tablespoons vegan margarine, softened
4 tablespoons vegetable shortening
3 cups powdered sugar, divided use
1 teaspoon peppermint extract
2–3 tablespoons soymilk
½ cup crushed peppermint candies

1. In a large bowl, beat margarine, shortening, and 1 cup powdered sugar on medium speed until smooth. Beat in peppermint extract and 1 tablespoon soymilk.
2. Add remaining powdered sugar and continue to beat until fluffy, adding additional soymilk as needed to achieve desired consistency. Stir in crushed peppermint candies.
3. Store in the refrigerator in an airtight container.

**PER 1-TABLESPOON SERVING** Calories: 55 | Fat: 2 g | Protein: 0 g | Sugar: 9 g | Fiber: 0 g | Carbohydrates: 9 g

# Peanut Butter Frosting

*This frosting tastes great with crunchy peanut butter, too.*

**INGREDIENTS | MAKES 3½–4 CUPS**

¼ cup vegetable shortening

¼ cup vegan margarine, softened

1 cup creamy peanut butter

2½ cups powdered sugar, divided use

¼ cup soy creamer

¼ teaspoon vanilla extract

1. In a large bowl, beat shortening, margarine, and peanut butter until blended. Beat in 1 cup powdered sugar, soy creamer, and vanilla extract.
2. Beat in the rest of the powdered sugar, adding additional powdered sugar or soy creamer until desired consistency is achieved.
3. Store in the refrigerator in an airtight container.

**PER 1-TABLESPOON SERVING** Calories: 75 | Fat: 5 g | Protein: 1 g | Sugar: 6 g | Fiber: 0 g | Carbohydrates: 8 g

# Strawberry Glaze

*Make your desserts extra special with this delightful glaze!*

**INGREDIENTS | MAKES APPROXIMATELY 1 CUP**

2 cups strawberries, hulled

¼ cup water

1½ tablespoons cornstarch

⅓ cup sugar

1. Purée strawberries in a blender. Strain strawberry purée to remove seeds by pressing through a fine mesh sieve with the back of a large spoon until you have 1 cup of strained purée.
2. In a small saucepan, whisk together purée, water, cornstarch, and sugar until well blended. Bring to a boil over medium heat, stirring constantly. Boil for 1 minute. Remove from heat. Cool completely.
3. Store in an airtight container in the refrigerator.

**PER 1-TABLESPOON SERVING** Calories: 25 | Fat: 0 g | Protein: 0 g | Sugar: 5 g | Fiber: 0 g | Carbohydrates: 6 g

# Pink Frosting

*This frosting is perfect for birthday cake or cupcakes at a springtime luncheon.*

**INGREDIENTS | MAKES 3–4 CUPS**

¼ cup vegetable shortening

¼ cup vegan margarine, softened

3 cups powdered sugar

1 teaspoon vanilla extract

2–3 tablespoons soy creamer or soymilk

Red food coloring, as desired

1. Cream shortening and margarine with an electric mixer on medium speed until creamy. Gradually beat in powdered sugar.
2. Beat in vanilla extract and soy creamer until light and fluffy. Blend in red food coloring a few drops at a time until frosting is the desired shade of pink.
3. Add additional soy creamer or powdered sugar to achieve desired consistency. Store in an airtight container in the refrigerator.

**PER 1-TABLESPOON SERVING** Calories: 48 | Fat: 2 g | Protein: 0 g | Sugar: 7 g | Fiber: 0 g | Carbohydrates: 8 g

## Bubblegum Days

Do you miss the long, carefree days of childhood? Add bubblegum extract to any basic vanilla frosting. Upon your first taste you'll find yourself frolicking once again through the forgotten fields of your youth!

# White Frosting

*Sweet and simple, this recipe is versatile and may be used to frost just about anything.*

**INGREDIENTS | MAKES 3–4 CUPS**

¼ cup vegetable shortening

¼ cup vegan margarine, softened

3 cups powdered sugar

1 teaspoon vanilla extract

2–3 tablespoons soy creamer or soymilk

1. Cream shortening and margarine with an electric mixer on medium speed until creamy. Gradually beat in powdered sugar.
2. Beat in vanilla extract and soy creamer until light and fluffy. Add additional soy creamer or powdered sugar to achieve desired consistency.
3. Store in an airtight container in the refrigerator.

**PER 1-TABLESPOON SERVING** Calories: 48 | Fat: 2 g | Protein: 0 g | Sugar: 7 g | Fiber: 0 g | Carbohydrates: 8 g

# Lemon Curd Filling

*This sweet, tart, and creamy filling doubles as a delicious dip for shortbread cookies!*

**INGREDIENTS | MAKES 1¼ CUPS**

½ cup soymilk

1 teaspoon cornstarch

½ cup sugar

½ cup lemon juice

1 tablespoon lemon zest

6 tablespoons vegan margarine

### Lemon Curd Makes a Great Gift!

During the holiday season, show your friends and family how much you care by giving them a gift of homemade short-bread cookies and fresh lemon curd. The lemon curd is the perfect dip for the cookies and will have everyone marveling at your culinary prowess!

1. Whisk together soymilk, cornstarch, sugar, lemon juice, and zest in a medium saucepan, until cornstarch is dissolved.
2. Cook over medium heat, stirring constantly until mixture is thick enough to coat the back of a spoon. Remove from heat and whisk in margarine. Whisk an additional 1½ minutes.
3. Pour into bowl and cool completely. Store in an airtight container in the refrigerator.

**PER 1-TABLESPOON SERVING** Calories: 54 | Fat: 3 g | Protein: 0 g | Sugar: 5 g | Fiber: 0 g | Carbohydrates: 6 g

# Cinnamon Glaze

*Drizzle this sinfully delicious glaze over spice cakes or zucchini bread.*

**INGREDIENTS | MAKES ¾ CUP**

2 cups powdered sugar

2 teaspoons cinnamon

½ teaspoon vanilla extract

3 tablespoons soy creamer

1. In a small bowl, stir together powdered sugar, cinnamon, vanilla extract, and soy creamer until smooth.
2. Stir in additional powdered sugar or soy creamer as needed to achieve desired consistency.
3. Store in an airtight container in the refrigerator.

**PER 1-TABLESPOON SERVING** Calories: 80 | Fat: 0 g | Protein: 0 g | Sugar: 20 g | Fiber: 0 g | Carbohydrates: 20 g

# Lemon Frosting

*This version of Lemon Frosting uses just the right amount of lemon without being too tart!*

**INGREDIENTS | MAKES 2 CUPS**

1 teaspoon lemon zest

2 tablespoons vegetable shortening

2 tablespoons vegan margarine, softened

2 tablespoons lemon juice

3 cups powdered sugar

1 tablespoon soymilk

1. Cream lemon zest, shortening, and margarine with an electric beater on low speed until smooth. Blend in lemon juice.
2. Gradually beat in powdered sugar on medium speed until smooth.
3. Add more powdered sugar or soymilk until the desired consistency is achieved.
4. Store in an airtight container in the refrigerator.

**PER 1-TABLESPOON SERVING** Calories: 58 | Fat: 2 g | Protein: 0 g | Sugar: 11 g | Fiber: 0 g | Carbohydrates: 11 g

# Raspberry Curd Filling

*For a brighter shade of pink, add red food coloring, one drop at a time, until the color is right.*

**INGREDIENTS | MAKES 1¼ CUPS**

1 cup raspberries

½ cup soymilk

1 teaspoon cornstarch

3 tablespoons sugar

2 tablespoons lemon juice

6 tablespoons vegan margarine

1. Purée raspberries in a blender and strain through a fine mesh strainer, pressing with the back of a spoon to extract the juice. Add a few more berries as needed, for a total of a ½ cup of raspberry juice.
2. Whisk together raspberry juice, soymilk, cornstarch, and sugar in a medium saucepan, until cornstarch is dissolved.
3. Cook over medium heat, stirring constantly until mixture is thick enough to coat the back of a spoon. Remove from heat and whisk in lemon juice and margarine. Whisk for an additional 1½ minutes.
4. Pour into bowl and cool completely. Store in an airtight container in the refrigerator.

**PER 1-TABLESPOON SERVING** Calories: 43 | Fat: 3 g | Protein: 0 g | Sugar: 2 g | Fiber: 0 g | Carbohydrates: 3 g

# CHAPTER 15

# **Bread Machine**

# Classic White Bread

*This recipe makes a straightforward, flavorful bread, perfect for everyday needs.*

**INGREDIENTS | MAKES 1 (2-POUND) LOAF (32 SERVINGS)**

1⅓ cups water

2 tablespoons vegan margarine, softened

1 tablespoon plus 2 teaspoons sugar

4 cups bread flour

2 tablespoons soymilk powder

1½ teaspoons active dry yeast

## Ingredient Order

Bread machine instructions are very specific about the order in which the ingredients are added. If you are planning on mixing and baking right away, it really isn't that important. If, however, you are using the delay setting to make your bread, the order becomes very important. Ingredients must remain inert until the machine turns itself on. This means liquid and yeast have to remain separate until the mixing and kneading begins. Be careful to keep yeast out of direct contact with salt and sugar, too.

1. Assemble bread machine with the dough paddle in place. Bring all ingredients to room temperature.
2. Add all ingredients to the pan in the order indicated in your machine's operation manual. Proceed according to manufacturer's directions for white bread.
3. Cool for 10 minutes, then remove from pan. Cool bread completely before slicing. Store in an airtight container or freeze.

**PER SERVING** Calories: 73 | Fat: 1 g | Protein: 2 g | Sugar: 1 g | Fiber: 0 g | Carbohydrates: 13 g

# Rosemary-Olive Bread

*Try this herby, salty bread toasted, with a generous smear of vegan cream cheese.*

**INGREDIENTS | MAKES 1 (1-POUND) LOAF (16 SERVINGS)**

1 cup water
1½ teaspoons sea salt
3 tablespoons olive oil
1½ teaspoons sugar
2 teaspoons dried rosemary
¼ teaspoon cracked black pepper
2½ cups bread flour
1½ teaspoons active dry yeast
⅓ cup kalamata olives, pitted and coarsely chopped

1. Assemble bread machine with the dough paddle in place. Bring all ingredients to room temperature.
2. Add all ingredients to the pan, except for the kalamata olives, in the order indicated in your machine's operation manual. Proceed according to manufacturer's directions for white bread, adding the olives when the machine beeps, indicating the time to add additional ingredients.
3. Cool for 10 minutes, then remove from pan. Cool bread completely before slicing. Store in an airtight container or freeze.

**PER SERVING** Calories: 176 | Fat: 3 g | Protein: 3 g | Sugar: 19 g | Fiber: 1 g | Carbohydrates: 35 g

# Carrot-Dill Loaf

*This is a creative take on the popular vegetable side dish, dilled carrots!*
*Serve as an accompaniment to a simple bean soup.*

**INGREDIENTS | MAKES 1 (1½-POUND) LOAF (24 SERVINGS)**

1 cup water
3 cups carrots, grated
3¼ cups bread flour
½ cup cornmeal
1½ tablespoons sugar
1½ teaspoons salt
1½ tablespoons dried dillweed
2½ teaspoons instant yeast

1. Assemble bread machine with the dough paddle in place. Bring all ingredients to room temperature.
2. Add all ingredients to the pan in the order indicated in your machine's operation manual. Proceed according to manufacturer's directions for white bread.
3. Cool for 10 minutes, then remove from pan. Cool bread completely before slicing. Store in an airtight container or freeze.

**PER SERVING** Calories: 89 | Fat: 0 g | Protein: 3 g | Sugar: 2 g | Fiber: 1 g | Carbohydrates: 18 g

# Maple-Oat Bread

*Oats give this recipe great texture, and that wonderful maple syrup aroma will fill the kitchen while it's baking.*

**INGREDIENTS | MAKES 1 (1½-POUND) LOAF (24 SERVINGS)**

1 cup plus 2 tablespoons water

1½ tablespoons vegan margarine

⅔ cup Grade B maple syrup

1 teaspoon salt

¾ cup rolled oats

3 cups bread flour

2 tablespoons soymilk powder

2 tablespoons active dry yeast

1. Assemble bread machine with the dough paddle in place. Bring all ingredients to room temperature.
2. Add all ingredients to the pan in the order indicated in your machine's operation manual. Proceed according to manufacturer's directions for white bread.
3. Cool for 10 minutes, then remove from pan. Cool bread completely before slicing. Store in an airtight container or freeze.

**PER SERVING** Calories: 99 | Fat: 1 g | Protein: 3 g | Sugar: 5 g | Fiber: 1 g | Carbohydrates: 21 g

# Whole-Wheat Sandwich Loaf

*Homemade, hearty whole-wheat bread just calls out for homegrown tomatoes and ripe avocado!*

**INGREDIENTS | MAKES 1 (2-POUND) LOAF (32 SERVINGS)**

1⅜ cups water

½ cup soymilk

5 cups whole-wheat flour

3 tablespoons sugar

2 teaspoons salt

4 tablespoons vital wheat gluten

2 tablespoons vegan margarine

2 teaspoons active dry yeast

1. Assemble bread machine with the dough paddle in place. Bring all ingredients to room temperature.
2. Add all ingredients to the pan in the order indicated in your machine's operation manual. Proceed according to manufacturer's directions for whole-wheat bread.
3. Cool for 10 minutes, then remove from pan. Cool bread completely before slicing. Store in an airtight container or freeze.

**PER SERVING** Calories: 80 | Fat: 1 g | Protein: 3 g | Sugar: 1 g | Fiber: 2 g | Carbohydrates: 15 g

# Fruit and Nut Bread

*Use the delay setting on the bread machine at night to have this bread hot and fresh-baked for breakfast.*

**INGREDIENTS | MAKES 1 (2-POUND) LOAF (32 SERVINGS)**

2 cups water

5 cups whole-wheat flour

3 tablespoons brown sugar

2 tablespoons soymilk powder

1½ teaspoons salt

2 tablespoons vegan margarine

½ teaspoon cinnamon

½ teaspoon allspice

5 tablespoons vital wheat gluten

3 teaspoons active dry yeast

⅔ cup mixed dried fruits, chopped

¼ cup walnuts, chopped

1. Assemble bread machine with the dough paddle in place. Bring all ingredients to room temperature.
2. Add all ingredients to the pan, except for the dried fruits and walnuts, in the order indicated in your machine's operation manual. Proceed according to manufacturer's directions for wheat bread, adding the dried fruits and walnuts when the machine beeps, indicating the time to add additional ingredients.
3. Cool for 10 minutes, then remove from pan. Cool bread completely before slicing. Store in an airtight container or freeze.

**PER SERVING** Calories: 93 | Fat: 2 g | Protein: 4 g | Sugar: 3 g | Fiber: 3 g | Carbohydrates: 17 g

## Fresh Versus Dried Fruits

Fresh or frozen fruits are too wet to add to a bread machine, which doesn't know to ease up on the kneading if necessary. If you really want to use fresh berries, set them aside and run the rest of the recipe on the dough cycle. When the cycle is complete, gently fold in the fresh berries by hand, and form into a loaf and bake in a traditional oven at 325°F for about an hour.

# Cinnamon-Raisin Bread

*You'll love this moist, chewy bread with plumped-up raisins and plenty of cinnamon!*

**INGREDIENTS | MAKES 1 (1½-POUND)
LOAF (24 SERVINGS)**

1 cup plus 3 tablespoons water

3¼ cups bread flour

2 tablespoons sugar

1½ tablespoons soymilk powder

1 teaspoon salt

1½ tablespoons vegan margarine

1 teaspoon cinnamon

1½ teaspoons active dry yeast

¾ cup raisins

1. Assemble bread machine with the dough paddle in place. Bring all ingredients to room temperature.
2. Add all ingredients to the pan, except for the raisins, in the order indicated in your machine's operation manual. Proceed according to manufacturer's directions for white bread, adding the raisins when the machine beeps, indicating the time to add additional ingredients.
3. Cool for 10 minutes, then remove from pan. Cool bread completely before slicing. Store in an airtight container or freeze.

**PER SERVING** Calories: 95 | Fat: 1 g | Protein: 3 g | Sugar: 4 g | Fiber: 1 g | Carbohydrates: 19 g

# Caramelized Onion–Rye Bread

*Fill two slices of this bread with sauerkraut, whole-grain mustard, and your favorite vegan meat substitute for a deliciously satisfying Reuben sandwich!*

**INGREDIENTS | MAKES 1 (1½-POUND)
LOAF (24 SERVINGS)**

1⅛ cups water

1 tablespoon plus 1 teaspoon olive oil

2 tablespoons agave syrup

1 teaspoon salt

1 tablespoon caraway seeds

1⅓ cups rye flour

2¼ cups bread flour

2 teaspoons vital wheat gluten

¼ cup soymilk powder

2½ teaspoons active dry yeast

¾ cup caramelized onions, chopped

1. Assemble bread machine with the dough paddle in place. Bring all ingredients to room temperature.
2. Add all ingredients to the pan, except for the caramelized onions, in the order indicated in your machine's operation manual. Proceed according to manufacturer's directions for white bread, adding the caramelized onions when the machine beeps, indicating the time to add additional ingredients.
3. Cool for 10 minutes, then remove from pan. Cool bread completely before slicing. Store in an airtight container or freeze.

**PER SERVING** Calories: 91 | Fat: 2 g | Protein: 3 g | Sugar: 0 g | Fiber: 2 g | Carbohydrates: 15 g

# Sweet Multi-Grain Bread

*This nourishing, earthy bread tastes great and is full of fiber!*

**INGREDIENTS | MAKES 1 (1½-POUND) LOAF (24 SERVINGS)**

1¼ cups water
2 tablespoons vegan margarine
1⅓ cups bread flour
1⅓ cups whole-wheat flour
1 cup multigrain cereal, uncooked
2 teaspoons vital wheat gluten
3 tablespoons brown sugar
1¼ teaspoons salt
2½ teaspoons instant yeast

1. Assemble bread machine with the dough paddle in place. Bring all ingredients to room temperature.
2. Add all ingredients to the pan in the order indicated in your machine's operation manual. Proceed according to manufacturer's directions for wheat bread.
3. Cool for 10 minutes, then remove from pan. Cool bread completely before slicing. Store in an airtight container or freeze.

**PER SERVING** Calories: 79 | Fat: 1 g | Protein: 3 g | Sugar: 2 g | Fiber: 2 g | Carbohydrates: 15 g

# Pickle Bread

*Like pickles? Then you'll love this unique loaf! Throw a grilled veggie burger between two slices of this surprisingly good bread.*

**INGREDIENTS | MAKES 1 (1½-POUND) LOAF (16 SERVINGS)**

1 cup dill pickle juice, warm (110–115°F)
1 large dill pickle, chopped
1 tablespoon vegan margarine
1 tablespoon dried onion
1 teaspoon parsley flakes
1 tablespoon dried dillweed
1 tablespoon sugar
3 cups bread flour
3 teaspoons instant yeast

1. Assemble bread machine with the dough paddle in place. Bring all ingredients to room temperature, except for warm pickle juice.
2. Add all ingredients to the pan in the order indicated in your machine's operation manual. Proceed according to manufacturer's directions for white bread.
3. Cool for 10 minutes, then remove from pan. Cool bread completely before slicing. Store in an airtight container or freeze.

**PER SERVING** Calories: 107 | Fat: 1 g | Protein: 4 g | Sugar: 1 g | Fiber: 1 g | Carbohydrates: 20 g

# Sweet Potato Bread

*This pretty bread makes great almond butter and banana sandwiches.*

### INGREDIENTS | MAKES 1 (2-POUND) LOAF (32 SERVINGS)

½ cup plus 2 tablespoons water

1 teaspoon vanilla extract

1 cup mashed cooked sweet potatoes

4 cups bread flour

¼ teaspoon cinnamon

¼ teaspoon nutmeg

2 tablespoons vegan margarine

⅓ cup dark brown sugar

1½ teaspoons salt

2 teaspoons active dry yeast

2 tablespoons soymilk powder

1. Assemble bread machine with the dough paddle in place. Bring all ingredients to room temperature.
2. Add all ingredients to the pan in the order indicated in your machine's operation manual. Proceed according to manufacturer's directions for white bread.
3. Cool for 10 minutes, then remove from pan. Cool bread completely before slicing. Store in an airtight container or freeze.

**PER SERVING** Calories: 87 | Fat: 1 g | Protein: 2 g | Sugar: 3 g | Fiber: 1 g | Carbohydrates: 17 g

## Sweet Potatoes or Yams?

They're similar, but are actually two different plant species. Unfortunately, markets often don't make that distinction. (Canned "yams" are frequently sweet potatoes.) They can be used interchangeably in most recipes, and can be replaced outright by pumpkin or squash purée.

# Potato Bread

*This light, fluffy bread will quickly become a family favorite.*

**INGREDIENTS** | MAKES 1 (1½-POUND)
LOAF (24 SERVINGS)

¾ cup soymilk

½ cup water

2 tablespoons vegan margarine

3 cups bread flour

½ cup instant mashed potato flakes, dry

1 tablespoon sugar

1½ teaspoons salt

⅛ teaspoon turmeric, for color (optional)

2 teaspoons instant yeast

1. Assemble bread machine with the dough paddle in place. Bring all ingredients to room temperature.
2. Add all ingredients to the pan in the order indicated in your machine's operation manual. Proceed according to manufacturer's directions for white bread.
3. Cool for 10 minutes, then remove from pan. Cool bread completely before slicing. Store in an airtight container or freeze.

**PER SERVING** Calories: 80 | Fat: 1 g | Protein: 3 g | Sugar: 1 g | Fiber: 1 g | Carbohydrates: 14 g

# Beer Bread

*As with making beer bread the old-fashioned way, experiment with a variety of brews in this bread machine recipe to get different flavor profiles!*

**INGREDIENTS** | MAKES 1 (1½-POUND)
LOAF (24 SERVINGS)

12 ounces flat beer

1 teaspoon salt

1 tablespoon vital wheat gluten

2 tablespoons olive oil

2 tablespoons dark brown sugar

3 cups bread flour

2¼ teaspoons active dry yeast

1. Assemble bread machine with the dough paddle in place. Bring all ingredients to room temperature.
2. Add all ingredients to the pan in the order indicated in your machine's operation manual. Proceed according to manufacturer's directions for white bread.
3. Cool for 10 minutes, then remove from pan. Cool bread completely before slicing. Store in an airtight container or freeze.

**PER SERVING** Calories: 85 | Fat: 1 g | Protein: 3 g | Sugar: 1 g | Fiber: 0 g | Carbohydrates: 14 g

# CHAPTER 16

# Gluten-Free Recipes

# Gluten-Free Onion Burger Buns

*Jazz up your next veggie burger with one of these homemade rolls. They're also great with fresh salads!*

### INGREDIENTS | SERVES 6

½ cup water, plus additional water as needed

⅛ cup dried onion

1½ tablespoons poppy seeds

¾ teaspoon salt, divided use

1½ teaspoons plus 2 tablespoons olive oil, divided use

2¼ teaspoons active dry yeast (1 packet)

1½ tablespoons sugar, divided use

½ cup rice flour

½ cup tapioca flour

½ cup cornstarch

½ tablespoon potato flour

1 teaspoon egg replacement powder

1 teaspoon xanthan gum

1 teaspoon guar gum

1½ teaspoons baking powder

1 teaspoon onion powder

1 teaspoon white vinegar

Egg replacement equal to 1 egg, prepared

1. Bring ½ cup water to boil in a small saucepan. Add dried onion and allow to rehydrate for 15 minutes, until soft. Drain onions, reserving soaking water. Add poppy seeds, ¼ teaspoon salt, and 1½ teaspoons olive oil to onions. Stir to combine. Set aside.

2. Combine reserved soaking water with enough fresh water to equal 1 cup. Bring water temperature to 110°–115°F. Combine warm water with yeast and 1 teaspoon sugar in a small bowl and allow to sit for 5–10 minutes to get bubbly.

3. In a medium bowl, whisk together the rice flour, tapioca flour, cornstarch, potato flour, egg replacement powder, xanthan gum, guar gum, baking powder, onion powder, and remaining ½ teaspoon salt. In a large bowl, mix the remaining sugar, vinegar, prepared egg replacement, and remaining oil together with an electric mixer on low speed until combined.

4. Add the yeast mixture to the wet ingredients. Gradually beat the flour mixture into the wet ingredients, adding one half at a time. Beat until mixture is smooth. Dough will be sticky.

5. Divide dough up between 6 greased burger bun molds, until each is about half full, or roughly form into rounded bun shapes on a greased baking sheet. Divide onion-poppy seed topping between the buns and gently press into the top of the dough to help topping stick. Cover with a kitchen towel and allow to rise until doubled in bulk, about 40–45 minutes.

6. Preheat oven to 375°F. Bake for 20–25 minutes until golden brown. Transfer to wire racks to cool. Cut in half to serve as burger or sandwich buns.

**PER SERVING** Calories: 213 | Fat: 7 g | Protein: 2 g | Sugar: 4 g | Fiber: 2 g | Carbohydrates: 37 g

# Gluten-Free Fruit Nut Squares

*Quinoa is rich in high-quality protein, making this sweet, chewy treat very nutritious and a great source of fiber.*

**INGREDIENTS | SERVES 12**

1 cup quinoa flakes
½ teaspoon cinnamon
½ teaspoon sea salt
1 cup walnuts, finely chopped
1 cup raisins, finely chopped
½ cup dates, pitted and finely chopped
½ cup figs, finely chopped
1 cup cooked brown rice
¼ cup canola oil
1 tablespoon orange zest
4–6 tablespoons water

1. Preheat oven to 325°F.
2. Place quinoa flakes, cinnamon, and salt in a food processor and process until finely ground. Add walnuts and process until also finely ground. Add raisins, dates, figs, brown rice, oil, orange zest, and 4 tablespoons water. Process until combined, adding more water if needed, so that mixture will be easy to spread in the baking dish.
3. Press mixture into an oiled 8" baking dish and bake for 30 minutes. Cool completely. Cut into squares to serve.

**PER SERVING** Calories: 232 | Fat: 12 g | Protein: 4 g | Sugar: 12 g | Fiber: 3 g | Carbohydrates: 31 g

# Gluten-Free Chocolate Chip Cookies

*Enjoy dipping this warm, gooey chocolate-chip goodness in your favorite cold glass of nondairy milk!*

**INGREDIENTS | MAKES ABOUT 5 DOZEN COOKIES**

2⅔ cups brown rice flour
1 teaspoon baking powder
1 teaspoon baking soda
¼ teaspoon salt
⅔ cup vegan margarine, softened
2 cups brown sugar, lightly packed
Egg replacement equal to 2 eggs, prepared
2 tablespoons water, hot
1 package (10–12 ounces) gluten-free vegan chocolate chips

1. Preheat oven to 375°F.
2. In a small bowl, combine flour, baking powder, baking soda, and salt. In a large bowl, beat together margarine, brown sugar, egg replacement, and water until well blended. Gradually add flour mixture to wet ingredients. Stir in chocolate chips.
3. Drop by heaping teaspoonful onto a lightly greased baking sheet about 1" apart. Bake 8–11 minutes until edges are golden brown. Allow to cool on baking sheet for 2 minutes. Transfer to wire racks to cool.

**PER 1 COOKIE** Calories: 91 | Fat: 4 g | Protein: 1 g | Sugar: 8 g | Fiber: 1 g | Carbohydrates: 14 g

# Gluten-Free Pie Crust

*This recipe makes a basic, gluten-free pastry crust that is also vegan.*
*Now you can have your pie and eat it too!*

**INGREDIENTS | MAKES 2 SINGLE, OR 1 DOUBLE 9" PIE CRUST**

1 cup rice flour

½ cup potato starch

½ cup sorghum flour

3 teaspoons sugar

¼ teaspoon salt

1 teaspoon cinnamon, optional

8 tablespoons vegan margarine, cold and cut into pieces

2 tablespoons apple cider vinegar

Egg replacement equal to 1 egg, prepared

¼ cup ice water

1. In a large bowl, combine rice flour, potato starch, sorghum flour, sugar, salt, and cinnamon. Cut margarine into flour mixture with a pastry cutter or large fork, until mixture resembles coarse crumbs. In a separate bowl, whisk together vinegar and egg replacement until blended. Add vinegar mixture to flour and stir until combined.
2. Begin adding ice water, 1 tablespoon at a time, until dough can be formed into a ball. Divide dough in half. Wrap each piece in plastic wrap. Gently press each wrapped piece of dough with the palm of your hand to slightly flatten into a disk shape. Refrigerate for at least 1 hour.
3. Remove dough from the refrigerator and allow to soften enough to roll. Roll dough out between 2 sheets of plastic wrap or parchment paper according to recipe needs.
4. For a single, prebaked crust, press 1 sheet of rolled dough into a pie pan, trim or fold up edges into a fluted pattern on the edge of the pan. Dock bottom with the tines of a fork to vent. Bake 15–20 minutes in a preheated 350°F oven.

**PER ⅛ SINGLE CRUST PIE** Calories: 125 | Fat: 6 g | Protein: 1 g | Sugar: 1 g | Fiber: 1 g | Carbohydrates: 17 g

# Gluten-Free Apple-Carrot Loaf

*Juicy apples and carrots make this a moist, sweet snacking bread.*
*Enjoy a warm, fresh-baked slice with vegan margarine and a cup of tea for a delicious rainy-day treat.*

**INGREDIENTS | SERVES 16**

1 cup sorghum flour

½ cup tapioca flour

2 teaspoons baking powder

½ teaspoon baking soda

¾ teaspoon xanthan gum

½ teaspoon salt

1½ teaspoons cinnamon

¼ teaspoon nutmeg

¼ teaspoon cloves

½ cup sugar

½ cup brown sugar

⅓ cup canola oil

1 teaspoon white or apple cider vinegar

Egg replacement equal to 2 eggs, prepared

¼ cup coconut milk

2 teaspoons lemon zest, chopped

½ cup apple, grated

½ cup carrot, grated

½ cup raisins

½ cup walnuts, chopped

1. Preheat oven to 350°F. Grease a 9" loaf pan.
2. In a large bowl, whisk to combine the sorghum flour, tapioca flour, baking powder, baking soda, xanthan gum, salt, cinnamon, nutmeg, cloves, sugar, and brown sugar.
3. With an electric mixer on medium speed, beat the oil, vinegar, egg replacement, coconut milk, and lemon zest into the flour mixture for about 2 minutes, or until well blended. Blot apple and carrot shreds with paper towels to remove excess moisture. Use a fork to separate shreds and stir into batter. Stir in raisins and walnuts.
4. Pour batter into the loaf pan. Bake for 50–60 minutes, or until the top is golden brown and a toothpick comes out clean when inserted into the center of the bread. Cool in pan for 10 minutes. Transfer to a wire rack.

**PER SERVING** Calories: 186 | Fat: 8 g | Protein: 2 g | Sugar: 17 g | Fiber: 2 g | Carbohydrates: 29 g

# Gluten-Free Sandwich Bread

*Flour made from the ancient teff grain replaces the wheat flour in this yummy yeast bread.*

**INGREDIENTS | SERVES 12**

2¼ teaspoons active dry yeast (1 packet)

1½ cups water, warm (110–115°F)

1 teaspoon sugar

¼ cup canola oil

3 tablespoons agave syrup

2 tablespoons flaxseed meal

2 cups teff flour

½ cup cornstarch

½ cup tapioca flour

1½ teaspoons xanthan gum

1¼ teaspoons sea salt

1. Combine the yeast with the warm water and sugar in a medium bowl. Stir to mix and allow to sit for 5–10 minutes to get bubbly. Whisk in the oil, agave syrup, and flaxseed meal. Continue to whisk until the mixture begins to thicken and feels a bit slimy.
2. In a large bowl, whisk together the teff flour, cornstarch, tapioca flour, xanthan gum, and salt. Continue to whisk as you pour the wet ingredients into the flour mixture.
3. Once the ingredients are combined, mix for an additional 1 minute, or until the dough becomes smooth and thickened. Transfer dough to a greased 8" × 4" loaf pan, using a spatula to form dough into a loaf shape. Place dough in a very warm place and allow to rise until doubled in bulk, about 1 hour.
4. Preheat oven to 350°F. Bake for 35–40 minutes until golden brown around the edges. Allow bread to cool in the pan for 10 minutes, then remove from pan and transfer to a wire rack. Cool completely before slicing and serving. Store in an airtight container.

**PER 1 SLICE** Calories: 139 | Fat: 5 g | Protein: 2 g | Sugar: 0 g | Fiber: 2 g | Carbohydrates: 18 g

# Gluten-Free Nutty Banana Cupcakes

*These banana cupcakes get a double boost of flavor from Peanut Butter Frosting and peanut bits!*

**INGREDIENTS | SERVES 14**

½ cup soymilk

1 cup sugar

¾ cup canola oil

2 teaspoons vanilla extract

1 cup plus 1 tablespoon sorghum flour, divided use

¼ cup potato starch

¼ cup tapioca flour

1 teaspoon xanthan gum

1 teaspoon baking powder

½ teaspoon salt

3 tablespoons white vinegar

⅔ cup diced bananas

⅓ cup crushed peanuts, plus extra for topping

¼ batch Peanut Butter Frosting (see Chapter 14)

## Exploring Nut Butters

Peanut butter is a great source of protein and kids love it, but shop around for other nut butters for variety. Cashew nut butter is a rich and creamy treat, and soy nut butter is similar to peanut butter but with an earthy taste. If you've got a food processor, mix and match your favorites to make your own homemade nut butters.

1. Preheat oven to 350°F.
2. In a large bowl, combine soymilk, sugar, oil, and vanilla extract. Whisk until blended. In a separate bowl, whisk together 1 cup sorghum flour, potato starch, tapioca flour, xanthan gum, baking powder, and salt. Gradually add flour mixture to wet ingredients, stirring until mixed. Add vinegar, 1 tablespoon at a time, mixing well between additions.
3. Combine diced bananas with 1 tablespoon sorghum flour in a small bowl. Stir to coat. Add bananas to batter, stirring to combine. Mix in crushed peanuts. Place ¼ cup batter in greased or paper-lined muffin tins.
4. Bake 25–30 minutes, until lightly browned and firm. Cool completely and frost with Peanut Butter Frosting. Sprinkle crushed peanuts over the top. Store in an airtight container.

**PER 1 CUPCAKE** Calories: 261 | Fat: 17 g | Protein: 2 g | Sugar: 19 g | Fiber: 1 g | Carbohydrates: 26 g

# Gluten-Free Pecan Cookies

*This versatile cookie can be decorated to match any holiday, with frosting, icing, sprinkles, or decorating sugar. Baking them is a fun activity for the little ones who want to help in the kitchen!*

**INGREDIENTS | YIELDS APPROXIMATELY 30 COOKIES**

⅔ cup vegan margarine, softened

¾ cup plus 2 tablespoons sugar, divided use

1 teaspoon vanilla extract

Egg replacement equal to 1 egg, prepared

4 teaspoons soymilk

1⅓ cups sorghum flour

⅔ cup cornstarch

½ cup soy flour

1½ teaspoons baking powder

¼ teaspoon salt

½ cup pecans, chopped

1½ teaspoons cinnamon

1. Preheat oven to 375°F.
2. In a large bowl, cream together margarine, ¾ cup sugar, and vanilla extract with a pastry cutter or a large fork until fluffy. Stir in egg replacement and soymilk until well mixed. In a separate bowl, whisk together sorghum flour, cornstarch, soy flour, baking powder, and salt.
3. Gradually add flour mixture to wet ingredients until blended. Stir in pecans. Cover bowl and refrigerate for 1 hour. Place dough between 2 sheets of wax paper or parchment and roll out to ¼" thick. Use a cookie cutter to cut into 2" rounds, or other desired shapes. Place cookies on an ungreased baking sheet 1" apart. Combine remaining 2 tablespoons sugar with cinnamon in a small bowl. Sprinkle cinnamon mixture over cookies.
4. Bake for 7–9 minutes until lightly browned around the edges. Transfer to wire racks to cool. Store in an airtight container.

**PER 1 COOKIE** Calories: 108 | Fat: 5 g | Protein: 2 g | Sugar: 6 g | Fiber: 1 g | Carbohydrates: 14 g

# Gluten-Free Apple Crisp

*Sorghum flour works well as a replacement for wheat flour in the topping of this delicious apple crisp. Try swapping out the apple for other fruits, such as peaches or plums.*

**INGREDIENTS | SERVES 8**

4 cups apple slices

1 tablespoon lemon juice

¼ cup sugar

2 teaspoons cornstarch

1½ teaspoons cinnamon, divided use

½ cup brown sugar, packed

⅛ teaspoon salt

¾ cup sorghum flour

½ cup walnuts, chopped, optional

8 tablespoons vegan margarine, cold and cut into small pieces

1. Preheat oven to 350°F.
2. Toss apples with lemon juice, sugar, cornstarch, and ½ teaspoon cinnamon in a large bowl. Place apple mixture in an even layer in a greased 8" × 8" baking pan. In a medium bowl, mix together the brown sugar, salt, sorghum flour, and the remaining 1 teaspoon cinnamon until blended. Stir in the nuts, if desired. Using fingers, gently work the cold margarine into the flour mixture until pea-sized lumps are formed.
3. Top apples evenly with the flour mixture and bake until juices are bubbling and the top is golden brown, about 45 minutes.

**PER SERVING** Calories: 303 | Fat: 16 g | Protein: 3 g | Sugar: 25 g | Fiber: 3 g | Carbohydrates: 39 g

# Gluten-Free Chocolate Cake

*On a vegan, gluten-free diet, chocolate cake doesn't have to be
a thing of the past! This recipe will satisfy your craving.*

**INGREDIENTS | SERVES 9**

½ cup soymilk

1½ teaspoons apple cider vinegar

½ cup canola oil

Egg replacement equal to 1 egg, prepared

1 teaspoon vanilla extract

1¼ cups sorghum flour

1½ teaspoons xanthan gum

1½ teaspoons baking soda

¼ teaspoon salt

4 tablespoons unsweetened cocoa powder

1 cup sugar

½ cup water, boiling

1. Preheat oven to 350°F.
2. Combine soymilk and vinegar in a small bowl. Allow to sit for 10 minutes, then add oil, egg replacement, and vanilla extract. Beat with an electric mixer on low speed until well blended.
3. In a separate bowl, whisk together sorghum flour, xanthan gum, baking soda, salt, cocoa powder, and sugar. Add to wet ingredients in 2 or 3 batches, mixing well between additions. Add boiling water and beat until smooth.
4. Pour batter into a lightly greased 8" × 8" baking pan and bake for 35–40 minutes until a toothpick comes out clean when inserted into the center of the cake. Cool completely and frost as desired.

**PER SERVING** Calories: 274 | Fat: 13 g | Protein: 3 g | Sugar: 23 g | Fiber: 3 g | Carbohydrates: 39 g

# CHAPTER 17

# Leftover Bread Recipes

# Panzanella Bread Salad

*The bread in this salad soaks up the juices of the tomatoes and the flavors of the olives and vinegar.*

**INGREDIENTS | SERVES 6**

4 (½"-thick) slices French Bread (see Chapter 5) from the center of the loaf

½ cup extra-virgin olive oil, divided use

1 teaspoon sea salt, divided use

½ teaspoon cracked black pepper, divided use

1 large clove garlic, peeled

¼ cup onion, thinly sliced

3½ cups ripe tomatoes, cut into ½" dice

1 medium cucumber, peeled, seeded, and diced

4 tablespoons fresh basil leaves, cut into ribbons

¼ cup green olives, pitted and chopped

3 tablespoons red wine vinegar

1. Brush sliced bread with ¼ cup olive oil and sprinkle with ¼ teaspoon salt and a few pinches of black pepper. Brown both sides of the bread on a grill over medium heat. Once bread is toasted, rub the garlic clove on both sides of bread. Garlic will melt and infuse the bread with garlic flavor. Tear bread into pieces and set aside.

2. In a large bowl, combine onion, tomatoes, cucumber, basil, and olives. For the dressing, whisk together the remaining ¼ cup olive oil, salt, pepper, and red wine vinegar in a small bowl.

3. Toss the pieces of bread with the tomato mixture. Add the dressing and mix well. Allow salad to sit at room temperature for about 30 minutes before serving.

**PER SERVING** Calories: 477 | Fat: 38 | Protein: 6 g | Sugar: 5 g | Fiber: 3 g | Carbohydrates: 30 g

## Homemade Flavored Oils

A flavored oil will beautify your kitchen and add flavor to your food. Simply combine several of your favorite herbs, whole garlic cloves, peppercorns, dried lemon or orange zest, or dried chiles with a quality olive oil. For safety's sake, avoid fresh herbs and zests, and always use dried. Oils infused with dried herbs will keep for up to one year, while fresh herbs can cause spoilage after less than a week.

# Gazpacho de Andalusia

*This Spanish version of gazpacho incorporates bread into a refreshing, cold tomato and vegetable soup. Check your local farmers' market for the most delicious, ripe tomatoes around!*

## INGREDIENTS | SERVES 6

4 slices French Bread (see Chapter 5), 1" thick

1 cup water

8 medium tomatoes, chopped

1½ cups cucumber, peeled and seeded

1½ cups red bell pepper

2 large cloves garlic, crushed

½ cup olive oil

2 tablespoons apple cider vinegar

¾ teaspoon cumin seeds

1½ teaspoons sea salt

Garnishes to taste, including diced cucumber, jalapeño pepper, red or green bell pepper, sweet onion, avocado, tomato, and cilantro leaves

1. Place bread in a medium bowl. Add water and set aside to soak for 30 minutes. In a blender, combine tomatoes, cucumber, bell pepper, and garlic. Blend until smooth.
2. Press some of the water out of the bread. Combine bread with olive oil, vinegar, cumin, and sea salt in a medium bowl. Add to tomato mixture and blend until smooth. Blend in batches if blender is too full.
3. Adjust seasoning as desired and refrigerate for at least 2 hours. Serve chilled, with garnishes.

**PER SERVING** Calories: 329 | Fat: 19 g | Protein: 7 g | Sugar: 7 g | Fiber: 4 g | Carbohydrates: 34 g

# Ribollita

*This Tuscan kale and bread soup is a rich, hearty dish that can be served as a meal. Lacinato kale, also known as black or dinosaur kale, is very dark green in color with leaves that are not curled like regular kale leaves. You can substitute regular kale in a pinch!*

### INGREDIENTS | SERVES 14

4 cups hearty bread, cubed, such as ciabatta or French Bread (see Chapter 5)

4 tablespoons olive oil, divided use

1 cup onion, chopped

¼ cup celery, chopped

3 cloves garlic, minced

12 cups vegetable broth

4 cups Lacinato kale, chopped

4 cups savoy cabbage, chopped

4 cups Swiss chard, chopped

3 cups broccoli rabe or Brussels sprouts, shredded

2 cups Yukon Gold potatoes, diced

1 medium carrot, diced

1 medium zucchini, diced

1 (28-ounce) can diced tomatoes, do not drain

2 (15-ounce) cans cannellini beans, divided use

1 tablespoon sea salt

1 tablespoon dried thyme

½ teaspoon crushed red pepper

½ cup fresh basil leaves, packed, cut into ribbons

1. Preheat oven to 375°F.
2. Lightly brush both sides of bread with 1 tablespoon olive oil, cut into 1" cubes, and place on a baking sheet. Bake for 15 minutes, stirring occasionally until bread is toasted. Set aside.
3. Heat remaining olive oil in a large pot over medium heat. Add onion and celery and cook for about 5 minutes, until onion is translucent. Add garlic and cook for 1–2 minutes. Add vegetable broth, kale, cabbage, chard, broccoli rabe, potatoes, carrots, zucchini, and tomatoes. Cover, reduce heat to medium-low, and simmer until greens are wilted, about 20 minutes. Drain 1 can of beans, reserving the juice. Place beans into a small bowl and mash with a potato masher, adding a small amount of canning juice, if needed. Add mashed beans to the soup.
4. Reduce heat and simmer until all vegetables are tender, about 30 minutes. Drain the remaining can of beans. Add drained beans, sea salt, dried thyme, crushed red pepper, and toasted bread cubes to the soup. Bring soup to a boil, reduce heat, and simmer for 10 minutes. Allow to cool for 10 minutes. Serve topped with fresh basil ribbons.

**PER SERVING** Calories: 234 | Fat: 5 g | Protein: 10 g | Sugar: 5 g | Fiber: 7 g | Carbohydrates: 40 g

### Fresh Is Always Best

Cans are convenient, but dried beans are cheaper, need less packaging, and add a fresher flavor. And if you plan in advance, they aren't much work at all to prepare. Place beans in a large pot, cover with water (more than you think you'll need), and allow to sit for at least 2 hours or overnight. Drain the water and simmer in fresh water for about an hour, then you're good to go! One cup dried beans yields about 3 cups cooked.

# Peach Bread Pudding

*This is a sweet twist on the classic bread pudding.*
*Try serving it with a drizzle of Caramel Topping (see Chapter 14).*

**INGREDIENTS | SERVES 12**

½ cup silken tofu

1 cup soy creamer

2 cups soymilk

¼ cup vegan sour cream

½ cup sugar

1 teaspoon vanilla extract

1 teaspoon cinnamon

⅛ teaspoon nutmeg

Pinch salt

4 cups day-old bread, cut into 1" cubes

¾ cup raisins

1½ cups peaches, ripe but firm, diced

2 tablespoons vegan margarine, cold, cut into small pieces

1. Preheat oven to 350°F.
2. In a blender, combine tofu and creamer. Blend until mixture is smooth. Add soymilk, sour cream, sugar, vanilla extract, cinnamon, nutmeg, and salt. Blend until smooth. Set aside.
3. In a large bowl, stir together the bread cubes, raisins, and diced peaches. Pour tofu mixture over the bread and fruit, stirring to thoroughly combine. Pour into a lightly greased 9" × 13" baking dish in an even layer. Dot surface with margarine pieces and allow to stand for 10 minutes.
4. Bake for 50–60 minutes, until pudding seems set and edges are lightly browned. Serve warm or cold.

**PER SERVING** Calories: 233 | Fat: 6 g | Protein: 7 g | Sugar: 14 g | Fiber: 2 g | Carbohydrates: 39 g

# Caesar Salad

*Enjoy warm, garlicky croutons with cool, crunchy lettuce, all tossed in a creamy Caesar dressing. Top with a few slices of blackened tofu for a complete meal.*

**INGREDIENTS | SERVES 6**

½ teaspoon vegan Worcestershire sauce

1½ tablespoons fresh lemon juice

½ teaspoon Dijon mustard

2 cloves garlic, crushed

¼ teaspoon sea salt

¼ teaspoon cracked black pepper

1 teaspoon capers

¼ cup silken tofu

⅓ cup extra-virgin olive oil

6 cups romaine lettuce, chopped

1½ cups Garlic Croutons, warm (see recipe in this chapter)

Vegan Parmesan cheese, optional

1. In a blender, combine Worcestershire sauce, lemon juice, Dijon mustard, garlic, salt, pepper, capers, and tofu. Blend until smooth. Continue to blend while drizzling in olive oil until combined.
2. In a large bowl, toss romaine lettuce with dressing. Add warm croutons and toss to combine.
3. Serve on chilled plates with vegan Parmesan and additional cracked pepper, if desired.

**PER SERVING** Calories: 226 | Fat: 16 g | Protein: 4 g | Sugar: 2 g | Fiber: 2 g | Carbohydrates: 18 g

# French Onion Soup

*The rich, deep flavors of slowly caramelized onions and garlic are the stars of this wonderful peasant soup. The crunchy, grilled bread soaks up some of the broth, adding texture and body to the dish.*

**INGREDIENTS | SERVES 6**

4 tablespoons olive oil, divided use

6 large yellow onions, sliced

¼ teaspoon sugar

4 cloves garlic, divided use

8 cups vegetable stock or broth

½ cup dry white wine

¼ teaspoon dried thyme

1 bay leaf

1½ teaspoons sea salt

½ teaspooon cracked black pepper

3 tablespoons vegan margarine

¼ cup all-purpose flour

6 slices day-old French Bread (see Chapter 5)

## Varieties of Veggie Broths

A basic vegetable broth is made by simmering vegetables, potatoes, and a bay leaf or two in water for at least 30 minutes. While you may be familiar with the canned and boxed stocks available at the grocery store, vegan chefs have a few other tricks up their sleeves to impart extra flavor to recipes calling for vegetable broth. Check your natural grocer for specialty flavored bouillon cubes such as vegetarian "chicken" or "beef" flavor, or shop the bulk bins for powdered vegetable broth mix.

1. Heat 3 tablespoons olive oil over medium heat in a large saucepan. Add onion and sauté for 10 minutes. Add sugar and continue to cook for 35–40 minutes, or until onions are very browned, without being burned. Crush 2 cloves of garlic. Add to onions and sauté for 2 minutes. Add the vegetable stock, wine, thyme, and bay leaf. Partially cover the pan with a lid and simmer for about 30 minutes. Discard bay leaf and stir in salt and pepper.

2. Melt vegan margarine in a small saucepan over medium-low heat. Add flour and cook for 5–10 minutes, stirring constantly until flour is browned. Add ½ cup of the soup broth to the browned flour and whisk until smooth. Stir flour mixture into the soup until well blended. Simmer soup for 5–10 minutes.

3. Brush French Bread with remaining olive oil and grill or toast bread on both sides. Rub warm bread on both sides with remaining raw garlic cloves. Garlic will melt into the bread. Ladle soup into bowls and top with bread.

**PER SERVING** Calories: 330 | Fat: 15 g | Protein: 6 g | Sugar: 10 g | Fiber: 3 g | Carbohydrates: 40 g

# Herbed Cornbread Dressing

*This dressing makes a terrific holiday side dish! You may use more cornbread and a lesser amount of bread crumbs if you wish . . . just be careful to adjust the amount of liquid if needed!*

## INGREDIENTS | SERVES 12

1 recipe (4 cups) Corn Bread (see Chapter 4)

4 cups vegan bread crumbs

3 tablespoons vegan margarine

2 tablespoons olive oil

¾ cup onion, chopped

¾ cup celery, chopped

½ cup green bell pepper, diced (optional)

1 clove garlic, crushed

1 teaspoon poultry seasoning

½ teaspoon sage

2 tablespoons fresh flat-leaf parsley, chopped

¾ teaspoon salt

¼ teaspoon cracked black pepper

2–3 cups vegetable stock or broth

1. Preheat oven to 350°F.
2. In a large bowl, break up Corn Bread into rough ½" chunks. Add bread crumbs. Set aside.
3. In a large skillet, melt margarine and oil together over medium heat and sauté onion, celery, bell pepper, and garlic for 5 minutes, or until softened. Add vegetable mixture to cornbread, including the margarine and oil used for cooking. Stir to combine. Mix in poultry seasoning, sage, parsley, salt, and pepper.
4. Add 2½ cups vegetable broth, stirring until just moistened. If dressing seems dry, add another ¼ to ½ cup vegetable broth. Spoon dressing into a greased 9" × 13" baking dish, pressing down slightly to fill in any gaps.
5. Bake for 50–60 minutes until golden brown and cooked through.

**PER SERVING** Calories: 424 | Fat: 17 g | Protein: 8 g | Sugar: 16 g | Fiber: 3 g | Carbohydrates: 60 g

# Apple Brown Betty

*Falling somewhere between an apple crisp and an apple cobbler,*
*this combination of fruit, sugar, and bread crumbs is a humble yet classic dessert!*

**INGREDIENTS | SERVES 9**

2 cups soft bread crumbs (White Bread or Whole-Wheat Rolls, see Chapter 5)

4 tablespoons vegan margarine, melted

⅓ brown sugar, packed

⅓ cup sugar

½ teaspoon ground cinnamon

Pinch salt

6 cups Granny Smith apples, peeled, cored, and sliced

¼ cup orange juice

1. Preheat oven to 350°F.
2. In a medium bowl, combine bread crumbs with melted margarine. Stir in brown sugar, sugar, cinnamon, and salt. Arrange half of the apples in the bottom of a greased 8" × 8" baking dish. Spread half the bread crumb mixture over the apples. Drizzle with half of the orange juice. Add the rest of the apples, top with the remaining crumbs, and drizzle with the remaining orange juice.
3. Bake until bubbly and browned, about 1 hour. Serve warm or at room temperature with vegan ice cream, if desired.

**PER SERVING** Calories: 169 | Fat: 5 g | Protein: 1 g | Sugar: 23 g | Fiber: 1 g | Carbohydrates: 30 g

# Seasoned Bread Crumbs

*Here is a perfect use for stale bread as well as the heels of the bread that always seem*
*to be left behind. Vary the spices according to your needs and tastes.*

**INGREDIENTS | MAKES 4 CUPS**

8 slices stale bread (White Bread or Whole-Wheat Rolls, see Chapter 5)

1 teaspoon salt

½ teaspoon black pepper

¼ teaspoon ground red pepper

1 teaspoon dried parsley

¼ teaspoon dried oregano

¼ teaspoon dried basil

1 teaspoon onion powder

1 teaspoon garlic powder

1. Preheat oven to 400°F.
2. Place bread on a baking sheet and toast in the oven for 10–15 minutes, or until completely dry. Break bread into pieces and grind into crumbs in a food processor or blender. Add the rest of the ingredients and pulse to combine.
3. Store in an airtight container.

**PER ¼ CUP SERVING** Calories: 58 | Fat: 0 g | Protein: 2 g | Sugar: 1 g | Fiber: 0 g | Carbohydrates: 11 g

# Garlicky Bread Soup

*Enjoy a hot bowl of this farm-style soup with a squeeze of fresh lemon!*
*Add a cup of cooked white beans when the broth is added for an even heartier meal.*

### INGREDIENTS | SERVES 6

1 tablespoon vegan margarine

2 tablespoons olive oil

2 cups onion, sliced

10 cloves garlic, peeled and sliced

2 quarts vegetable stock or broth

6 cups stale French Bread (see Chapter 5) or Sourdough Bread (see Chapter 7), cubed

2 teaspoons sea salt

½ teaspoon cracked black pepper

¼ cup flat-leaf parsley, chopped

1 tablespoon fresh thyme leaves

Extra-virgin olive oil for garnish

1. Heat margarine and oil in a heavy-bottomed stockpot over medium-low heat. Add onions and garlic. Sauté for 25–30 minutes, stirring frequently, until onions are caramelized.
2. Add the vegetable broth, bread cubes, salt, pepper, parsley, and thyme. Simmer 20 minutes.
3. Carefully purée the hot soup with an immersion blender, or in batches in a regular blender. Serve hot with a drizzle of extra-virgin olive oil.

**PER SERVING** Calories: 285 | Fat: 8 g | Protein: 8 g | Sugar: 6 g | Fiber: 2 g | Carbohydrates: 46 g

# Garlic Croutons

*These croutons are crunchy on the outside, but not too hard. It will be difficult*
*to resist the temptation to snack on these tasty tidbits, so make plenty!*

### INGREDIENTS | MAKES 4 CUPS

4 cups day-old French Bread (see Chapter 5), cubed, without crusts

2 tablespoons vegan margarine

2 tablespoons olive oil

1 clove garlic, minced

⅛ teaspoon sea salt

1. Preheat oven to 350°F. Line a rimmed baking sheet with foil.
2. Place bread cubes in a bowl. Place margarine, olive oil, and garlic in a small saucepan and heat over medium-low until garlic is lightly browned. Add margarine mixture to bread cubes and quickly toss to coat. Place coated bread cubes on baking sheet and sprinkle with salt.
3. Bake for 15 minutes, or until croutons are golden brown. Cool and store in an airtight container.

**PER ¼ CUP SERVING** Calories: 97 | Fat: 4 g | Protein: 3 g | Sugar: 1 g | Fiber: 1 g | Carbohydrates: 14 g

# Bruschetta

*Crunchy grilled bread and luscious, juicy tomatoes taste great together. Serve this as an appetizer or for a light lunch. Use a variety of colorful heirloom tomatoes for a gorgeous presentation!*

### INGREDIENTS | MAKES 18 PIECES

1½ pounds ripe tomatoes

2 tablespoons red onion, minced

2 tablespoons fresh basil, chopped

2 tablespoons plus ¼ cup extra-virgin olive oil, divided use

1 teaspoon balsamic vinegar

½ teaspoon sea salt

¼ teaspoon black pepper

3 cloves garlic, peeled, divided use

1 Italian Loaf (see Chapter 5)

## A Tuscan Tradition

A true Italian chef will prepare the bread for bruschetta by toasting homemade bread over hot coals, then quickly rubbing a sliced clove of garlic over both sides of the bread before drizzling with just a touch of the finest olive oil. In lieu of hot coals, a toaster, grill, or 5 minutes in the oven at 350°F will work just fine.

1. Chop tomatoes in a ¼" dice and place in a large bowl with red onion, basil, 2 tablespoons olive oil, balsamic vinegar, sea salt, and black pepper. Mince 1 clove garlic and stir into tomato mixture.
2. Slice bread diagonally into 24 pieces, about ½" thick. Grill on each side until browned, about 1 minute per side. Use the remaining 2 cloves garlic to rub directly on one side of the grilled bread and brush with remaining olive oil.
3. To serve, place the tomato mixture in a serving bowl and center on a serving platter. Arrange bread with the garlic and oil side up, on the platter around the bowl.

**PER 1 PIECE** Calories: 133 | Fat: 6 g | Protein: 3 g | Sugar: 2 g | Fiber: 1 g | Carbohydrates: 18 g

# English Summer Pudding

*This is a strikingly beautiful fruit and bread dessert, perfect for a barbecue or picnic!*

**INGREDIENTS | SERVES 6**

8 ounces blackberries

8 ounces raspberries

4 ounces blueberries

4 ounces strawberries

⅔ cup sugar

10 slices White Bread (see Chapter 5), crusts removed

Additional berries for decorating, as desired

1. Place fruit in medium saucepan, add sugar, and bring to a boil over medium-high heat. Reduce heat and simmer for 5 minutes. Set aside.

2. Lightly oil a 4-cup capacity mixing bowl. Line the bowl with a piece of plastic wrap long enough to overhang the edges of the bowl. Cut 8 of the bread slices in half to form rectangles. Dip one side of each rectangle in the juice of the cooked fruit and place along the sides of the bowl with the juice side to the outside. Slightly overlap the rectangles. Cut out a circle of bread to fit the bottom of the bowl. Dip the bread circle into the juice and place in the bottom of the bowl, juice-side down. Make sure the bread is completely lining the bowl with no gaps.

3. Pour the fruit into the bread-lined bowl. Cut the last 2 pieces of bread to fit the top of the bowl. Arrange the bread pieces to cover the top so that there are no gaps. Place a piece of plastic wrap over the top of the bowl. Place a plate on top that will fit just inside the rim of the bowl and set something heavy on the plate, such as a can of soup, to weigh it down. Refrigerate overnight.

4. To serve pudding, remove the weight and plate. Remove the top plastic wrap. Invert the pudding onto a serving plate and remove the plastic wrap. Decorate with fresh berries, if desired.

**PER SERVING** Calories: 192 | Fat: 1 g | Protein: 3 g | Sugar: 30 g | Fiber: 5 g | Carbohydrates: 45 g

# Mushroom-Tofu Strata

*Tofu substitutes for eggs in this savory dish. Serve it at your next brunch, or on a weekend morning.*

**INGREDIENTS | SERVES 9**

1½ tablespoons vegan margarine

1½ tablespoons olive oil

1 large onion, diced

3 cloves garlic, minced

2½ cups mushrooms, sliced

3 tablespoons dry white wine

⅓ cup fresh chives, chopped

1 teaspoon dried thyme

10 slices stale Potato Bread or White Bread (see Chapter 5), but not completely dry, cubed

1½ cups silken tofu

4 cups soymilk

¼ cup tahini

¼ teaspoon turmeric

1½ teaspoons salt

½ teaspoon cracked black pepper

1 cup vegan Cheddar cheese, shredded, optional

1. In a medium skillet, heat margarine and olive oil over medium heat. Add onions and sauté for 4–5 minutes, until translucent. Add garlic, mushrooms, and wine. Continue to sauté, about 10 minutes, stirring frequently, until mushrooms are browned and most of the liquid has evaporated. Stir in chives, thyme, and bread cubes. Remove from heat and transfer to a large mixing bowl. Set aside.

2. In a blender, combine tofu and 1 cup of the soymilk. Blend until smooth. Add the remaining soymilk, tahini, turmeric, salt, and pepper. Blend 15–20 seconds until mixed. Pour liquid ingredients over bread mixture. Stir to mix. Cover and refrigerate for 1 hour, stirring occasionally.

3. Preheat oven to 350°F. Pour mixture into greased, 9" × 13" baking dish. Stir in vegan Cheddar cheese, if desired. Bake 50–60 minutes until golden brown and set.

**PER SERVING** Calories: 152 | Fat: 6 g | Protein: 6 g | Sugar: 3 g | Fiber: 1 g | Carbohydrates: 18 g

## In Search of Tahini

Tahini is a sesame seed paste native to Middle Eastern cuisine with a thinner consistency and milder flavor than peanut butter. You'll find a jarred or canned version in the ethnic foods aisle of large grocery stores, or a fresh version chilling next to the hummus if you're lucky. Check the bulk bins at co-ops and natural foods stores for powdered tahini, which can be rehydrated with a bit of water.

# Roasted Olives and Cauliflower with Bread Crumbs

*This is an unusual yet elegant side dish that will impress!*
*Roasting intensifies the flavor of the olives and sweetens the cauliflower.*

**INGREDIENTS | SERVES 8**

2 medium heads cauliflower, cut into bite-sized pieces

¼ cup plus 2 tablespoons olive oil, divided use

¼ cup garlic-stuffed olives

¼ cup pitted kalamata olives

¼ cup pitted black olives

1 cup cherry tomatoes, whole

3 cloves garlic, unpeeled

4–5 slices Italian Loaf (see Chapter 5) or ciabatta bread, ½" thick

¼ cup lemon juice

¼ cup flat-leaf parsley, chopped

¼–½ teaspoon cayenne pepper flakes

1. Preheat oven to 450°F.
2. Combine cauliflower and ¼ cup olive oil in a large bowl and spread evenly on a large baking sheet. Divide cauliflower between two baking sheets, if necessary. Place in the oven and roast for 10 minutes. While cauliflower is roasting, combine olives, tomatoes, and garlic cloves in a large bowl with the remaining 2 tablespoons olive oil. Add the olive mixture to the cauliflower, again dividing between both baking sheets if using two. Reduce the oven temperature to 425°F and continue roasting for another 15–20 minutes, until cauliflower is browned and tender. Remove from the oven.
3. Grill or toast the sliced bread until browned on both sides. Tear bread into pieces and place in a food processor. Process bread into coarse crumbs. Set aside. Peel the roasted garlic cloves and mash together with the lemon juice in a large bowl.
4. Add the roasted cauliflower mixture, parsley, bread crumbs, and pepper flakes to the garlic mixture and toss to combine. Taste and adjust for salt, as desired.

**PER SERVING** Calories: 190 | Fat: 12 g | Protein: 5 g | Sugar: 4 g | Fiber: 5 g | Carbohydrates: 18 g

# Glossary

**Acesulfame potassium** An non-caloric, artificial sweetener, also known as acesulfame K. Acesulfame potassium is a potassium salt, with twice the sweetening power of sugar.

**Add-ins** A term referring to garnishes folded into dough and batter, such as chocolate chips, nuts, or raisins.

**Adding alternately** A mixing technique in which dry and wet ingredients are divided into 3 or 4 portions each and added to a batter, a little at a time, alternating first dry, then wet. The purpose is even and thorough incorporation.

**Agave syrup** A liquid sweetener extracted from the blue agave plant. Also called agave nectar.

**Amaranth** An ancient grain, high in protein, that has been a food source for several thousand years. Amaranth is a small yellow grain that can be served as a cooked cereal or as a grain side dish, like rice. Amaranth contains no gluten, making it useful as flour in gluten-free baking.

**Amaretto** An Italian liqueur with the distinctive flavor of bitter almonds.

**Antioxidants** Molecules that slow oxidation of other molecules. Oxidation can produce free radicals, which trigger chain reactions that damage cells. In addition to preventing these reactions, antioxidants can inhibit them, once begun.

**Arepa flour** A corn flour that is precooked for use in making a corn cake called arepa, common to the cuisines of certain South American countries.

**Artificial sweeteners** Synthetic, non-nutritive sugar substitutes that are usually calorie-free or very low calorie. Includes aspartame, saccharin, acesulfame potassium, and sucralose.

**Baking powder** Baking powder is a combination of cream of tartar (acidic) and sodium bicarbonate (alkaline). May be single-acting or double-acting.

**Baking soda** A powdered alkaline compound known as sodium bicarbonate, which reacts with acidic ingredients in baking, to form carbon dioxide bubbles, giving rise or volume to baked goods.

**Balsamic vinegar** An Italian vinegar made since the Middle Ages from the Trebbiano grape, and while commonly aged up to twenty-five years, may also be aged as long as 150 years.

**Black gram lentils** A legume with a black skin and white interior. Also known as urad dal, black lentil, and kali dal.

**Bread flour** Flour containing less starch and more protein than all-purpose flour, perfect for bread making, when a strong elastic dough structure is needed.

**Brown rice syrup** A sticky, liquid sweetener made from brown rice. It is similar to honey in consistency.

**Buckle** Similar to a coffee cake, with fruit added to the batter, and streusel added to the top.

**Buckwheat** The seed from a plant in the rhubarb family, ground into flour or cooked the same way as rice, in which case it is called "kasha."

**Cake flour** A soft flour containing less protein and more starch than all-purpose flour, perfect for cakes and other delicate baked goods that don't need a strong, elastic dough structure.

**Caramelized** To cook food until the sugar, naturally occurring or added, darkens to an amber "caramel" color. Caramelization brings out the food's deep, sweet, rich flavors.

**Chana dal** A small, beige legume related to the chickpea or garbanzo bean.

**Chickpea flour** Also known as gram flour or besan flour; made from chickpeas, which are also known as garbanzo beans.

**Chutney** A chunky condiment from Southern Asia and India, sometimes cooked and jam-like, made with fruits or vegetables and often spiced with chilies.

**Coconut cream** Refers to the higher fat component of coconut milk that rises to the top of a container of coconut milk when it is allowed to sit.

**Coconut milk** Refers to the milky liquid made from the flesh of the coconut.

**Confectioners' sugar** Another name for powdered sugar.

**Cream of tartar** An acid salt commonly used to stabilize whipped egg whites. Also used in combination with baking soda in cookies and biscuits as a substitute for baking powder.

**Creaming** A term used to describe the blending of two ingredients into a creamy, smooth, paste-like texture.

**Crumble** A dessert also known as a crisp, consisting of fruit with a streusel topping.

**Currants** Tiny raisins made from the miniature zante grape. Do not confuse them with red, white, or black currants, which are small berries used for preserves, pastries, and the liqueur cassis.

**Curry powder** A spice blend originated by the British during their colonial rule of India, so they could bring home the flavor of the regional curry dishes. The flavor of the powder found in supermarkets is fairly generic, but throughout India and other parts of Asia, there are dozens of unique curry sauce variations.

**Cut in** A method of incorporating fat into dry ingredients by breaking it into small pieces. With heat, moisture is released from the fat, creating a flaky texture. Used in recipes such as biscuits and pie dough.

**Demerara** A large crystalled sugar that is minimally processed from cane juice, which is boiled to a syrup.

**Egg replacements** Refers to ingredients or combinations of ingredients used as a substitution for eggs in cooking and baking. May be a commercial product, such as EnerG Egg Replacer, or homemade, such as baking soda mixed with vinegar.

**Emulsified** The blending of two ingredients by suspension of small globules of one inside the other, so that the resulting blend becomes one homogenous substance.

**Enrich** In food, "enrich" refers to the replacement of a portion of the inherent nutrients that are lost from a food during processing.

**Evaporated cane juice** Refers to sugars made through the evaporation of the juice or syrup of whole sugar cane.

**Fenugreek seeds** Also known as methi seeds, fenugreek is a small, amber seed, commonly used in Indian cooking.

**Folding** A mixing method used to combine two substances of different texture. The gentle motion of folding, as opposed to beating or stirring, is meant to prevent light airy mixtures from deflating, which would inhibit leavening or reduce the airy quality of the finished product.

**Fortify** In food, refers to the addition of nutrients not inherent in a food to boost the nutritional value. Often done with the intent of preventing specific nutrient deficiencies in a population.

**Fructose** Fructose is a monosaccharide sugar that is 20–50 percent sweeter than table sugar.

**Fuji** A crisp, sweet Japanese apple variety introduced in the 1960s, popularized in the United States in the 1980s.

**Gala** A New Zealand apple variety, developed in the 1920s.

**Garam masala** The most common spice blend from Northern India. The word *garam* means "warm" or "hot." While the blend can be spicy, the name denotes the toasting of the spices prior to grinding.

**Gluten** The protein in wheat endosperm that promotes elasticity in bread dough. When moistened and agitated, gluten proteins tighten, creating a smooth, firm dough that can stretch to hold the gas of fermentation.

**Guar gum** A thickening agent made from the seeds of the guar plant.

**Herbes de Provence** A blend of herbs commonly used in Mediterranean cuisine, including lavender, thyme, sage, marjoram, basil, rosemary, fennel, and savory.

**Infuse** To steep two foods or flavors together.

**Instant-read** A thermometer designed to determine the internal temperatures of food.

**Julienne** A classic knife-cut that looks like long, thick matchsticks.

**Kalamata** Greek black olives marinated in wine and olive oil.

**Kamut** An ancient strain of wheat, thought to be one of the original strains of grain. Found in Egyptian tombs, kernels of this grain were brought to the United States, where it is currently cultivated. It is high in protein, and much larger in size than modern wheat.

**Kasha** See Buckwheat.

**Knead** The action of manipulating dough by hand or machine, in folding and massaging motions, for the purpose of encouraging the development of gluten strands. Gluten strands add strength and structure to leavened doughs.

**Leavening** An agent in dough that causes fermentation and rising, giving volume to baked goods.

**Legumes** Dried beans from seed pods that split open along the side when ripe. Legume varieties include soybeans, peas, garbanzo beans, and peanuts.

**Lemon curd** A tart lemon custard used as a spread or a filling.

**Macerate** To soak food, usually fruit, in liquid to infuse flavor.

**Maillard reaction** Refers to the browning of foods caused by a non-enzymatic reaction that occurs when the amino acids from proteins combine with the sugars on the surface of food in the presence of heat, usually between 300°F and 500°F.

**Masa harina** Flour made from dried hominy corn, used for corn tortillas and tamales.

**Millet** Known mainly as bird seed in the United States, this tiny, high-protein grain is popular throughout Asia and Africa, and used for breads, pilaf, and porridge.

**Muscovado** A moist, unrefined raw sugar, similar to brown sugar. Muscovado has a strong flavor from a high molasses content. Can be used like brown sugar.

**Oat** Available as groats, rolled, quick cooking, and steel cut, oats are known as one of the most nutritious grains. High in soluble fiber and vitamins B1, B2, and E, oat bran is generally believed to reduce cholesterol.

**Organic** Foods raised, grown, and manufactured without artificial ingredients, preservatives, hormones, antibiotics, certain pesticides, fertilizers, radiation, or food additives.

**Oven spring** Refers to the rapid increase in volume of yeasted doughs in the oven in the first few minutes of baking, due to the expansion of gasses.

**Parchment** Heavy paper that withstands heat, water, and grease; used to line pans and wrap foods.

**Pastry blender** A U-shaped tool consisting of several wires with a handle, used to cut fat into dry ingredients.

**Purée** Any food pulverized to a smooth paste of varying consistencies.

**Quinoa** An ancient grain of the Incas, and one of the few vegetable sources of complete protein. Suitable for use in gluten-free diets.

**Rancidity** Oxidation of oil that results in foul flavor and odor.

**Rapadura** An unrefined sugar that retains the molasses of the whole cane. Similar to Sucanat; however, rapadura is more finely ground than Sucanat.

**Reduce** A culinary term meaning to cook the water out of a dish, reducing its volume, intensifying its flavor, and thickening its sauce.

**Rhubarb** Rhubarb is an herbaceous plant having large green leaves at the end of long stalks. Culinary use of rhubarb is limited to the sour-tasting stalks, which are prepared in the manner of fruit, in preserves, pies, and tarts. The leaves are toxic and therefore not used as food.

**Roast** A dry heat cooking method in which foods are usually cooked to a degree of browning, or caramelization.

**Rye** This sturdy grass was historically given to the lower classes, while wheat, with much higher gluten content, was reserved for the rich. Closely related to barley and wheat, rye is also available rolled and as rye berries, in which the grain is whole with the bran removed.

**Sauté** To cook food quickly, over high heat, constantly stirring for even browning. The term means "to jump"; sauté pans are designed with a curved lip, making constant motion as easy as a flick of the wrist.

**Scone** A savory or sweet, biscuit-like bread originating in early 1500s Scotland.

**Self-rising flour** Refers to flour that has been precombined with chemical leavening agents, such as baking powder.

**Shorteners** Refers to ingredients, such as vegetable shortening and other fats, that inhibit the formation of gluten strands in dough, resulting in a tender baked good.

**Simple syrup** A pastry staple ingredient, made by boiling equal parts sugar and water. Used for moistening cakes, sweetening sauces and fruit purées, and as a recipe ingredient.

**Sorghum** Sorghum is a gluten-free grain with a neutral flavor. Used as a cereal grain and as flour for gluten-free diets.

**Sourdough** Refers to bread made with a fermented leavener, or starter.

**Spelt** This ancient strain of wheat, native to Southern Europe, is protein-rich and suitable for use as flour, pilaf, and porridge.

**Sponge** A thin predough or yeast batter that is made prior to making bread in order to prolong fermentation for improved flavor and texture.

**Stevia** A natural sweetener, 300 times the sweetness of sugar, derived from the leaves of the stevia plant.

**Stone fruit** A tree fruit that contains a pit, or stone, such as peaches, apricots, cherries, and plums.

**Sucanat** An unrefined sugar in which the molasses is separated and then added back during processing. Similar to rapadura, but with a coarser grain.

**Sucralose** Sucralose is a low-calorie, artificial sweetener that is 600 times sweeter than sugar. The chemical structure of sucralose is a chlorinated sugar molecule.

**Tahini** A paste made of ground sesame seeds.

**Tandoor** Used in Indian cuisine, this cylindrical clay charcoal oven cooks food at extremely high temperatures, retaining moisture, flavor, and nutritional benefits. Some breads, such as naan, are made by slapping the dough onto the side of the tandoor oven to be baked.

**Tapioca flour** Also known as tapioca starch, a fine powder ground from the roots of the cassava plant. Used as a thickener.

**Teff** This tiny grain from Africa is high in protein, calcium, and iron, and is cooked similar to rice, as well as ground into flour for breads.

**Tofu** Tofu, or soybean curd, is made by curdling soymilk with an acidic ingredient. The curd is pressed into blocks which are high in protein. Tofu has a bland flavor, and takes on the flavor of other ingredients in a dish, making it suitable for use in both sweet and savory dishes.

**Turbinado** Light brown coarse sugar, also known as raw sugar.

**Turmeric** A spice derived from the root of a plant in the ginger family, used for its bitter flavor and bright yellow color.

**Vanilla** The seed pod of a climbing orchid (*vanilla planifolia*), vanilla has been treasured for centuries. Look for beans that are thick and tough but pliable. To use vanilla beans, pound them first before splitting them lengthwise to crush the millions of inner mini-seeds and activate as much oil as possible. Once scraped, spent pods can be stored in sugar or steeped in rum to harness as much of the oil as possible.

**Vegetable shortening** Vegetable shortening consists of vegetable oil that has been hydrogenated for the purpose of staying solid at room temperature.

**Vital wheat gluten** High protein, hard-wheat flour in which most of the starch has been extracted, leaving a very high gluten content. Used to increase gluten content in bread recipes. Also known as gluten flour.

**Xanthan gum** In food, xanthan gum is used as a thickener, often in salad dressings. In gluten-free baking, xanthan gum helps doughs rise, giving volume to baked goods.

**Yeast** A single-celled organism from the genus *Saccharomyces*, used as a leavening agent in baked goods. Also used in the fermentation of alcoholic beverages.

**Zest** The colorful outermost rind of a citrus fruit, containing a high concentration of the essential oils and flavor compounds that flavor the fruit itself.

**Zester** A small tool designed to strip the aromatic, colorful, oil-rich skin from citrus fruit.

# Resources

## Bakeware

### KitchenEmporium.com
Offers a large selection of mini pans, including bundt, muffin, pie, tart, and popover pans, all available in several materials. In addition, this site offers appliances, cookbooks, coffee, tea, and wine products.
*www.kitchenemporium.com*

### Kitchen Universe
Offers paper pans, silicone pans, and fantastically shaped specialty pans.
*www.kitchenu.com*

### King Arthur Flour
Offers a huge selection of bakeware, including mini pans of all kinds, seasonal pans, as well as bake-and-give paper pans.
*www.kingarthurflour.com*

### Pans.com
Offers cookware, utensils, small appliances, and bakeware made from several materials, including silicone, aluminum, nonstick, cast iron, and glass.
*www.pans.com*

## Ingredients

### Barry Farm Foods
Provides candied lemon and citron, as well as more unusual candied tropical fruits.
*www.barryfarm.com*

### DelKanic Greenhouse & Farm Market
A fantastic assortment of extracts, including strawberry, black walnut, and maple.
*www.bulkfood.net*

### Home Grown Harvest
Provides a variety of grains, seeds, nuts, beans, and even bread machines and grain mills.
*www.homegrownharvest.com*

### King Arthur Flour
Not just bakeware, King Arthur carries a wide selection of baking ingredients, including flours, gluten-free flours, nuts, oils, and flavoring extracts.
*www.kingarthurflour.com*

### The Spice House
Offers a great variety of salts and spices, plus extracts including coffee, almond, chocolate, and vanilla.
*www.thespicehouse.com*

## Vegan Shopping

### Vegan Essentials
Whether you're looking for a non-leather belt, a T-shirt proclaiming your love of tofu, or just some nondairy cheese, you'll find it here. Check out the excellent selection of vegan baking mixes and chocolates.
*www.veganessentials.com*

### Food Fight Grocery
Vegan shopping with a sense of humor. With a storefront location in Portland, Oregon, this is not your average vegan shop. The emphasis is on fun and hard-to-source foods, with a heavy bias toward junk food. If you're looking to try vegan haggis or vegan s'mores, this is the place to look.
*www.foodfightgrocery.com*

### Bob's Red Mill
For those living in rural areas without access to a natural foods store, Bob's Red Mill has just about everything you need, including whole grains, egg replacer, vital wheat gluten, and nutritional yeast.
*www.bobsredmill.com*

**Frontier Natural Products Co-op**
Frontier specializes in natural and organic products, including spices, teas, and herbs, as well as Fair Trade products.
*www.frontiercoop.com*

**Mountain Rose Herbs**
Mountain Rose Herbs offers sustainable organic herbs, spices, teas, and botanicals.
*www.MountainRoseHerbs.com*

# Advice and Support

**About.com**
About.com offers a wealth of easily digestible information (and recipes!) as well as an Internet forum moderated by the author.
*www.vegetarian.about.com*

**People for the Ethical Treatment of Animals**
PETA (styled as PeTA) is an international nonprofit organization dedicated to establishing and defending the rights of all animals. The website is a hub for information, activism, shopping, cooking, networking, and everything vegan.
*www.PeTA.org*

**Post Punk Kitchen**
The Post Punk Kitchen began as a Public Access Cable show created by Isa Chandra Moskowitz, which evolved into a funky, genius website with recipes, shopping, blogs, videos, books, and an extensive user forum.
*www.theppk.com*

**VeganBaking.net**
VeganBaking.net is a community of like-minded individuals sharing recipes, articles, videos, and a wealth of great vegan baking resources.
*www.VeganBaking.net*

**VeggieBoards**
With membership in the tens of thousands, the Veggie Boards are an active place to discuss everything from urban composting to the best-tasting veggie burgers.
*www.veggieboards.com*

# Health and Nutrition

**Physicians Committee for Responsible Medicine (PCRM)**
PCRM is a leader in the field of preventive medicine, presenting cutting-edge research into the benefits of a plant-based diet and providing reliable and comprehensive nutritional information for vegans.
*www.pcrm.org*

**The Vegetarian Resource Group**
Just about everything you need to know about plant-based nutrition is available online from the Vegetarian Resource Group.
*www.vrg.org*

# Vegan Restaurants

**HappyCow**
Find out where to get a vegan meal anywhere on the planet, from Toledo to Timbuktu. This comprehensive Internet directory includes contact information and brief reviews of natural foods stores, vegan restaurants, and vegan-friendly establishments across the globe.
*www.happycow.net*

# Standard U.S./Metric Measurement Conversions

## VOLUME CONVERSIONS

| U.S. Volume Measure | Metric Equivalent |
|---|---|
| ⅛ teaspoon | 0.5 milliliters |
| ¼ teaspoon | 1 milliliters |
| ½ teaspoon | 2 milliliters |
| 1 teaspoon | 5 milliliters |
| ½ tablespoon | 7 milliliters |
| 1 tablespoon (3 teaspoons) | 15 milliliters |
| 2 tablespoons (1 fluid ounce) | 30 milliliters |
| ¼ cup (4 tablespoons) | 60 milliliters |
| ⅓ cup | 90 milliliters |
| ½ cup (4 fluid ounces) | 125 milliliters |
| ⅔ cup | 160 milliliters |
| ¾ cup (6 fluid ounces) | 180 milliliters |
| 1 cup (16 tablespoons) | 250 milliliters |
| 1 pint (2 cups) | 500 milliliters |
| 1 quart (4 cups) | 1 liter (about) |

## WEIGHT CONVERSIONS

| U.S. Weight Measure | Metric Equivalent |
|---|---|
| ½ ounce | 15 grams |
| 1 ounce | 30 grams |
| 2 ounces | 60 grams |
| 3 ounces | 85 grams |
| ¼ pound (4 ounces) | 115 grams |
| ½ pound (8 ounces) | 225 grams |
| ¾ pound (12 ounces) | 340 grams |
| 1 pound (16 ounces) | 454 grams |

## OVEN TEMPERATURE CONVERSIONS

| Degrees Fahrenheit | Degrees Celsius |
|---|---|
| 200 degrees F | 95 degrees C |
| 250 degrees F | 120 degrees C |
| 275 degrees F | 135 degrees C |
| 300 degrees F | 150 degrees C |
| 325 degrees F | 160 degrees C |
| 350 degrees F | 180 degrees C |
| 375 degrees F | 190 degrees C |
| 400 degrees F | 205 degrees C |
| 425 degrees F | 220 degrees C |
| 450 degrees F | 230 degrees C |

## BAKING PAN SIZES

| American | Metric |
|---|---|
| 8 × 1½ inch round baking pan | 20 × 4 cm cake tin |
| 9 × 1½ inch round baking pan | 23 × 3.5 cm cake tin |
| 11 × 7 × 1½ inch baking pan | 28 × 18 × 4 cm baking tin |
| 13 × 9 × 2 inch baking pan | 30 × 20 × 5 cm baking tin |
| 2 quart rectangular baking dish | 30 × 20 × 3 cm baking tin |
| 15 × 10 × 2 inch baking pan | 30 × 25 × 2 cm baking tin (Swiss roll tin) |
| 9 inch pie plate | 22 × 4 or 23 × 4 cm pie plate |
| 7 or 8 inch springform pan | 18 or 20 cm springform or loose bottom cake tin |
| 9 × 5 × 3 inch loaf pan | 23 × 13 × 7 cm or 2 lb narrow loaf or pate tin |
| 1½ quart casserole | 1.5 liter casserole |
| 2 quart casserole | 2 liter casserole |

# Index

# We Have EVERYTHING® on Anything!

**With more than 19 million** copies sold, the Everything® series has become one of America's favorite resources for solving problems, learning new skills, and organizing lives. Our brand is not only recognizable—it's also welcomed.

The series is a hand-in-hand partner for people who are ready to tackle new subjects—like you!

For more information on the Everything® series, please visit *www.adamsmedia.com*

The Everything® list spans a wide range of subjects, with more than 500 titles covering 25 different categories:

| | | |
|---|---|---|
| Business | History | Reference |
| Careers | Home Improvement | Religion |
| Children's Storybooks | Everything Kids | Self-Help |
| Computers | Languages | Sports & Fitness |
| Cooking | Music | Travel |
| Crafts and Hobbies | New Age | Wedding |
| Education/Schools | Parenting | Writing |
| Games and Puzzles | Personal Finance | |
| Health | Pets | |